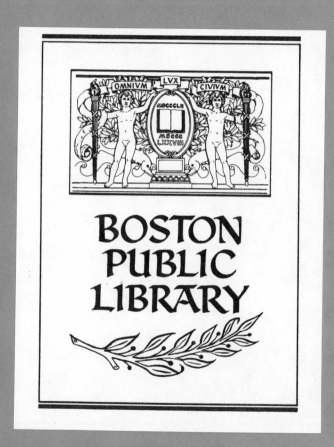

Reading Faulknerian Tragedy

Also by Warwick Wadlington:

The Confidence Game in American Literature

Reading Faulknerian Tragedy

WARWICK WADLINGTON

CORNELL UNIVERSITY PRESS

ITHACA AND LONDON

CORNELL UNIVERSITY PRESS GRATEFULLY ACKNOWLEDGES
A GRANT FROM THE ANDREW W. MELLON FOUNDATION
THAT AIDED IN BRINGING THIS BOOK TO PUBLICATION.

First published 1987 by Cornell University Press.

International Standard Book Number 0-8014-2011-3
Library of Congress Catalog Card Number 86-29166
Printed in the United States of America
Librarians: Library of Congress cataloging information
appears on the last page of the book.

The paper in this book is acid-free and meets the guidelines for
permanence and durability of the Committee on Production Guidelines
for Book Longevity of the Council on Library Resources.

Contents

Preface

Phil Stone once remarked to Faulkner that the trouble with some writers was that they wrote with one eye on the ball and the other on the grandstand. Faulkner answered that it seemed his own trouble as a poet was having one eye on the ball and the other on Babe Ruth. The exchange evokes and minimizes formidable anxieties, classic distractions for the writer. But Faulknerian tragedy attempts by expansion and elaboration to transform otherwise enervating distractions into enabling powers. It writes large the classic anxieties—over public recognition, over emulation and rivalry, and over some means, like heroic fame, of outfacing mortality—as themselves the subject of his performance. Further, the performer's place and the audience's become unfixed and overlap, shaping a contest for mortal stakes.

This book examines Faulknerian tragedy as an act in which the author at once says No to mortality and yet defiantly solicits the reader's collaborative performance. It relates this refusal and solicitation to the corresponding dynamics of human relations in culture. Because *tragedy* is an honorific term, an acknowledgment that must be bestowed by the reading public, Faulkner's achievement of modern tragedy requires that his performance as a writer be completed by its counterpart, his audience's realization of such tragedy through reading. This dependence is particularly fraught because Faulkner claims the right to the honorific while modifying the generic conventions that enable the claim to be made. His writing is best understood with the assumption that tragedy is neither fixed nor arbitrary but is fashioned in the course of cultural dialogue. And if we take seriously

7

the modern understanding that human being is likewise social, not simply given but continually made, maintained, and reachieved, then we may begin to see that an audience performing Faulknerian tragedy into reality is in a strong sense being helped to read itself into reality.

My study seeks to provide a coherent account of the aesthetics of tragedy in Faulkner by addressing the fresh questions about reading and writing which arise when we locate these practices within the constant cultural drama that constitutes persons. To see the reader's and writer's performances within the context of this broader drama is to free the academic conception of reading performance from its present restriction primarily to epistemology. Reading Faulknerian tragedy, I argue, potentially epitomizes the performance and acknowledgment of the scripts of culture itself, an activity that reproduces persons by furnishing them with the capacities necessary for existence. My concern is with this potential empowering activity along with its intrinsic opposite possibility. For the drama that forms persons does so at a risk that is sometimes deadly. Faulknerian tragedy springs from the hazardous possibilities for heroic existence in his particular version of an honor-shame culture as well as from the critique of this cultural script. With specific urgency in Faulknerian tragedy, the acts of reading and writing exist within a network of personal reproduction, including a distinctively human opposition to personal mortality, which troubled, excited, preoccupied a writer as mindful of literary immortality as Faulkner was.

This book continues my effort to contribute to the study of literature as the symbolic action of beings whose interdependence is fundamental and constitutive. Writing it has renewed my appreciation of interdependency. I thank above all T. Walter Herbert, Jr., and Wayne Lesser for their thoughtful reactions to the manuscript. John T. Matthews and Gary Lee Stonum made additional valuable suggestions. For advice or commentary on parts of the manuscript, I also thank Jeffrey Barnouw, Lynda Boose, Evan Carton, Larry Carver, John P. Farrell, Alan Warren Friedman, Peter M. Green, Joan Lidoff, Jane Marcus, and Robert V. Wess. I owe thanks as well to Judith Bailey for skillful editing. I gratefully acknowledge my students and others who responded to talks in which I developed versions of this book's ideas. Institutional support from The University of Texas at Austin provided time for some of the writing.

Preface

A portion of Chapter 3 appeared as "*The Sound and the Fury:* A Logic of Tragedy" in *American Literature* 53 (1981), 409–23.

I am grateful to Random House, Inc., for permission to quote from *Selected Letters of William Faulkner,* ed. Joseph Blotner (copyright 1977, by Jill Faulkner Summers); to Random House, Inc., and Curtis Brown, Ltd., for permission to quote from *The Sound and the Fury* (copyright 1984, by Jill Faulkner Summers), *As I Lay Dying* (copyright 1930, renewed 1957), *Light in August* (copyright 1932, renewed 1959), *Absalom, Absalom!* (copyright 1936, renewed 1951); and to Random House, Inc., and Chatto & Windus, Ltd., for permission to quote from *A Fable* (copyright 1954), *Requiem for a Nun* (copyright 1951), *Sanctuary* (copyright 1931, renewed 1958), and *Essays, Speeches and Public Letters,* ed. James B. Meriwether (copyright 1965).

WARWICK WADLINGTON

Austin, Texas

9

Reading Faulknerian Tragedy

Introduction:
On Saying No to Death

> Thou art the thing itself: unaccommodated man is no more but
> such a poor, bare, forked animal as thou art.
>
> *King Lear*

When Faulkner was asked about the possibility of creating a modern tragic hero, he did not respond to the implicit gambit—the supposed unheroic pettiness of modern humankind—but instead stipulated an unexpected requirement: an audience who could hear.

Q. You spoke a little while ago of Greek themes. I was wondering if you think that modern literature . . . could feature the truly tragic hero that you would find in Greek times, or do you think the characters should be meaner or more simple? . . . A. . . . I think the writer has got to write in terms of his environment, and . . . his readers are part of that environment too, . . . and probably a writer, whether he intends to or not, or knows it or not, is going to shape what he writes in the terms of who will read it. So maybe when there are fine listeners, there will be fine poets again. (*University* 41–42)

We are now used to the critical view that readers must supply Faulkner's work with a consummating interpretation, as in the reader's way of "looking at the blackbird" which completes the several narrative perspectives of *Absalom, Absalom!* (*University* 274). Here, however, we will be concerned with a more inclusive completion invited by Faulkner's tragedy: the consummation by performance— for instance, to use Faulkner's not uncharacteristic example, by speaking and thus hearing, as fine listeners. Let me stress from the first that by reading I mean not only an interpretive but a comprehensive performative act, engaging the unfolding possibilities of literary role-enactment and giving full reality to the perceived authorial performances.

We are not concerned here with the most general abstraction, *the* implied (or "ideal") reader or reading. Nor will we consider empirical reports of actual readings. Our framework is in one sense narrower, in another much broader: Reading Faulknerian Tragedy. These terms raise mutually implicated questions: what *reading possibilities* does the perspective of Faulknerian tragedy disclose? Or what is Faulknerian tragedy from the standpoint of certain reading practices it anticipates? Let me in turn anticipate. The most tragic Faulknerian prospect is unaccommodated man and woman. Opposing this are the processes, themselves potentially tragic, of accommodating—furnishing—the bare, forked animal. It will take the whole book to demonstrate this prospect and process, but the attempt to do so carefully will from the first open up the widest implications for the study of literature.

To engage the questions just indicated is to reunderstand both the act of reading in general and the revisionary activity of a great novelist writing modern tragedy. The reunderstanding of reading and Faulknerian tragedy I propose here has one broad informing focus: the cultural acts engendering human being by furnishing the very power to exist. Accordingly, the first chapter offers an anthropology of rhetoric centered on the terms *performance, persons,* and *reproduction.* With these we will pursue the general question of how reading is more-than-interpretive, and thus how a discipline that seeks to grasp reading must study more than either the act of interpretation or the conventions in which these interpretations are inscribed. To establish the grounds for this expansion, we will need to see that the interdependency of fine listeners and fine poets is an example of a larger one. We will need, that is, to classify writing, reading, and genre conventions with the creating and consummating of the formative scripts of culture itself. This step will give us a schema for understanding literature which is more encompassing than the presently dominant epistemological model, a larger schema of human relations, comprising the activity of knowing (to include reflecting on knowledge) as one among the powers constitutive of human being. Taken together, these powers are performances that enable and reproduce persons. Put briefly: Faulknerian tragedy pinpoints the mutual interference as well as the mutual enabling of these powers. And it focuses the consequences of exercising them.

In this examination of Faulkner, by the "reader's enactment" I mean, more precisely, the diverse ways audiences can take on roles in reading Faulknerian tragedy, and the various consequences of role-taking which they enjoy or suffer, ranging from sensuous pleasure and possible affront to daunting entanglement with otherness. Finally, to analyze the mutually enabling and acknowledging performances of "fine listeners" and "fine poets" will be to establish that for our purposes acknowledgment is more salient than knowledge. I will trace the dialogue of enactment: performative claims and performative acknowledgments, and the consequences of these acts. In the words of one of Faulkner's people, "Man performs, engenders, so much more than he can or should have to bear." These words highlight the act-consequence experience within reading performance which reanimates a major tradition of tragedy.

Emphasizing the reciprocity of performance in the terms just sketched will be a step toward filling two voids in Faulkner criticism. One is that no adequate description of Faulknerian tragedy exists. The other is that there is no sustained discussion of performing Faulkner's prose and in particular no examination of his voice as an invitation to reading performance.

The first void is partly understandable, inasmuch as it took three centuries for commentators to adjust theory to the practice of Shakespeare, to recategorize him from deviant to tragedian par excellence. Critical attention to tragedy and Faulkner has taken two general forms, which, seen in the long view, constitute part of a campaign within the perennial battle of the books. In its twentieth-century incarnation, the pitting of ancients against moderns has prominently deployed notions of tragedy for attack and defense. On the one hand, Faulkner criticism has measured his novels against putatively fixed yardsticks of definitive tragedy, either discovered in a classical statement or formulated by the critic, and found the works fit or unfit for the accolade *tragic*. On the other hand, Faulkner's admirers have simply invoked *tragedy* without defending the usage, as a self-evident prestigious term to convey the admirer's sense that, in Faulkner, disaster and suffering have been captured in a great and moving art.[1] Both these approaches were indispensable in rescuing Faulkner from charges of indecency and worse, which portrayed him as an example of modern degeneracy. At appropriate points in the following chapters, we will reflect on the need for the critical redemption of Faulkner by this twofold reference to tragedy and by other means. Suffice it to say here that this effort, or more exactly this phase of a continuing effort, has largely done its work. Moreover, as recently exemplified by Alastair Fowler, careful students of genre have ceased to measure literary specimens against purported fixed genres. We need to describe Faulknerian tragedy without either measuring it against Tragedy, as if this were immobile or monolithic, or paying vague compliments merely testifying to the importance of his work to us. Yet simultaneously, we need to take into account the actual force of these very impulses in reading works like Faulkner's which, the critical record attests, urgently raise the question of tragedy.

The recurrent, if not definitive, theme of tragedy which concerns us here is what Faulkner called the No to death: the confrontation with mortality which tests as it enacts the power to exist. To examine this sustaining No of Faulknerian tragedy requires a sense of the dialectical process by which tragedy is culturally sustained. In the ideal case of this process, a work and *certain aspects* of a generic tradition are continuously adjusted to each other through the reading public's trial of, and education by, the work as it develops and illuminates the tradition it is tested against. The complexity of this process increases when the genre has the prestige tragedy has enjoyed in cultural arguments since the Renaissance. As is implicitly evidenced, for instance, in the studies of J. M. Bremer, Lucien Goldmann, and Timothy J. Reiss, tragedy develops as each era, while appealing to traditional statements like Aristotle's, redefines the concept through both practice and theory to help formulate current momentous concerns. Thus the eighteenth-century controversy about why audiences derive pleasure from tragedy focused a wider argument about essential human selfishness or altruism (Wasserman). Continuing the sociopolitical implications of this question, much of the nineteenth-century preoccupation with tragedy expressed anxieties over revolution (Farrell). By Faulkner's time, in the general critique of modernity, the very possibility of writing modern tragedy was questioned.

The most succinct critique of the view that tragedy has a typological, ahistorical essence is Clayton Koelb's. But by virtue of the insight that tragedy is best understood developmentally, in historical—institutional, genealogical—terms, we must still take into account the notions of tragedy specifically obtaining in various periods in order to say anything meaningful. We must not simply discard a typological understanding of tragic genre. Rather, we reintroduce it within the historical context we have chosen, as that era's typology or one of its proposed, contending typologies, a large part of whose significance is that many have thought it to be a general definition of tragedy. To do so allows us, first, to grasp the coherence of such cultural modeling and therefore the transformations that writers like Faulkner propose, working within the logic of their era's purported general definition. (Thus my third chapter is titled *a,* not *the,* logic of tragedy.)

Further, this procedure takes into account that to understand the concept "tragedy" is to understand precisely that it has long constituted a claim to general significance. Koelb appeals for a rigorous use of *tragedy* which employs the concept only in restricted contexts, properly qualified: "The temptation to use a term conveying such a wealth of meaning is easy to understand. But 'tragedy' carries so much meaning that it actually communicates nothing. Better, then, to resist the temptation and keep to critical terms which, while more modest, are more precise" ("Problem of Tragedy" 264). I have tried to follow this practice, modified by an awareness that tragedy's periodic, and present, honorific character generates a paradox. The paradox is that, in the somewhat improbable event that professor-critics were to succeed in imposing Koelb's strict usage on society in general, the term would lose most of the interest it has had. To recall the earlier point: *tragedy* carries so much meaning because it is a contested term of cultural sanctification. From the time of Aristotle's dispute with Plato over the far-reaching issue of regulating the passions, and commencing anew with the Renaissance, *tragedy* has been a highly value-laden, protean term, which various parties to cultural disputes have sought to capture for their causes by defining or implying its supposed essence. *Tragedy,* consequently, is what W. B. Gallie has called an essentially contested concept. To understand it means to understand the contest or contests in which it participates.

Perhaps the basic question of the "tragedy debate" since the nineteenth century is whether human beings, or moderns, are capable of genuine action, as required by an "Aristotelian" view of tragedy, or condemned only to passive endurance of suffering, to "mere pathos," in life or literature. This debate in turn implies the question of how the concept of genuine action itself is to be understood. Even if Faulkner scholars do not always name tragedy as their governing concept, essentially the same disputes regarding his characters have long informed judgments of his art.[2] In this study we will see how Faulkner's work raises and transforms to his own ends certain traditional issues of tragedy, all of them irradiated by the general issue of action and passivity which modernism has given special urgency: hubris, pathos, catharsis, recognition, and the formal completion of action in plot. In treating these matters, we will find indispensable Kenneth Burke's concept of symbolic action, particularly the strategies of the negative, the No.

As I hope to have suggested so far, my general premise is that a better understanding of such matters as tragedy is achieved not by attempting to abandon one's historical situation but by recognizing previously obscured resources within the situation, which is to say within the ongoing cultural tradition of which tragedy is a part. One proceeds by means of successive cross-illuminations between present and past phases of the process. Interdisciplinary investigation can be of great service here because it provides a series of platforms from which we can discern what may otherwise be "too close" or "too far" to recognize clearly in our own ongoing situation. Thus, anthropological investigations into certain other cultural traditions have been aided by, and in turn assist, the increasing awareness of the honor-shame code in our own continuing tradition. When, as in the work of the classicist E. R. Dodds, anthropology is used to illuminate certain dynamic honor-code features of the ancient Greek culture that fostered tragic art, and when the historian Bertram Wyatt-Brown develops similar insights in his study of the traditional American South, we are offered an enlarged opportunity to discover the action of Faulknerian tragedy.

Addressing this action in the opening paragraphs, I began by noting that the corresponding reading enactments are diverse, as are the consequences of performance. The primary term I will use in examining enactments is *voice,* which will serve as a bridging concept between certain key elements of these enactments as well as between writer's and reader's performances. The term is both literal and figurative, and successive chapters will gradually unfold what it includes. For now, it will suffice to press its literal meaning, which covers the range from speaking aloud to mental voicing. Even a century ago, to say that speaking the text might be important would be merely to express a commonplace assumption. Now, this claim has point because reading practices have changed, for reasons and with consequences that Walter Ong and others have explicated. In fact, the claim had point when Faulkner implicitly made it himself.

Speaking Faulkner's language has not had much more than passing mention in the voluminous commentary on a writer whose repertoire of sonority extraordinarily invites speaking and hearing. This is not so much a remarkable oversight as a result of prevailing ideas about reading. Both generally and in Faulkner criticism, the reader has emerged as a figure with considerable powers to interpret, but silenced, most recently by poststructuralist skepticisms about voice. Possessed of competence but not performance, the critic's reader has taken a curious center stage. We have long had good analyses of Faulkner's style, including such matters as prose rhythm. (And despite our interest here in Faulkner's No, we will do little more than note that his stylistic "negative ultimates," which critics like Florence Leaver and Richard Poirier have variously treated, are relevant to Faulkner's conception of life as a resistance to mortality. The speaking reader of Faulkner's prose is constantly pronouncing various forms of No.) But when, in recent criticism, "the reader" and "reading" are the topics, stylistic matters go by the board or are reformulated as merely interpretive cruxes. The same is true of the topics of voice and sound: they are ably treated, but only treated, as themes or epistemological problems by critics like Karl Zender and Stephen Ross. The prevailing assumption is that the reader's text is an object to be studied alertly and mutely, but the reader's enactment of the sonorous language that invites our voicing is to be treated with indifference or suspicion, as outmoded belletrism. How, the assumption goes, can such a thing matter to serious criticism? I hope to answer this question. I deal with it both generally, in the first chapter, and specifically, in the subsequent chapters concentrating on voice as not only theme but rhetoric in four novels of Faulkner's major phase. In a further study, I hope to complete the discussion of the major phase begun here.

This, then, is a book about Faulknerian tragedy as the representation and scripting of hazardously reciprocating performances. Faulkner's tragedy broods over the prospect of unaccommodated man, the bare, forked animal divested of human requirements. In Faulkner, reciprocating voices constitute a crucial human requirement, so that the voices of his texts solicit the mutual accommodation of performance.

Performance and *accommodation* are close in meaning. As one of the best students of performance observes, the term derives from the Old French *parfournir*—*par* ("throughly") plus *fournir* ("to furnish")—and literally means to complete something by furnishing or supplying it thoroughly (Turner, *Ritual to Theatre* 79, 91). The overlapping meaning of *accommodation* is to furnish that which is suitable, hence to adjust something to suit something else. In *The Classic,* Frank Kermode argues that classics maintain their immortality because they are amenable to a series of accommodations, in the sense of interpretive adjustments that allow the works to speak meaningfully to successive generations. This book also addresses the significant role accommodation plays in literary immortality. But we will be concerned with more than Faulkner's immortality, since this is implicated with, literally, im-mortality, the No to death. And again, rather than solely the adjustments of interpretation, we will accentuate the more inclusive furnishings of performance—among other things, the reader's furnishing the text with the living voice it needs to exist completely as a literary voice and the text's accommodation of the reader's No.

The contrary influential idea that silence is, as Paul Lilly put it, Faulkner's impeccable language, has not been so much wrong as it has been conceived too simply, outside the reader's performative process, which gives "silent" *audition* its reality and meaning. I suspect that recent deconstructionist notions of unvoiced reading (voice as mere epistemological metaphor) have reinforced an older desire whose motives are quite different but compatible: to protect Faulkner's prose from charges of sacrificing sense to sound. This deconstructive reinforcement of a protective instinct follows upon, and surpasses, the similarly unwitting or half-conscious reinforcement accomplished by the neglect of the speaking reader in formalist criticism. More broadly still, with the submergence of oral performance, reading as a more-than-cognitive acting of the text, either outwardly *or* inwardly, has been submerged as well. Because the reader's making-real of voice is weakened sensuously and experientially, the sense of an authorial voice is attenuated. (In this respect, poststructualist skepticism gave a vigorous shove to a door already ajar.)

With whatever theoretical justification, critical curiosity about the speaking reader, as well as Faulknerian tragedy, has been held in check by a decorum that is now more of a barrier than a help. Even the basis for understanding the subject is in considerable disarray, since various apparently conflicting implications have never sufficiently been made to confront each other. For example, a completely different view from Lilly's appears to be derivable from Faulkner's widely recognized debt to oratory and oral narrative.[3] A closer look should make the issue clearer, and its full dimensions will appear in the chapters that follow.

Lilly proposed that, for Faulkner as for Mallarmé, actual utterance degrades pure "poetic" communication. Following Lilly, Ross and Zender have strongly implied that reading Faulkner is a silent activity. This assumption fails to take sufficiently into account that everything important to Faulkner, including voice and voicing, is a subject of contention for him, which is why his statement that the writer records the conflicts of the human heart, despite the stock quality of the conception, quite appropriately has been made a watchword by his commentators. Zender respects Faulkner's many-mindedness and usefully highlights various meanings and values sound has for Faulkner. But with regard to reading, Zender captures only one part of the field of contention which is voice by citing Faulkner's preference for prose over music: "I prefer silence to sound, and the image produced by words occurs in silence. That is, the thunder and the music of the prose takes place in silence" (*Lion* 248). What is noteworthy in this formulation is the sonorous, "loud" quality of language Faulkner ascribes even to the inner audition that is "silence." That is, the silence in question, as compared to music, is an absence or cessation of *acoustical* sound, but is emphatically not the full silence of nonaudition. Faulkner's very sensitivity to the sound of language accounts for the distaste for modern noise which Zender demonstrates.

But to leave the matter even at this misses the important assimilative process that takes place through the utterance of language, the speaking through which sonority is internalized. Silence, it will be shown, names one part of a dialectic in Faulkner, as well as, in a special sense, the end of the process that may depend upon actual speech.

To ignore this process is not only to dismiss Faulkner's debt to oral tradition. It is to disregard his habits of recitation from memory and of listening to the recitations of others, such as his daughter, Jill, and Phil Stone (e.g., Blotner, *Biography* 1:169, 203; Sensibar 78, 85, 86). It is to ignore the suggestive discrepancy between his own thin, high speaking voice and the amplification, vigor, and range he gave it in his sounding fictional language. It is to overlook the deep relationship between voicing and breathing, particularly in a writer who stated that an intense "passion of breathing" motivated the writer (*University* 145) and in whose work breathing is constantly invoked. It is to slight as well Faulkner's recordings, in which his reedy voice, suffused by the sound of breathing, performs his works aloud—an unaccountable activity for a writer for whom the profanation of language by speech is supposed to be the last word. And finally, it is to disregard those actual readers of Faulkner who have not been deafened and silenced by an education devoted to silent perusal, readers who know a striking invitation to vocal performance when they hear one.

A major reason for the particular contending impulses in Faulkner's writing is that he sees everything valuable as liable to impurity and corruption, so that catharsis is an imperative of his creativity. Yet we will see that catharsis too becomes the field of contrary forces. If, for Faulkner, language is to be made impeccable, it is by immersion in the deadly element of speech as it exists potentially in its scripted, printed form, and by stylizing it and working through the conflicts of utterance whose push and pull readers have often noted in Faulkner's prose.

Faulkner the modernist-Symbolist, partly environed by the modernist desire to strangle "eloquence," also hearkens back to a tradition of eloquence underwritten by an honor-culture in which one declared who one was and the honor one claimed through the competitive, transactive drama of speaking, hearing, and being judged. We will consider at length the honor-culture principles at work in Faulkner's rhetoric. Here I abstract the central transactive principle common to the major topics of our study—the hazarding of a claim in the hope of winning recognition. Honor "stands as a mediator between individual aspirations and the judgment of society. . . . The facts of honor may be viewed as related in the following way: honor felt becomes honor claimed, and honor claimed becomes honor paid. . . . Public opinion, in its sympathy for the successful, betrays the notion of honor as a purely moral concept" (Pitt-Rivers, "Honor" 503–4). So too the bid for the public opinion that is immortal fame betrays the notion of either voice or tragedy as purely formal or "textual" reality. That is, not only tragedy but voice is constituted by a transactive process: it is realized within a circuit of bold claims that are either acknowledged and fulfilled by others or ignored or rejected. Faulkner's ambitious bid for the honorific of tragedy bespeaks his commitment to a code of honor, one which, we will see, he nevertheless critiqued as part of his very claim to the greatest accolade of his time. Voice helps him to make this bid and in itself comprises an ambitious claim to the reader's speech in the face of the modern reader's silence. Only with the reader's acknowledgment through voicing, mentally or aloud, does voice exist in the full sense. Essentially the same holds for voice as for honor, for tragedy, and for immortality. In Faulkner, all imply each other, and all are hazardous claims to the highest cultural aspirations, but remain only aspirations without accommodation, the active acknowledgment of others.

I have implied that the present needs of Faulkner criticism converge with those of reader-oriented criticism. As the first chapter argues, literary immortality is continuous with the No to death that is on-going human life. That life depends upon the cultural dramas in which we supply each other the mutual lendings and furnishings of the power to exist. Reading condenses and illuminates this process. Reading Faulknerian tragedy does so doubly. By reflecting on Faulkner's tragic dramatization of such hazardous accommodations, I want to refresh and deepen our understanding of important themes whose shopworn appearance threatens them with critical neglect—or critical despair at treating what can seem, as Faulkner knew, worse than shopworn, merely sentimental pieties. Chief among Faulkner's own statements deserving a more careful rehearing is this: "The poet's voice need not merely be the record of man, it will be one of the props, the pillars to help him to endure and prevail" (*Essays, Speeches* 120). We can similarly revive a critical theme no less significant for its familiarity to Faulknerians: the necessity of the community to the very existence of individuals who nevertheless feel alienated from or vulnerable to it.

One anecdote helps to pinpoint the conflict involved in the accommodations of both immortality and human life. Faulkner once claimed that at the end of his legendary great-grandfather's life "the county raised a marble effigy which still stands" (*Letters* 212). In fact, the monument had been bought prospectively by the Old Colonel himself. The contradiction between the fact and Faulkner's account sums up his competing impulses: the hope of a lasting public recognition that would furnish him immortality and, replacing this hope or proudly outbidding it, a self-sufficient determination somehow to supply his own No to mortality.[4]

The writer creates out of a foreknowledge and hatred of death, to mark his "Kilroy was here" on the door of oblivion (*Essays, Speeches* 114, 143)—we have yet to grasp the amplitude of such passionate assertions by Faulkner. Faulkner's best-known and most comprehensive statement about the potency of engendering the No to death characteristically associates the mutual enunciation of the No, the necessary confirmation thereby of one's humanity, and the writer's overcoming of a potential vulnerability:

> To uplift man's heart; [that is the aim of all writers:] the ones who are trying to be artists, the ones who are trying to write simple entertainment, the ones who write to shock, and the ones who are simply escaping themselves and their own private anguishes.
>
> Some of us don't know that this is what we are writing for. Some of us will know it and deny it, lest we be accused and self-convicted and condemned of sentimentality, which people nowadays for some reason are ashamed to be tainted with; some of us seem to have curious ideas of just where the heart is located, confusing it with other and baser glands and organs and activities. But we all write for this one purpose.
>
> This does not mean that we are trying to change man, improve him, though this is the hope—maybe even the intention—of some of us. On the contrary, in its last analysis, this hope and desire to uplift man's heart is completely selfish, completely personal. He would lift up man's heart for his own benefit because in that way he can say No to death. He is saying No to death for himself by means of the hearts which he has hoped to uplift, or even by means of the mere base glands which he has disturbed to that extent where they can say No to death on their own account by knowing, realizing, having been told and believing it: *At least we are not vegetables because the hearts and glands capable of partaking in this excitement are not those of vegetables, and will, must, endure.*
>
> So he who, from the isolation of cold impersonal print, can engender this excitement, himself partakes of the immortality which he has engendered. Some day he will be no more, which will not matter then, because isolated and itself invulnerable in the cold print remains that which is capable of engendering still the old deathless excitement in hearts and glands whose owners and custodians are generations from even the air he breathed and anguished in; if it was capable once, he

24

knows that it will be capable and potent still long after there remains of
him only a dead and fading name. (*Essays, Speeches* 181–82)

The connection between potent immortality and tragedy, as literary genre or more-than-literary reality, runs deep in Faulkner's
thought. Accompanying it is the recurrent fear that his effort as an
artist was pointless, and this in turn is opposed by a lifelong preoccupation with survival, ranging from subtle resistance against fundamental unaccommodations of humanity to the open repudiation of
apocalypse in his speeches of the fifties.[5] Near the beginning of his
major period Faulkner stated that "the printed word that lasts over
centuries has for its skeleton tragedy or despair" (*Lion* 14). Near the
end of his career he declared that "man's immortality is that he faces a
tragedy he can't beat and he still tries to do something about it" (*Lion*
89). Immortality is sometimes an achieved result noted or pre-
dicted—tragic expressions have lasted, man will endure and prevail—and sometimes an effort and process alone—tragedy cannot be
beaten, but man is immortal because he tries, because the very effort
entails a recurrently revived No. Indeed, the nearly all-purpose
"proofs" of immortality Faulkner cited in his speeches and interviews
reflect the tremendous conflict in the human heart which is
Faulkner's. The conflict is between hope and despair, words that
resound through his writings. The hope of endurance is in fact built
upon despair, just as Faulkner, hopefully, implies that his own art
takes the materials of tragedy and despair as its "skeleton," since
these are the materials that last over centuries. Despair in its intensest
form in Faulkner sounds like nihilism, hope in its intensest form
sounds like firm belief, but fundamentally the contest is not that of
nihilism and belief but of empowering hope set against, and poised
upon, its potentially enervating opposite.

Although I will only briefly refer to the biographical dimension of
Faulkner's writing, those who know the biography will recall that
Faulkner learned on his own pulses what power and incapacitation
were as he enacted extremes of these conditions, swinging, especially
in his earliest years, from periodic inertia and shiftlessness to the
energy that propels his major achievements by lavishly staging and
resisting the threats to such power. For some readers it may matter
less whether the prose is "about" an embattled enduring and prevailing than that the mutually animating performances of Faulknerian
tragedy constitute the things themselves.

CHAPTER I

Reading and Performance:
Reproduction and Persons

> *To be* means *to communicate*. Absolute death (non-being) is the
> state of being unheard, unrecognized, unremembered. . . . To be
> means to be for another, and through the other, for oneself. . . .
> Monologue is finalized and deaf to the other's response, does not
> expect it and does not acknowledge in it any *decisive* force. . . .
> The single adequate form for *verbally expressing* authentic human
> life is the *open-ended dialogue.*
>
> Bakhtin, *Problems of Dostoevsky's Poetics*

Jonathan Culler's rallying cry, "beyond interpretation" accurately
marks a stage in the study of reading, but now needs to be directed at
the basic conception of reading itself. In our conception of reading,
we have gone hardly a step beyond interpretation, whether we seek
the conventions "dictating" particular interpretations or debunk interpretation as necessary chimera or celebrate subjectivism. Mave-
ricks outside the academy, such as Susan Sontag and, at times,
Roland Barthes, have for some time questioned or played scan-
dalously with the academic equation of reading with interpretation or
knowledge, but this equation nonetheless persists as academic
orthodoxy. The basic premise of hermeneutics, that the text is, first
of all, difficult to understand, guides both academic criticism and
teaching of reading. This premise has had the effect of depleting the
idea of performance, so that, for instance, the idea that poetic forms
act out their meaning has become a dead metaphor, seemingly innocuous, as in "This novel enacts Henry's distrust of abstractions."
Clearly enough, as Louise Rosenblatt has pointed out, poetic forms

26

can act nothing. Only persons can act and, as writers or readers, enact poetic forms and act through them. When such performance by the reader has been acknowledged, however, enactment is given a consistently reduced scope. Thus, many proponents of the newly "liberated" reader describe readers who are performing, creating, and transacting with various degrees of "freedom," but what these readers create, transact, and perform are interpretations.[1]

Jane Tompkins's "The Reader in History" tellingly argues against the notion that *criticism* is simply equivalent to interpretation by showing how recent, and institutionally based, is the idea. Equally telling is Tompkins's confusion of reader and critic, since, her title notwithstanding, her aim is to give criticism, not reading, a renovated understanding by returning it to the ancient rhetorical tradition in which discourse is power. If we would indeed understand reading by a recovery of this tradition, we must first abandon the effective equation of reading with criticism/interpretation, since this persistent identification has simultaneously served the academy's power and purposes while obscuring the broader cultural empowerment comprehended in reading. A key term for beginning to undo the equation is *voice*.[2]

Current debates over reading can influentially portray voice as merely an issue of the author's cognitive authority because for a long time our profession has assumed "the reader" to be a cognitive entity. This reader's voicing, vocal performance, of the text has been considered almost wholly a supplementary means to experiential knowledge or has been ignored entirely. The question of voice forms the principal current means by which the more inclusive issue of reading as performance is at once ambiguously raised and domesticated by an academic criticism preoccupied with cognition. By attending to performance here, I will seek to move toward a conceptual foundation for the reunderstanding of reading as an element of humanly creative culture. In other words, my aim is to grasp reading's *distinctiveness* from the academic goal of knowledge in such a way that we can then properly seek knowledge about it.

The literary text is currently understood as a sort of puzzle or mystery case whose hermeneutic solution by readers is declared feasible by some and radically problematic by others. From the viewpoint of the academy, the motive for the emphasis on reading as interpretation is of course benign and valid. The conception is useful in developing students' powers of analysis or in teaching them to demystify

27

the ideological confidence games of society. As long as we consider reading simply or mainly a means to a ratiocinative end, such worthy aims will monopolize our attention. But there are powerful reasons to believe that reading is much more. The model of the text I will propose is that of a script or score to be performed by readers in an enacted creation and regeneration of persons fundamental to human being. Interpretation enters into this performance as one constituent, but only as one constituent. Thus the proposed model is both an additional paradigm and a corrective and inclusive one.

Accordingly, the *reproduction* of my chapter title is meant to wedge professional discussion over from the mesmerizing question of referentiality, and "reproduction" of reality in that sense, to consider a broad cultural analogy between the motives of reading and sexual recreation. *Performance,* in a similar vein, will mean more than "performative" does in J. L. Austin and the deconstructive critique of his distinction, and it will have a more theatrical sense than it does in Kenneth Burke's dramatism. I mean by it the actual enactment of reading roles that the individual takes on even in private reading, since the individual, as Burke says, is a "corporate we" (*Attitudes* 264), an internalized social multiplicity of voices engaged in a complex inward and outward dialogue—what M. M. Bakhtin terms "dialogical heteroglossia." Consequently the concept *person,* indicating the social nexus of reproduction and performance, is not a synonym for the individual, nor is *personal* equivalent to what Gerald Graff has called the "New Sensibility" (31–32, 138).

If in its moments of critique this chapter accentuates certain limitations of deconstruction, it is partly because this criticism has influentially investigated performatives and voice in such a way that these concepts appear to be enfeebled for the examination we will undertake here. But my primary point is that the limitations I identify are symptomatic of our current general professional situation.

I

What are the grounds for reunderstanding reading?

Gender criticism has provided a significant incentive and example, even if it too has remained circumscribed by limiting interpretive preoccupations. Gender criticism makes it undeniable that readers are persons who can be outraged, in, for example, being solicited by an academically prestigious text to assume a sensibility unacceptable or offensive to women. Some time ago, Walker Gibson and Wayne Booth gave notice that there are some roles that a given reader will refuse to play, but gender criticism has given this insight the edge of really personal and not simply theoretical outrage. What has been outraged is precisely an individual or collective *person* (here, a woman or women), not an epistemological subjectivity or a set of reading conventions.[3]

Second, by one of its characteristic themes, feminist scholarship can alert us that what is involved in this outrage, or its possibility, is a civilized but genuine general struggle over the means of reproduction—that is, the prepotent shaping of others after one's own image.[4] A specifically human enterprise, this reproduction is the personal impulse that is coinstrumental with the continuation of culture through *its* attempted self-replication over generations. In biology, prepotence refers to the greater capacity of one entity (individual, strain, etc.) among competing entities to transmit its characteristics to offspring. The feminist problematic spotlights the distinctively human counterpart.

The third related point to note here is that the institutional conventions that position people in literary as in extraliterary sexual roles must be activated by flesh-and-blood readers in a performance, a role taking, and that this performative activation in itself is crucial. It may be bracketed off methodologically from one's consideration, to serve the ends of formalism or structuralism, but the methodological brackets bid fair to become rigid and would-be permanent boundaries (e.g., Culler, *Poetics* 29–30, 258). In a specific act of reading, the reader's performance puts at stake a complex set of personal values that variously counteract, reinforce, and transmute the specifically gendered ones. When a feminist reader is affronted or delighted by a perceived reading role, a larger network of personal and interpersonal commitments is activated and affected than that of gender. The result of this interplay of values is thus not simply describable in gender terms. It is important to try to distinguish what is gender-specific, but it is most valuable to do this in a more general dialectical framework.[5]

In pursuing a general social framework for literary study, however, much contemporary criticism has tended to obscure individual distinctiveness with concepts like Stanley Fish's reading communities. Or else, concentrating like David Bleich and Norman Holland on the particularly subjective, criticism has lacked a persuasive means for bridging to the social dimension, which it nonetheless recognizes to some degree. In the first case, the individual person must be smuggled into an impersonal notion of society; in the second, society must be smuggled into an asocial notion of the individual person. We need a schema that inherently articulates psyche with society, changes with continuities, in a dynamic process of making. In the current fascination of criticism with how interpretations, texts, or readers are constituted psychologically or socially, there is concealed the embracing question of constituting human being. To deal with it takes more than an epistemology, more than what Steven Mailloux has called constitutive hermeneutics. We require a pragmatics of constitutive social relations.

To understand reading, we need a conception of persons which is psychosocial or anthropological. Our point of departure is an important body of thought represented by such thinkers as Burke, Bakhtin, and a third not yet mentioned, Clifford Geertz—none alone wholly adequate to our purposes but together richly suggestive. From Burke we take, and refurbish, the idea of reading/writing as in an important sense a single symbolic action with two components. In its simplest form the concept of symbolic action addresses the question: what does the work *do* for the writer, and what does it do for the reader? The question considers literature as a means for writer and reader simultaneously to understand and to "cope with" the world and act in it. From Burke's key conception, dramatism, we take the reminder that "person" (from *persona*) is fundamentally a dramatistic term, or, as I would presently stress, a performative one. As does Burke implicitly, the first dictionary definition of *person* further reminds us at the outset that person is a diacritical value concept: an entity distinguished from a thing or lower animal (e.g., Burke, *Language* 52–53). Like Bakhtin, with his increasingly influential concept of dialogism, and like Burke, Geertz is in the tradition of George Herbert Mead and Lev Vygotsky, which conceives persons as the products of social exchange—specifically, as in Mead, role playing.

From an evolutionary perspective, Geertz emphasizes, moreover, that the biological unfinishedness and malleability of human beings makes such cultural completion a necessity.[6] The implications of Geertz's emphasis are large, although the point can be stated, or taken, simply. Typically, critics have helped to turn the idea that "man is the role-playing animal" into a routine observation by mak-

30

ing it a staple of thematic interpretation, while they have shielded the act of reading from anything like its full impact. Geertz's perspective serves as a counter to Holland's idea that the individual's interpretive replication of an unchanging core identity is all that is pertinent to the activity of reading. Above all Geertz provides us with the broadest grounds for understanding art as a special and illuminating case of the cultural reproduction of persons.

In contrast to the structuralist view that the reader is merely the site of reading conventions, Geertz's view of personality also counters the simple wholesale reduction of interactive persons to either cultural system or social structure, since the "personality system" is "indispensable to the other two in the sense that without personalities and culture there would be no social system and so on around the roster of logical possibilities. But this interdependence and interpenetration is a very different matter from reducibility, which would mean that the important properties and processes of one class of system could be theoretically *derived* from our theoretical knowledge of one or both of the other two" (145–46).

Over a decade ago, Geertz counseled other anthropologists to study and adapt the advances in interpretation made by literary critics (above all, Burke). Now that Geertz and others like him have enriched what they have borrowed with anthropological applications and extensions, it is fitting that we continue the dialogue by borrowing back our own in its augmented form and expanding it further by refraction once more through literary criticism.[7] Nothing in the views represented by Burke, Bakhtin, and Geertz is new anymore. What is important is that their combined implications be drawn for a sufficiently broad-based understanding of reading as a reflection of and contribution to human being.

To sum up these implications provisionally, human beings are biologically incomplete and, without culture, helpless animals who become capable persons, and *continue* to become capable persons, by enacting personae selected by imitation from the repertoire offered by their culture and social structure. But the repertoire exists only within the specific varying performances of others, imprinted with their particular styles and "accents." All, then, are engaged in concrete, mutually shaping enactments in a complex dialogue with others as well as with their own already acquired internalized roles. One simultaneously becomes and influences others to become a confederation of persons by "trying on," selecting, and habituating oneself to roles.

In this actively seeking, evaluative, and self-defensive process of becoming and reproduction, no one identity, "voice," can be duplicated exactly. All are handed on to another, to the degree they are, in forms transmuted by idiosyncratic accents. As in sexual reproduction, identity in its transmission is mediated and thereby modified by another.

Reading, as part of the dyad writing/reading, is a performance of persons continuous with this reproductive, transforming enactment. In effect, current theory, controlled by the cognitive issue, looks at the question of how faithful the transfer can be. Or else it unmasks the informing cultural-social institutions without appreciating that the institutions are not only powerless but nonexistent unless people incorporate them as a repertoire to simultaneously create and reproduce persons. Specific institutions, languages, conventions—none can act or exist except by and in the persons who must act a specific script in order to exist. For interpretation, the *personal* dimension tends to be merely something that gets in the way, to be either reduced to institutions or understood only as a quirky eccentricity that (distressingly or delightfully) prevents epistemological fidelity. But we cannot thus dispose of an absolute human necessity of self-creation. The overemphasis on interpretation in the critical conception of reading myopically blurs the large drama—the human making of persons—that reading/writing wonderfully condenses.

The sense in contemporary criticism that reading has immense implications is, I agree, correct. On the other hand, if we wish to check the current confusion of the *study* of reading with its subject, reading per se, then it will help if we do not on any basis, including that offered here, pretend that reading is the essence and revealer of everything, as certain critical enthusiasms strongly imply. Reading is one thing people do, in some cultures, that mutually illuminates some things but not everything people do in all cultures just to be human, just to exist at all.

Just to exist at all. That is what we are talking about, and although it is genuinely portentous to recognize this, there are many things we, and all living things, must do and have just to be at all. Each of them is necessary but not sufficient.

Just to be at all, however, needs to be stressed, because as Geertz notes, the false assumption is widespread even among the educated that without their cultural scripts human beings would still be human beings of some diminished sort—very much like clever apes, still viable creatures. Geertz, however, has spelled out the quite contrary implications of our current understanding of evolution and present human cultural existence. Prehuman beings in evolving culture willy-nilly invented themselves *as* human and evolved a dependency on culture in order *to be*. Without culture, human beings would be not some sort of clever apes but, in Geertz's phrase, "basket cases" (49). Human being is not possible without culture, is incapacitated without it, would vanish without it as a *lusus naturae*.

Because our species does not have the elaborate and much more complete biological programs that other species do, we simply cannot function unless something gives us the intricate set of marching orders which even the simplest organism has. Culture, that network of symbols, is that substitute "program," though for our purposes, and I think for most, it will help to distinguish cultural enabling directions from biological ones if we call them scripts or scores. Other "higher" species of course must learn much, but human beings have an extraordinarily high requirement to cobble together capacities through and from symbolic forms. Other species are innately empowered just to live, in ways we are not at all. Our human strengths are intertwined with this weakness.

Three features of this odd strength have everything to do with reading: our flexible capacity to entertain possible roles, either (rarely) as wholes or in bits and pieces borrowed from others; our complementary capacity to commit ourselves inflexibly to a role with a tenacity that other species reserve for matters of life or death; and our necessity to exercise capacities in order to have them. All three help to distinguish reading significantly from interpretation or from critical analysis *of* reading.

To consider the third feature: Since our capacities are so little underwritten innately and somatically, we must repeatedly "write" them. Only in their reenactment and reexperiencing can they be maintained, and our lives with them. The reproduction we have been discussing is thus not simply the more or less unconscious transmission of our personae to others by means of a remarkable mutual influencing. It is simultaneously the re-production of oneself in repeatedly exercising what one has assimilated and is assimilating. In human life, it is "use it or lose it." The repetitiousness of human life—of habit, communal ritual, convention, drudgery—is not the repetition of a programed behavior, in the respect that a program precedes some behavior or activity and will still exist unimpaired if

33

the behavior is not repeated. Human exercise of capacity is repetition of a script that indicates and maintains the very power scripted, and it maintains the script in existence as well. If, as Schiller wrote, it is characteristically human to play, to exercise abilities "for no purpose" in play and art, this behavior is not in fact a Kantian purposefulness without purpose. It is one revealing manifestation of the requirement for biologically incapacitated creatures to become capable by always exercising capacity, if only for the satisfaction of *being* capable. To feel that capacity is not just satisfying; it is satisfying because it is, broadly speaking, necessary.

To follow an old tradition, we may call this constant possibility of not being at all, death. Human beings are given an absolute biological mandate to fashion and reproduce themselves culturally by an ever-precarious enactment as persons. This is human life. Human death can thus take several forms as these enactments decline, fail, or become self-defeating, and the apprehension of any of these personal fatalities can impel a counterstrategy of reproduction, in Faulkner's phrase, an effort to "say No to death." Doing so in writing/reading can be a way of displaying capacity, power, in the face of one's always-possible incapacity. To say such a No is not just bravado; in that very exercise of power there is the negation, since it is precisely in the exercise that one *is* capable.

The post-Kantian realization that knowledge is not just given but taken has had considerable impact on literary criticism, especially the criticism of reading. Even more true is that for us capability is not given but must be taken; the real absorption by criticism of this realization has yet to occur.

The idea that writing attempts the reproduction of identity in defiance of death is not new. Its major reference point in our culture, Shakespeare's sonnets, alternate between pleading that the beloved patron reproduce himself and continue his identity by siring children and covertly and overtly assuring him that by the patron's inspiration, the poet's lines, even in default of lineage, will keep the patron alive: "Neither marble nor the gilded monuments / Will outlast this powerful rhyme." But if the poet is thus the patron's mate, the patron is also the writer's stand-in, for Shakespeare, like Keats, Woolf, and Faulkner after him, also subscribes forthrightly to the ancient ideal of preserving himself in his art, harking back to Horace: "I have erected a monument more lasting than bronze. . . . I shall not entirely die" (*Odes* 3.30). Woolf, identifying the writer's patron with

34

his or her audience, presses a further identification between writer and audience as "twins indeed, one dying if the other dies, one flourishing if the other flourishes" (292).

The sensibility-bearing signs of rite and art solicit in a relatively systematic way the innate capacity for performative translation of other valued sensibilities into the individual participant's repertoire. Seen in these terms, interpretations, articulable or not, are only rough indicators of a set of personal capacities actually educed in readers through, and only through, the acting out of sensibility-symbols. Criticism here has the task of identifying these capacities in a given case and the artistic means for concretely proposing their elicitation to readers.[8]

Note once more the crucial difference. Merely designating an interpretation suffices to fulfill the goal of interpretation. But designating personal capacities, no matter how subtly, no more establishes them in the reader's aggregate of valued powers to act than merely knowing that jogging can increase certain physical capacities suffices to create them. Someone wishing to have these physical capacitites must actually jog to produce them. Similarly, one must actually and repeatedly exercise personal capacities in order for them to exist. That exercise, that shaping performance, is not reducible to either prescriptions for or descriptions of it. Criticism and pedagogy talk about; reading does. Criticism may arrive at interpretation; reading *actively* entertains the possibility of modifying the audience's sensibility or reinforcing it.

Readers entertain the possibility by actually trying out and auditioning for the role of reader which the text as score or script implicitly offers through the rhetoric of voice, structure, character, and thematic focus. Reading is performatively axiological, since one actively tests what one is willing to enact, even as an audition.[9] Thus one auditions the role scripted by the text as well as auditions for it: the text tries out for a part in the reader. The reader's own unique repertoire of personae, which is bounded and made possible by the assimilated resources of the cultural and historical moment, enables him or her to accept or reject, wholly or in part, a sensibility to be adopted/adapted for the time of reading, and perhaps beyond it. These resources are not merely and in a given instance may not be primarily literary. How much of these resources will be what the culture customarily calls literary at a given historical time, with a given text, and with a given reader's personal situation, is simply incalculable. This is not to say that discerning the contribution of literary conventions to the reading experience is unimportant. It is to say that toting these up and calling them reading is rather like reciting the American Constitution and calling that the practice of American law.

For all these reasons, critics and teachers of reading might well pay renewed attention to the features of texts that most directly engage performance—and repeated performance.[10]

II

Against this backdrop of reading as a cultural praxis, we can now distinguish our current academic practices and the initiatives involved in the concept of reading performance more sharply.

When Paul de Man claims that "it is not only possible but necessary to read *Julie* in this way, as putting in question the referential possibility of 'love' and as revealing its figural status" or, more sweepingly, that "no reading is conceivable in which the question of its truth or falsehood is not primarily involved," he is erecting not only his professional analytic procedures but his professional identity as an ontological essence (*Allegories* 200; Foreword xi). The power of the profession's impulse to arrogate legitimate reading to itself is demonstrated when an extremely able critic thus goes counter to his stated principles and establishes *reading* as a proper name safe from "inconceivable" impropriety. De Man takes on the exemplary role not so much of Reader as of Reading, in a sense of performance which his discourse even more than Derrida's suppresses and marginalizes. To say that this perfected group self-portrait is attractive to many in the profession is an understatement. It is an aspiration to rehearse, try out, try out for, absorb. (A more particular brief discussion of deconstruction is available in Appendix A.)

Deconstructionists and "traditionalists" are engaged in a family quarrel within our shared ideology of academic life—that is, our committed role of one-concerned-with-searching-for-knowledge, positively or critically. The question one has learned to ask automatically in the constant practice of teaching and study within this ideology is some polite or blunt version of "How do you know?" If everyone basically agrees that reading means the search for knowledge, that it is essentially the same as our professional activity, then it is reasonable to think that "How do I know?" will always be a significant question for any true reader. Seen in this way, reading is not only cognition but epistemology.

For those with an insatiable relish for arguments of and with skepticism, this founding portrait of the true reader/reading will seem self-evidently true. But for those who can seriously conceive that there are other issues in reading besides knowledge which we can, quite professionally, seek knowledge about, that furtive self-delineation within reading will have to go; it is no longer very interesting in the way it is intended to be. To deny that the act of reading is necessarily best understood in epistemological terms is not to say that one is uninterested in knowing exactly what readers are up to. In general, what they are up to is power—the basic cultural practice of securing, by exercising, the power to exist. This is not to ignore cognition but to place it. In the more inclusive perspective, reading cognition and epistemology are understood as existing among other performances furnishing humanity with existence. And therefore cognitive questions will not automatically have a privileged place as we consider the enabling possibilities of role enactment within the variousness of reading.

One can in fact read in several ways, and in several ways at once, with no necessity of seeing contradiction and epistemological gaps in this multiple functioning. In daily life I can and usually do pay attention to several things at once, with widely varying degrees of conscious focus. Just as consciousness is multiple in daily life, just as a skilled pianist or conductor can play different parts simultaneously, I can play not just two but several kinds of readers and reading as I read along at several layers of consciousness. If I am, say, captivated by the interaction of a novel's characters I can focus on that while carrying along or gliding past a subsidiary global awareness of what seems an important thematic point, which I don't stop to work out, though I may dimly sense it may have to do with analytic understanding of the characters. I may carry it along, along with, perhaps, my feel for the prose texture, my murmuring or subvocalizing of the text's moving sonority, my sense of the possibility of being irritated or affronted or amused by some idea or by some role into which the novel seems to want to cast its readers but which I don't actually want to take on or "stop for" now and toward which I take this metarole of "subliminally sensing a possibility" while I am preoccupied by the characters. And so on. Or I *may* stop and focus on any of these other levels or systematically on as many as I can encompass at once.

In contrast to such options of empowerment, one representative version of the deconstructive notion of reading describes a different power, an inescapable double movement in the "structural necessity" that requires a switching back and forth between the "text's dominance" and the "reader's dominance" (Culler 72). In a related context, the more general demystification of cultural rhetoric, although healthy in many respects, makes it easy to assume that all rhetorical effect is a malevolent tyranny of Orwellian mind control. The reader-as-interpreter has been liberated from the "tyranny" of the author and established in his own imperium by those who conceive reading as a zero-sum game wherein to give readers their due one must ignore or categorically oppose the author's invitation of a particular readership. That is, according to this view we try *not* to audition for the roles offered by the text but simply to unmask these personae. Thus we simply persist in being what we are, and what we all are in such a reading orientation is a clone of one unbudgeable ratiocinative identity.

Present criticism often alternates, even in the same critical statement, between seeing the literary text as a dangerous power and seeing it as something for the reader to overwhelm. The relationship between text and reader is characterized as dominance and submission. A good example is Terry Castle's fine recent discussion of *Clarissa,* which demonstrates the interpretive pliability of Richardson's novel and yet deploys language like this: "*Clarissa* repeatedly *strips* us of our complacent faith in its own representational illusion. The result is that we are *forced* to revise our concept of the text itself" (152, my emphasis). Contemporary criticism is full of textually stripped and forced readers who are yet declared to be prepotent interpreters, violated Clarissas who are yet formidably intact undoers of the text. The reduction of reading possibilities to issues of cognitive force and dominance is a double movement of reading with a vengeance.

The subject of discourse as power is too complex and important to be thus simplified. What is needed is a study of writing/reading in terms of the dialectical possibilities lying between, at one extreme, the sheer sharing of potency through exercising certain capacities and, at the other, the imposition of a tyrannical power. For even what seems intended as an imposition of power by a writer may be *taken* by certain readers as a transmission of capacitation to them, for example, if the readers identify themselves with the writer's purpose vis-à-vis some other implied audience.

One element of reading variability only touched on so far deserves a few more words, since the frequent reminder given by contemporary critics that reading is a learned activity forgets to consider that human being is a learned status in which childhood learning sets an ineluctable keynote. Recalling Faulkner's Joe Christmas can help us to remember.

Since the cultural scripts that establish our humanity can be written and assimilated in astonishingly various ways, to be human is in an important sense to be some specific kind of human being. To be at all is to be relatively idiosyncratic in certain key ways, at the level of the individual as well as at the level of one group in comparison to others. We all came in at different times and places in the ongoing cultural conversation; we catch only parts of it and catch some parts and inflections when we are at more malleable stages. There is no one holy of holies where one can go to assimilate an unchanging single entity, the Culture, all at once, though certain rites of passage, such as formal schooling, attempt to provide something like the feel of having done this.

Rhetoric, as Kenneth Burke says, is the attempt to induce cooperation among all the resulting relative idiosyncrasies. Ideology, in Alvin Gouldner's sense, is another name for this regularizing, and the schoolteaching of reading conventions is another. But rhetoric, or its cognates, always both powerfully draws upon and is frustratable by the idiosyncracy of what Gouldner calls the paleosymbolic level (224–26).

The result is that reading will always be *readings*. Reading is first shaped paleosymbolically, for most of us; that is, it is a learning woven into the earliest learned relationships with those whom sociology bleakly calls "significant others." It is bound up with the first persons who become "positively" or "negatively" part of us and empower us to function, the parents or siblings whose laps we sit on, whose bosoms or mustaches or knobby knees impress us in ways we forget but never lose, along with their personal ways of speaking and acting out the stories they read or tell with voice, gesture, demeanor—all of which the child reacts to or against within the context of their general attention, affection, abstraction, scorn, or abuse. Even for those whose sole learning experience with reading is in school, reading comes from childhood trailing clouds of paleosymbolism, and since in this case there is no possible single Wordsworthian home, neither is there anything we can absolutely declare as *the* way to read. The paleosymbolic continues, of course, in the individual associations certain reading styles, characters, etc., accumulate for us privately or within a small group.

(I am speaking here only peripherally of the variability of interpretation per se, though this is understandably a prime concern for teachers seeking to establish a justifiable authority to interpret. Able students who have internalized "reading-as-cognition," at least for classroom purposes, can vary their interpretations and ways of interpreting with comparative ease, once they discern what the teacher wants, as indicated neatly in the question "Is there a text in this class?" made famous by Stanley Fish.)

One can thus gesture toward the dimensions of formative reading that have been institutionally marginalized and can recall that according to the deconstructionist maxim such supplements are dangerous to claims for centrality, especially when the margin turns out to be larger by several orders of magnitude than what it supposedly merely frames.

III

What we observe in contemporary criticism, then, is a magnification of what we might call the academic reader: someone preoccupied with the issue of knowledge and the attainment of professional mastery, someone inattentive to the character of these concerns as roles (in this case, professional ones), someone with a regulating interest (no matter how legitimate for certain purposes) in defining reading in conformity with these preoccupations. By making the interpretive component of reading all there is of reading, we academics go forth and multiply ourselves according to a constricted notion of our professional being. In so doing, we are in competition with common readers (as Samuel Johnson and Virginia Woolf named them) in their influence on writers and with writers who attempt to re-create scripted versions of their usual and provisionally enacted identities in their readers.

An academic notion of reading which is, as Huck Finn would say, so dismal regular and decent, is not only unnecessary but fails of exactly the rigor it claims. What we offer is analysis and heuristics (or criticism), and these are important enough to be designated as such. Analysis will have to learn to justify itself without assuming its coincidence with the inherently various human activity of reading, as has been excessively plausible in academic criticism. With this procedural modesty the way is open for greater clarity about what purposes we conceive for a particular analysis or theory, and we can ask better questions about the perusal of certain texts within certain settings and consider how particular features of texts invite different readings from within the body of readers qualified to do them. The myth of the "competent reader," which surreptitiously posits omnicompetence, can then yield to the consideration, "Competent reader for what purpose and within what context? Competent for what kind of reading?"

The personal quality of the literary experience has long been bracketed by academic critics, according to an unspoken critical protocol that we will take for granted the in some sense undeniably personal character of reading. Otherwise stated, *for the purposes of interpretation,* the enabling postulate is that our experience of the personality scripted by the text is sufficiently shared that we can consider it a constant in order to attend primarily to interpretive matters. This is obviously a legitimate postulate.

But similarly, to attend to the reading activity I indicate, we must assume as our postulate an interpretation, in the words of *Absalom, Absalom!,* "true enough" for our purposes. The arguments over interpretive validity have much to teach us about both the interpretive moment and the particular level we may want to declare "true enough" in a given analysis of personal performance. Every endeavor of thought must hold constant one or more elements in the mental field so as to examine others reciprocally contingent upon them. Interpretive discussion postulates common personal performance. Similarly, analysis of the reading performance postulates common interpretation, or at least its possibility sufficient for a given case.

This book seeks neither to refine further nor to resolve the epistemological dispute over reading nor to follow the philosopher Richard Rorty in scoffing at it as a belated mimicry of an expiring philosophical contention (155–56). Correspondingly, the explanatory trope of performance should not be conceived as all-embracing, totalizing. How limited it would be, after all, to consider all we do and are as *merely* within the province of theater (or ritual, or fiction), which itself is only one aspect of human life. The circle of attention I invoke is drawn around more than human life, for a smaller circle often does lead the inquirer unconsciously to take some one aspect of human life as the key to it all. The large circumference calls attention to a remarkable difference between our species and the others and, within this comparative context, to our species' defining feature: its self-creation. I know of no better figure for this than performance, in both senses of *to do* and *to enact roles,* performing (intentionally or not) for others and for the others we have assimilated who are us, and in the process both exercising what others script for us and presenting to others implicit scripts to enact in turn, without end. The evolutionary perspective on this constant exchange helps to elucidate that human performance is not only a cognition or a deed but a self-creation and reproduction finally irreducible to any of its constituents.

At a minimum, there are three related, mutually illuminating, yet distinguishable subjects of study deriving from the preceding discussion of reading within the dyad writing/reading: (1) the text as the writer's symbolic action, performance; (2) the text as a script or score proposing certain reading performances; (3) actual readers reading the text as part of the general enactment of their lives. Clearly, the aims and methods of the criticism of reading as performance require more extensive formulation. This chapter so far has sought to establish the credentials of this dialogistic criticism. Now it is time to return specifically to Faulkner and the first two topics named above, the second of which will claim our primary attention. The third topic defines the limit toward which this study moves.

IV

Our acts make human being. We make persons by selectively emulating, impersonating, others. These ideas secure the basis for shifting our attention to literature as performance and acknowledgment. The inclusive performance category of acknowledgment encompasses reading-knowledge and the many other specific enactments by specific readers. And with Faulkner, any performance—whether represented thematically, displayed as author's tour de force, or enacted in reading—may put in play several interlocked capacities that both

42

support and baffle each other. As a result, this book will follow the development of Faulknerian tragedy through several striking turns. But in brief, this is the dialectic before us: the process in which culturally furnished enactments and capabilities mutually enable as well as mutually subvert one another.

Since my present purpose is not to survey actual readings empirically, in all their varying accommodations, I will control our detailed study of reading performance by critically reconstructing the text as the author's symbolic action, which seeks particular kinds of revivifying reading enactment. The act of understanding is one capacity that Faulkner's symbolic action of course seeks. But it seeks understanding itself, as a life-giving No to death to which fine listeners and fine poets help each other. The performative capacity of understanding—knowing—is involved, on what we might now call humanly constitutive grounds, in a tragic dialectic exemplified in Mr. Compson's troubled relation to Quentin: Because of its very importance, *knowing* other persons can become a fixation that blocks the different particular forms of acknowledgment others may need and solicit and so can depersonalize others. Or—in the formula of the dialectic I have outlined—because knowing suffuses and enables a host of other human capabilities and is likewise dependent on them, it may interfere with them and so expose and compound their fragility. And the reverse is true: other needs and capabilities can interfere with knowing. But since this reverse case has had plentiful critical attention, though on epistemological grounds alone, my discussion will subordinate it.

The capacity of voice also involves a particularly complex combination of strengths and attendant fragilities. Voice is profoundly linked with knowing, since it is the primary means through which we learn and exercise language, the symbol system enabling knowledge. By the same token, as living speech complementary to hearing, it is a major means by which we both transformingly absorb the aspects of others who become ourselves and project the marked intonations of our own distinctive being. At once opening onto "constitutive" questions of knowledge, personal distinctiveness, and personal otherness, voice opens onto the terrain of Faulknerian tragedy.

More specifically, among the diverse acts of acknowledging Faulkner, as noted before, one will claim our attention more than others: voicing Faulkner's prose, either mentally, subvocally, or aloud. Vocalization of Faulkner's writing is a potentially important part of the reading experience because, first, literal recitation is what Burke would call the "perfection" of performative reading (which is not a way of saying it's necessary). That is, it serves as a synecdoche for the elements of reading performance, in terms of their extreme, most fully developed tendencies. Voicing, to put it another way, highlights the performative nature per se of the cognitions, emotions, and attitudes reading activates. For dramatistically to consider the "perfection" of reading is to consider it as if done on a stage. But to consider Faulknerian tragedy in this way is to be reminded constantly not only that it is an act but that it is a fraught activity, since (to give the simplest example) pleasurably sounding out his prose encounters its exhausting complexity. Faulkner can be both enticingly speakable and forbiddingly unspeakable. Mentally or orally enacting this and other doubleness concretely vivifies in us Faulkner's embattled utterance, the risk of attempting both eloquence and tragedy in a modern environment, as well as the potential conflict in acknowledging persons both as distinctive beings and as complex assimilations of others.

Voice as contingent performance keys into Faulknerian tragedy as a contingent act. This interconnection leads to the second general reason for the prominence voice will have here: literally and figuratively, it will be an indispensable bridge between important tragic themes and the reading enactments that variously realize these in our experience and make us liable to their consequences. It will encompass, for example, thematically pertinent Faulknerian strategies of recruiting the reader's body, such as overloading the sensorium to produce an inner audition that houses the transitory voice. And voice will provide for the quasi-oral conventions of Faulkner's discourse, as in the discussion of transcriptive conventions in Chapter 6.

In the following chapters, then, we will be concerned primarily with the performances of and in Faulknerian tragedy constitutive of human being. This emphasis follows generally from the concerns expressed in the preceding discussion. But the emphasis also follows from Faulknerian tragedy itself as a meditation on human being as a process at once strong and paradoxically fragile, or fragile and paradoxically strong, subject to loss but, like Cecilia Farmer's name scratched on the pane of glass to be spoken evocatively by a stranger, potentially open to an active reception that will recover and preserve it: "*Listen, stranger; this was myself: this was I*" (*Requiem* 261–62). I noted that because personal existence is not a given but consists of capacities that must be reachieved and maintained, both mortality and the active negation of mortality are potentials of every moment, so that human life is in this respect a recurrent "as I lay dying" countered by a No to death. (Mr. Compson, weary of this process, imagines a lost simplicity in which heroic figures were "distinct, uncomplex . . . loving once and dying once" [Absalom 89].) To consider Faulkner's death-preoccupied, death-resistant writing as a symbolic action of immortality is to consider a powerful element and entailment of his tragic art. To examine his invitation to perform, his "Listen, stranger," is to do the same. The possibility of preserving another, and so ourselves, in our enactments can be a condition of artistic immortality because it is a condition of life.

It is thus as a key principle of tragic symbolic action that Faulkner sets a strong example of voice for our emulative performance. He does so comprehensively, in theme, style, character, structure, and conventions. The oral conventions, I have just instanced. The theme, put briefly, is the importance and difficulty of both speech and silence. The distinctive style accentuates enactable speech registers from rural vernacular to ceremonious sonority, and concomitantly, The Sound and the Fury, As I Lay Dying, and Absalom, Absalom! feature characters who in the main are voices. More exactly, they appear as scripts for the reader's actual voicing, since what these works seem to envision is a hybrid of drama and novel somewhat anticipated in Faulkner's apprentice closet drama The Marionettes and in a different form made explicit again in Requiem for a Nun. The scriptlike presentation of the characters is indicated not only by the stylistic invitation to speak their voices and minds for them but also by the fact that each novel is constituted as a sequence of notably discrete virtual enunciations (Benjy, Quentin . . . ; Darl, Cora . . . ; Rosa Coldfield, Mr. Compson . . .). These are as much like contrapuntally arranged collections of parts in a drama as a novelistic narration.

Moreover, it will become clear that Faulkner accentuates the exercise of mental or oral voice in reading by tacitly proposing various allocations of power between author and speaking reader to complete the novels as literary tragedies, insofar as completion is traditionally understood in "Aristotelian" terms to be requisite to a tragic effect. To put this another way, the issue of closure is variously treated in terms of plot structure and voice during Faulkner's major phase.

We now arrive at a last, fundamental point: the sense in which the author's or text's enactment of power, as in Faulkner's formidable voice, exists only in the reader's performance. To some this may seem obvious, but I am not so sure that it is, and it has an implication that defies deep-rooted assumptions and practices.

The best way for me to preclude a misunderstanding on this score is to examine the response one helpful reader of my manuscript made. Agreeing that the idea of the audience's acknowledgment through various performances was important and that the manuscript convincingly explicated Faulkner's tragic No to death, he pointed out, with a distinction as revealing as it is witty, that Faulkner's No to death does not require the audience to sing along; following the bouncing ball is enough. To begin with the simplest foreseeable misconception, it is indeed not necessary habitually to read Faulkner aloud, literally. (I will argue that at times this is how Faulkner's text seeks to be read, but not as a simple act.) To take up the more serious implication: we are discussing literature as the mutual conveyance of power, which is to say a complex collaboration that, for any number of reasons, may not occur. Examining this contingent cooperation requires that we repeatedly shift our perspective from one end of the collaborative axis to the other, now examining the text in terms of the author's action (Faulkner's claim to tragic immortality) and now in terms of the reader's possible fulfillment of this claim. The metaphor of the bouncing ball, offering a reader's perspective, describes a supposed nonperformative situation of merely observing and following an action being performed for us in and by the text itself. But even if mere observation is meant, this situation is impossible, as noted before: texts per se do not act. Only persons act. From this reading end of the axis, as readers look at the printed page, effectively there is not even a bouncing ball unless a determinate reader or act of reading will have it bounce, by mentally activating the appropriate shared cultural conventions. The ball too must be put in play by a reading performance. If readers observe a bouncing ball, it is because they have actually performed what they observe.

On the other hand, if the bouncing ball represents not an activity supposedly done independently by the text but the textual cues for performance, then the statement means that it is enough for readers to follow these cues. But if cues are indeed followed, then following simply is performing them. Performing them, if you like, at a minimal level, as a proto-performance. But especially if, to stay with our metaphor, the ball is really bouncing—the cues of Faulkner's No are perceived as strong—this reading is an enactment. (And in this regard, it makes no difference whether readers believe they find or only ascribe the cues they follow.)

As I will do here, we can try to reconstruct the text as the author's symbolic action and so treat it as if we caught it in the act of being made. To consider literature as a hazarded cooperation, we must do so. But in effect, once the text is written and published, Faulkner does not perform unless another person, his reader, performs, in an impersonation of Faulkner (or an impersonation of Faulkner's textual impersonation). This is why I discuss voice by using such formulations as "speaking and thus hearing" Faulkner's prose. I mean that there is nothing to hear unless the reader at least mentally and minimally enacts by following cues. Such reading is not automatic. Some readers, it is clear, do not read this way, or do so only so sporadically that the voice is not really "there" for them. Or else it is only a vague barrier, a swarm of words fogging what should be "clear meaning." Since reading is learned, we must learn to follow and to hear. It is not enough to perceive in pure detachment that the text contains cues for enactment without following them, any more than it is enough to know abstractly that Faulkner's prose is, for instance, reputed to be sonorous. Similarly, it is not enough to know by repute that a musical score can be read performatively, with a full orchestra sounding in the mind of the properly skilled reader. In both cases, to achieve the effect transcribed, it matters greatly that an actual reading skill must be learned, exercised, and applied.

We can now conclude by rounding out the treatment of performance. Performance lays claim to a certain virtue, skill, knowledge, or "way of being." Implicit in this claim is the idea that others will acknowledge it. For social-symbolic beings, once performance is confirmed, one possesses the power that has been claimed, in a way one previously did not. So we make and maintain persons not only by exercising powers but by being confirmed in their performance.

This dependency of performance on acknowledgment preoccupied Faulkner, who created with Quentin Compson his most persuasive tragedy of nonrecognition. Of great complementary interest to Faulkner is self-acknowledgment, with tragic potential most powerfully dramatized in Thomas Sutpen. This form of acknowledgment is possible because the individual is a confederation of persons impersonated and assimilated, so that one may—for good or ill—play both performer and audience. Because a person is a theater of others, one in fact always does so in some degree, to the extent that all practices, including thought, entail a latent self-consciousness, and insofar as one can act with relative autonomy. From persons of integrity defying public disapproval, to solipsists, to writers testing the effects of their writing on themselves by playing their own anticipated audience—all variously enact the supplementary metarole of acknowledger to their own primary performance. So too, conversely, readers may conjure—that is, impersonate—the author who both performs what is read and presides over reading.

For social-symbolic beings, then, all acts, including mental acts, are social. That the private and interior is a special case of the public does not mean, however, that the difference between public and private is insignificant. The stories of Quentin, Sutpen, and others help us to appreciate that there can be a vital distinction between being satisfied with the acknowledgment of one's inner voices and requiring a flesh-and-blood recognition or, with literature, between anticipated readers and actual ones.

Nor does the social nature of reading performance mean that one necessarily feels double, as an inner performer and an inner audience. We have traced the basis of the experience, which is not necessarily how it immediately feels. When readers read, as we just saw, the usual impression is simply that it is somehow the text, or else its author, that is doing the performing. In short, in some way we personify what we read. We do so although only persons can act. But paradoxically enough, it is also true to say that we do so *because* only persons can act, since it is constitutive of being human that we take symbols as cues for mutually animating performance that is only rarely aware of itself as such. So formalists, structuralists, and poststructuralists indulge in the same dead metaphor when they refer to texts that enact or deconstruct themselves. So too, when we refer, as I will, to Faulkner's voice or his display of power or his No to death, the reference is an elliptical form of a more complex statement. It is a condensation not only practical, not only true to the immediately felt reading experience, but also true to the way we re-produce, by reanimating, ourselves and others. All of this is why this ellipsis can be an especially obscuring one for literary critics.

The discussion so far has sought to unpack the fuller general sense of such elliptical statements about voice and act. We will need to retain this general sense as the subsequent discussion unfolds more particular meanings of personal performance.

Everything in the performance that is Faulknerian tragedy converges on a movement of expansion and contraction: the possibility of personal expansiveness which depersonalization constricts like the suffocation that often threatens Faulkner's characters. The next two chapters will examine with increasing specificity the grounds for this systole and diastole. The first of these is a cultural code of dramatic self-dilation through voice and demeanor which has traditionally furnished the material for tragic persons.

CHAPTER 2

Faulkner and the Tragic
Potentials of Honor and Shame

> [Sutpen] wanted to establish the fact that man is immortal. . . .
> the Greeks destroyed him—the old Greek concept of tragedy.
> *Faulkner in the University*

The previous chapter argued that reading is grounded, generally, in the necessity that cultures create persons by empowering them in a dialogue of performances. The same argument requires that we specify the cultural dialogue Faulkner engages. We begin now to locate the possibilities of heroic achievement in Faulkner's culture which furnished impetus, theme, and method for his ambitions as a novelist. What we discover is a series of partial but significant parallels between the honor-shame code of two traditional major periods of tragedy and Faulkner's South, and between the personal self-presentation of traditional heroic figures as sources of cultural empowerment and a remarkable potential effect of Faulkner's rhetoric.

I

Great novels often deal in those incidentals of human exchange which can demonstrate the pervasiveness and continuities of a group's axioms. In *Absalom, Absalom!* Bon apparently finds it natural to begin his letter to Judith, after four years of silence during the war, with the words "You will notice how I insult neither of us" (129). Similarly, the authorial narrator apparently feels called upon to comment when Shreve briefly interrupts Quentin's narration with "strained clowning": "There was no harm intended by Shreve and no harm taken, since Quentin did not even stop" (280). There is nothing startling in either of these formulations; but by elaborating many such incidentals around more dramatic gestures and events that speak to the same issues of insult and harm, the novel meticulously links Sutpen's and Quentin's eras. They are shown to be phases of an honor-shame culture whose members always bear a readiness to take or give offense, as the insignia of their personal worth.

Although today we lack much of the religious and political structure that anciently supported the honor-shame code with comprehensive rewards and sanctions, Western peoples of course still maintain much of this ethos in more informal, diffuse, and in some ways at least less dominant forms than the traditional societies manifested. Erving Goffman's work often examines the contemporary everyday semiotics of the code and in a well-known passage reminds us that although the locus of the gods may shift, the practices that enforce mutual importance and seriousness remain:

> Many gods have been done away with, but the individual himself stubbornly remains as a deity of considerable importance. He walks with some dignity and is the recipient of many little offerings. He is jealous of the worship due him, yet, approached in the right spirit, he is ready to forgive those who may have offended him. Because of their status relative to his, some persons will find him contaminating while others will find they contaminate him, in either case finding that they must treat him with ritual care. Perhaps the individual is so viable a god because he can actually understand the ceremonial significance of the way he is treated, and quite on his own can respond dramatically to what is proffered him. (95)[1]

If this description is true of contemporary society, the historian Bertram Wyatt-Brown has demonstrated how much more extensively and consciously the tradition of southern honor revived the ancient code. Paralleling the ideal of *virtu* explicitly revived in the Renaissance, this ethos flourishing in the South of the late eighteenth and early nineteenth centuries reached deeper than commonplaces about the "cavalier legend" would indicate. The sense of rapport which allows Quentin and Shreve to identify themselves with and create Bon and Henry is based on the shared conviction that honor and shame matter greatly. It is "in their blood," and personal immortality lies in the anonymous circulation of that "blood" of shared conviction over generations. Thus it did not matter "what faces and what names they called themselves and were called by so long as the blood coursed—the blood, the immortal brief recent intransient blood which could hold honor above slothy unregret and love above fat and easy shame" (295). Those Faulkner has described here, the ancient Greeks would have called the *spoudaioi*.

Faulkner's world profoundly retains the category of *spoudaioi*, the "serious," preeminently dignified persons whom one does not slight with impunity and whose standards provided Aristotle and his era with the material of the "serious and complete" (*spoudaias kai teleias*) action of tragedy—that is, heroes. Gerald Else, in his commentary on the *Poetics,* fittingly uses the old southern term *the quality* and its opposite *the no-account* to gloss *spoudaioi* and *phauloi* (and thereby to combat the misleading Judeo-Christian moral implications of such common translations as "noble" in reference to the tragic hero). The no-account are not the vicious but those who do not take themselves and others "seriously" by pursuing *timé* (honor) and *areté* (excellence); instead, they spend their lives "making money, or 'having fun.'"[2] Personal dignity and honor existed in various degrees in the social hierarchy of Athens, but the realm of the honorable as a whole was absolutely distinguished from the territory of those who were not deemed serious, those who did not engage in the dramas of honor demanded by the code. In other words, an absolute division existed between the *spoudaioi* and the *phauloi,* the quality and the no-account. (When some of the young Faulkner's local contemporaries, irritated at his self-dramatizations, satirized him as Count No 'Count, the resounding collision of terms depended on just this absolute division.) The category of "serious persons" remains relevant and compelling to Sutpen and Quentin, whether or not their respective generations believe the status to be altogether achievable or unproblematic. Their shared code of honor and shame is one that the characters of much Greek and Renaissance tragedy would have understood immediately.

All that has been written about Faulkner's troubled heritage, both familial and historical, suggests that he regarded it somewhat as the major Greek tragedians did their own legendary "serious" forebears, the heroes of epic. John Irwin and David Wyatt have alerted students of Faulkner to the thematic importance of insult and revenge within the historical and generational context. It remains now to see within this traditional topos the more general code, as a heritage still culturally formative and yet partly estranged from its adherents within which his vision of immortality makes the strongest kind of sense.

In Faulkner's South, as in the great tragic periods of Greece and the Renaissance, a guilt culture competed with the ethos of honor-shame. This competing code did much to complicate quotidian honor-shame behavior and to furnish a perspective from which it might be viewed critically, if one looked past the everyday evasions and adjustments that managed cultural contradictions. Here, however, we will set aside such complications, as well as historical differences, to highlight certain relatively constant aspects of honor-shame cultures within the larger social fabric. The matters that concern us presently do not lie directly along the shame-versus-guilt axis except in one respect. According to the usual view, in a guilt culture it is emphasized that persons have that within them which passes show; in a shame culture, the play, the show, is the thing itself. Our concern is with the empowering dramas and displays typical of honor-shame and with a potentially tragic feature of this social performance and its rhetoric, whether on the social stage of public action, the tragedian's platform, or in Faulkner, the author's implicit address to his audience.

If *The Unvanquished* makes the ethos of honor-shame partisanship and revenge most schematically obvious and shows its conflict with and transformation by Judeo-Christian guilt-culture standards, *Absalom, Absalom!* will be our main example because here Faulkner gives the person-shaping elements of honor their most complete expression. (In the last chapter, we will consider *Absalom* at length.) In *Absalom,* the assumptions of the honor code are made so comprehensively available to readers through the network of incidentals and dramatic incident that it can make entire sense to us that a fourteen-year-old lower-class boy affronted by a plantation owner's servant should almost instantaneously begin a spectacular self-transformation by emulative rivalry with the powerful class. This is a world where it also makes sense that a woman like Rosa, with no male kindred to avenge her, would similarly, upon being mortally affronted by Sutpen, devote herself to the vengeance of watching over Sutpen's symbolic tomb in order repeatedly to evoke, accuse, and attempt to purge him away. If Sutpen can become one of "the serious" on the basis of heroically taking offense, then Rosa on the same basis can become an inverted priestess who keeps the demonic hero immortal through her ritual and who tries to pass her ritual on to Quentin to pass on to others. And if this ritual portends a cycle of destruction, it is also true that it began because young Thomas Sutpen, like young Rosa Coldfield, converted a potentially enervating shame into a saving self-transformation—at least according to Quentin.

That Faulkner can define and criticize the limitations of the heroic honor-shame culture should not belie that he also finds it a compelling means, not yet superseded, for empowering persons to live and endure. For him, as for the ancient Greeks, the moral depends significantly upon what conveys and strengthens morale; virtue largely springs from *virtu*. (What is striking about Quentin in *The Sound and the Fury* is how much his appeal to honor is a morality doomed because it has been demoralized.) A major charge in Faulkner's critique of the heroic ethos, at least as he sees it in his time, is that it in fact often fails to generate communal morale and the capacity to act and endure except in the grotesque forms variously represented by Sutpen and Rosa.

The Renaissance ideal of *virtu* is perhaps the readiest reminder that to display for others' emulation one's self-respecting personal power is not only expected but necessary in the psychic economy of a heroic honor-shame culture. Body and voice are the chief realizations of person, through demeanor, speech, and action, because in such a culture what is real is what can be made external for minutely discriminated judgments of honor or shame, imitation or disparagement. Virtue felt must become virtue claimed so it can be realized as virtue acknowledged.[3] The culture that placed a premium on character as something to be enacted for others to see and hear was clearly a fertile ground for the development of literary drama from the social type well represented by Sutpen's "pristine aptitude for platform drama" (246). In this cultural theater, ideally the most honored are at the top and center of a pyramidal structure, radiating a magnified personhood outward and downward in stages to others.

Traditionally, power and dignity are supposed to be emulated and passed on by others surrounding the "glass of fashion and the mould of form" in degrees according to their station and merit, just as in the traditional warrior ethic the spoils of war and honor were ideally supposed to be shared in proportion to rank and honors won. Faulkner's critique of the structure is related to the traditionally understood tragic critique of the Greek hero on the grounds of hubris. Hubris may be understood as an affront given by someone and/or taken by others when the individual's radiating display of self-worth becomes an invasion of their proper dignity (cf. Peristiany 16). This radiation of capacity always risks affronting others exactly in proportion to the amount of power that could be conveyed. The more personal power is radiated, the more hubris is in the offing. Although of course the giving and taking of offense can have a variety of sources, the point here is that the hero's behavior inherently tends toward the gray area comprehended in the double meaning of the word *pique,* as offense and stimulation. If the rhetoric of Faulkner's major phase is understood from the perspective of the underlying honor-shame code, it begins to be clear how his characteristic piquing of his audience's sense of outrage significantly contributes to his shaping of a reading community of adherents for whom he is in fact heroic. Faulkner's is not a critique of a social practice merely external to his own rhetorical practice.

Kenneth Burke's discussion of the epic and tragic hero furnishes a complementary perspective on much that we have reviewed so far and will allow us to extend the points specifically to Faulkner's writing:

Each of the great poetic forms stresses its own peculiar way of building the mental equipment (meanings, attitudes, characters) by which one handles the significant factors of his time. . . .

The epic is designed, . . . under primitive conditions [of constant warfare and "tribal" raids], to make men "at home" in these conditions. It "accepts" the rigors of war (the basis of the tribe's success) by magnifying the role of warlike hero. Such magnification serves two purposes: It lends dignity to the necessities of existence, "advertising" courage and individual sacrifice for group advantage—and it enables the humble man to share the worth of the hero by the process of "identification." The hero, real or legendary, thus risks himself and dies that others may be *vicariously* heroic. . . . The social value of such a pattern resides in its ability to make humility and self-glorification *work together:* the sense of one's limitations (in comparison with the mighty figure of the legend) provides one with a realistic attitude for gauging his personal resources, while his vicarious kinship with the figure gives him the distinction necessary for the needs of self-justification.

The thought suggests what psychological devastation would follow from a complete adherence to the "debunking" school of biography whereby in destroying the dignity of great legendary or historical characters, we automatically destroy ourselves. The heroic legend is saying, in effect, as Goethe said to Schopenhauer: "We can only get from life what we put into it."

Greek tragedy, Burke believes, " 'welcomed' [hubris] by tragic ambiguity." The great playwrights, that is, partly retain the epic view of the hero but (short of debunking) complicate it by stressing the hero's limits, in a forensic dramatic structure of "offence, sentence, and expiation" (*Attitudes* 35–39).

In our present terms, again, the honor-shame code is both evoked and critiqued. We can further clarify this potent heritage of Faulkner's South and the rhetoric of its social performance by tracing the implications of the enabling mutual dependency between hero and audience which Burke indicates. The competitiveness and potentially hubristic aggressiveness of the honor-shame code entail that even such socially formative identifications as Burke mentions are infused with emulative rivalry. From the first, then, they are intrinsically forensic exchanges in the sense of involving judgments of performance, and attack and defense. In this respect, forensic is the rhetorical correlative to the ongoing dramas that pique honor. What we want to understand is how Faulkner develops the tragic potential of such a reciprocity, and capitalizes on its rhetorical possibilities for achieving the highest cultural aspiration.

The reciprocation whereby both parties in an exchange "get from" it what they "put into"—or take from—it, accounts for the mutual reinforcement and circulation of power which Faulkner luminously summarizes in describing Bon and Henry: "Each sought to preserve . . . what each conceived the other to believe him to be" (120). We are reminded of the limitations of the conventional hierarchical metaphor of the pyramid radiating power unidirectionally. As a corrective we might imagine the classical Greek ampitheater and the public power radiating downward to the figures on the central cultural stage. Their static quality aside, both images of the world and art premised by the honor-shame code are valid because power is reciprocal.

In this world the general public invests the heroes with their heroically *constituting* kudos and *kleos* (glory) on the condition that the dignity of the humbler social stations be in turn acknowledged and reinforced, just as heroes are made legendary only by being commemorated by their cults and admirers, and these followers in turn receive prestige and an enabling sense of power as followers of the heroes. As Faulkner's phrasing implies, this network of noblesse oblige usually works by tacit reciprocity, since too much explicitness would undercut the heroes' inspiring conviction of self-assurance. But the tacit reality often comes close to the surface as both social subordinates and superiors implicitly bargain for a reciprocity, a giving and taking, that ideally will maximally benefit all parties. The highest cultural aspiration is immortality through a community's commemoration of the hero after death. Here the reciprocation model is extended into the afterlife; for instance, heroes are thought still to demand kudos—even, as with the dead Achilles' demands in Euripides' *Hecuba*, human sacrifice in his honor. The reciprocity of the hierarchy, the heroes' actual dependency on social subordinates, can break out into the open when the affront of hubris is given or taken, as when Wash learns that Sutpen does not hold him in the proper regard as devoted follower or as in the quarrel of Agamemnon and Achilles. Or as sometimes in Euripides, clamorous public opinion quite openly controls the putative leaders, and a sacrifice is demanded, we may surmise, only apparently to satisfy a dead hero or the gods but really as a symbolic demonstration of the crowd's power.

Indeed, in a honor culture, where to be a person is very much to be a public actor, public opinion is always pivotal, and one is constantly under scrutiny—under the eyes Faulkner's characters feel watching or invading them. Pierre Bourdieu puts the consequence succinctly: "Existence and honour are one. He who has lost his honour no longer exists. He ceases to exist for other people, and at the same time he ceases to exist for himself" (in Peristiany 212). Conversely, the conception of achieving immortality in the minds of posterity carries the greatest conviction under the honor-culture assumption that one lives one's life directed *to* the perceptions of others and must win sustaining personal value in their perception. As for losing this vital recognition, the reversals and precipitous falls of much classical tragedy correspond to the fragility of honor in this judgmental environment and to the rapidity with which public shaming can replace public honoring.

Although, as Burke observes, such "debunking" and shaming are potentially dangerous to the group deriving its identity from the previously honored figure, the danger can be compensated for by an invigorating communal solidarity precisely in the rendering of adverse judgment, the venting of envy, or the resecuring of a just sense of personal worth after the perceived hubris of the preeminent person has injured it. With such options in mind, and since we have been considering these cultural dynamics with the help of terms like *code,* this is a good place to discount these terms with Wyatt-Brown's wise cautions about the contingencies of customs:

> The ancient philosophers and their humanistic interpreters, in early modern England and in the South as well, often spoke of the "laws of honor" as if they were as readily apparent as the Ten Commandments. They were not. Honor was accorded on the basis of community decision. The method of reaching that conclusion involved many contingencies. Any action, *ex post facto,* then seemed logical if it was regarded as conforming to those "laws." . . . [However, such a] process of necessary ordering distorts, because, as Faulkner intimates, much of human existence is really inchoate even if it lives on in memory. We speak of rules of behavior in the past. They were not rules, not immutable or even logical. At best they were acceptable options. The strategies and priorities were more like trails across a field. . . . One had to improvise. Yet the main objective of fidelity to custom could not be cavalierly repudiated. (113–14)

This contingency of decisions of honor has significant consequences. The previously cited comment on Shreve's interruption of Quentin's narration ("There was no harm intended by Shreve and no harm taken") recalls that affront can be given but not taken or taken though not given. This option is one of the grounds for both stability and instability in the cultural circulation of power by conferring and receiving honor and shame. The pivotal decision is whether to take offense at a potentially hubristic act or to accept the potency that is its complement and accompaniment. How much the recipient desires to share, to take, the potency of the socially recognized figures will often govern whether or not the powerful person's word or deed is grasped as an insult or as a part of the expected radiation of power, perhaps commingled with a "chastisement" that one feels must be deserved or that one unconsciously takes as a spur to a reflex-sensation of one's worth. (Everyday present examples range from the behavior of followers whose leaders treat them with ambiguous familiarity-condescension or jocular aggressiveness to the behavior of certain religious groups toward the supernatural. Anse Bundren supplies one version of the latter when he observes that God chastises those he most loves.)

The reciprocity involved in the giving and taking of power immediately points to the choice of *if* and *how* and *what* to take in reading powerful fiction like Faulkner's, particularly since his writing foregrounds the working of an honor value-system of social empowering and, most significantly, presents potentially outrageous matter in challenging, unsettling experimental forms. Reading offers an additional refinement of the reciprocity between social performer and audience which we have traced, because readers may answer the Faulknerian text's pronounced solicitation to perform, mentally or aloud, the very voice that may finally outrage them. Such readers, dismayed by what they find themselves saying, may feel as if exercising a desired potency by identification with a power of speaking has made them, as it were, insult themselves with their own speech. This is an extreme version of emulating a social source of personal power and the (at least threatened) collapse of this identification. The question is, how will readers choose to "defend" themselves?

One defense is to close the book and read no more. It is good for seasoned readers of Faulkner to remind themselves of this obvious option of the outraged and to recall that it has been exercised by many readers both before and after Faulkner's rise to literary fame. In freshening our sense of Faulkner's outrageousness, we deliver him, or at least deliver his major phase, from that excessive respectability he accused one of his villainous impersonations, Flem Snopes, of succumbing to; he made the accusation, and chronicled Flem's taming, during the closing phase of Faulkner's career, when he was comparably succumbing (*University* 33). The stage of criticism has passed in which, as Richard Brodhead has recently noted, Faulkner did need simply to be defended against those who reviled him as degenerate and willfully obscure. In Brodhead's words, "we can say, smugly but with much justice, that Faulkner's early readers failed to recognize his greatness. Our own problem is more likely to be that we take his greatness as a given, that we find him important because he is important" (3). The irony is that in the very act of having made Faulkner respectable (albeit partly with his connivance) and thus having offered him within the academy the possibility of the literary immortality he sought, critics are in some danger of frustrating it by cosmetically obscuring the real intimations of outrageousness which are among the conditions of his power to stir the "immortal brief recent intransient blood" of a reading posterity.[4] For although an outraged closing of Faulkner's major texts is a possibility that helps us to define their conditions for success, there are other optional strategies within the forensic pattern we find ourselves considering—a pattern of perceivable attack and defense. These options do not constitute "laws of reading," but we can chart preliminarily one of the most important "trails across a field" anticipated by Faulkner's work, in the potential linkages among provocation, emulation, and empowering.

Recall that Sutpen's perception of the plantation owner's hubris goaded him into emulatively magnifying his own personal dignity in a self-transforming accession of enormous power.[5] Rosa's self-defensive transformation from a naïvely romantic young woman into the much more formidable outraged priestess of a demon-harrying cult is the mirror image of Sutpen's reaction to affront. Faulkner's apocalyptic rendering of Wash's reaction to Sutpen's affront to him is of course a further parallel. The response of Bon's college-mates to his provocative *virtu* is still another telling variant on the convertibility of insult, or potential insult, into a self-conversion. Here it means strong identification and partisanship with Bon, whose behavior was "a source not of envy, because you only envy whom you believe to be, but for accident, in no way superior to yourself . . . —not of envy but of despair: that sharp shocking terrible hopeless despair of the young which sometimes takes the form of insult toward . . . the human subject of it, or in extreme cases like Henry's, insult toward and assault upon any and all detractors of the subject" (95). Although Faulkner could both sympathize with and criticize the underlying relationship of provocation and emulated power, his inferable aim as a writer is to harness it as one accentuated element of rhetoric and voice.

Faulkner's evident rhetorical instinct was to tempt outrage. This impulse is obvious enough in the "decadent" strains of apprentice pieces like *The Marionettes* and, especially seen from the standpoint of Faulkner's immediate Mississippi mores, a certain provocativeness in the early novels. With *The Sound and the Fury, As I Lay Dying,* and *Sanctuary,* Faulkner's major phase sharply escalates the outrageousness. Not only the challenging techniques but the subject matter prominent in Faulkner's major phase (the now-familiar inventory of incest, rape, fratricide, idiocy, castration, bodily corruption, and tragic miscegenation which can still unsettle the new or unjaded reader of Faulkner) make affront a constant possibility. According to the logic wherein imitable power is allied with or stems from the risk of hubris, this possibility is one means of making salient the imitable, performable power of his art. Thus, if we reconstruct the rhetorical postulates of his major phase from the perspective of the honor-shame code it dramatizes, Faulkner's writing summoned up an ancient, now somewhat subterranean ethos of the heroic which would have to "shock," to pique, in order to test whether the old dynamic of hazarded affront and enabling was still sufficiently alive, or could be revived, in a reading audience. Technique was an element of potential affront designed simultaneously to be a tour de force, a display of virtuosity, which could elicit something like Arnold Bennett's comment that Faulkner wrote like an angel—more accurately, perhaps, a "fallen angel, the unregenerate immortal" (*University* 2).

The act of reading Faulkner thus becomes an engagement with a proto-tragic rhetoric and voice. Other related, and qualifying, features of this engagement will claim our attention in future chapters. This "hubristic" rhetorical feature is so characteristic of Faulkner's major phase, besides being immediately relevant to our present topic, that I consider it here as a general point applicable to the principal works of this period. The theme of affront, revenge, and personal empowering which becomes increasingly pronounced during the major phase, and climaxes in *Absalom,* explicitly crystallizes a rhetorical resource Faulkner had been mining. Faulkner was exceptionally alert to the potentials of this resource for selecting out of the reading public a particular audience bound to him the more strongly—as Henry becomes a partisan of Bon's—for having psychologically converted the author's possible "demonic" insult of subject matter and form into an "angelic" reciprocation of power.

II

There is an important distinction to be made here, growing out of the considerations of the preceding chapter. It is the distinction between, on the one hand, using such terms as *powerful* and *compelling* to reflect a *reader's* possible experience of being moved, aroused, or captivated and, on the other hand, employing such common phrases as "Faulkner *forces* the reader. . . . " This is not to quibble over a *façon de parler,* for even taken as such, the latter phrasing is not innocent, nor is the similar prevalance of the unfortunate term *reader-response* criticism, which indulges a simplistic stimulus-response model. Such insufficiently careful phrasing concedes at once too much and too little. It concedes too little because criticism too often neglects to examine exactly what the power consists in and how it works. Given the imperatives of our professional commitments, to say nothing of the abuses of political power to which our century has made us sensitive, academic critics are often suspicious of literary power and reluctant to consider it unless it can be treated as the power of knowledge effectively conveyed to the minds of an audience or as an authority subject to the hermeneutics of suspicion. The common phrases concede too much because words like *force* drastically overstate the case. It is as if we were oversensitively registering power in any form as coercion, or perhaps exaggerating it because of a secret collective inclination to identify ourselves, as purveyors of ideas to sometimes reluctant or indifferent audiences inside and outside the academy, with an imagined power that can *make* others see, learn, understand.

Torture can force people to do things. But when we speak of the influence of a particular fiction on its audience, we are dealing with the field of persuasion, more exactly with what Aristotle called the "artistic" means of persuasion, to distinguish them from torture, contracts, laws, and the like (cf. Burke, *Rhetoric* 50). "Artistic" persuasion, compared to this grimmer end of the spectrum, has, as a whole, more to do with the give and take of reciprocation, the inducing of cooperation through the invitations of language. Such a rhetoric may of course be *taken* as compelling by those who feel compelled by such invitations and obviously in many respects or instances may be quite worthy of suspicion. But there is no universal rhetoric like the one implied by words denoting coercion. Every rhetoric must choose some resources of appeal and neglect others and, consequently, reach some members of the public and neglect—or bore, puzzle, or merely irritate—others. If there were a universal rhetoric, there would be no torture, prisons, or laws (Aristotle's "inartistic" means of "persuasion"). Since the matter is complex, it should be noted that we consider here a caution against the indiscriminate, insufficiently careful use of terms like *makes* or *forces* with respect to a particular writer or text, on the grounds that such usage obscures significant gradations of influence by treating them all with words redolent of real coercion. Clearly, a broader view of general enculturation or a careful "perspective by incongruity" such as Burke practices could usefully treat discourse as "torture" or coercion of a certain kind. But the wholesale use of *makes* and *forces* can trivialize such a project as well.

The language of *forces* and *makes* puts us always in the simple zero-sum game of dominance and submission we noted earlier, rather than allowing for a situation in which the power of one participant can empower and liberate the other. As in Faulkner, power can enable extraordinarily and reciprocally: the author is empowered by writing a score that the reader's own power makes realizable; the reader is solicited to perform by a score that feeds the reader's power. And the author is his or her own first reader and enabling performer, in an act that formally reflects human being as the dialogical performance for our "others," even in solitude. In publication, as in ordinary action in society, this pattern is extended outward to a further multiform give and take of performance and audition.

In its most benign form or aspect, this is not a tug-of-war but a concert of power, one in which the author's, like the composer's, score remains impotent unless a reader plays the role of both conductor and orchestra. It is the concert that Quentin and Shreve engage in, growing out of their initial tug-of-war in which Shreve goads a reluctant Quentin to tell him about "the aunt Rosa" and "the demon." It is a concert of mutual enabling in which Shreve's later "strained clowning" is not given or taken as an offense but rather is transformed into a shared "protective levity" for them both. This is one of the devices of self-defense which enable them to survive while summoning up Sutpen's shade for forensic accusation and apologia: "as though at the last ditch, saying No to Quentin's Mississippi shade" (280).

But the ghost or shade of affront is always there, so that the combined narration and listening that grew out of Shreve's goading and Quentin's sullen resistance and that reached an extraordinary "marriage of speaking and hearing" transforms on its own principles of empowering back into Shreve's insulting remarks, which are given and taken as threats as the novel ends.

A final remark on the hazardous yet necessary interdependence between a culture's empowering scripts and their enactment by persons will afford a preview of our course from here. Generally, Faulkner's writing dramatizes this relationship by claiming the right to the honorific term *tragedy* while transforming the generic conventions that support the claim and leaving its fulfillment to the reader's performance. One specific performance feature of interdependency in honor-shame forensic is especially relevant.

The difficulty of practicing forensic is that one's shame must be spoken, published. One must indicate the outrage one has endured in order to defend oneself or to attack the perpetrator. So in principle at least, to vindicate one's honor requires an admission, itself painful because shaming, of how one's honor has been injured. *Qui s'excuse, s'accuse.* Perhaps strong identification with the offender is one way to avoid this difficulty or something like it, so gestures that might have looked like unworthy submission become instead proofs of loyalty to the other, and like Henry with Bon, one defends oneself in the bearable form of defending the other.

A related form of this solution is the communal identification with stories of shame vindicated, which creates an ideological resource from which an individual apologia may draw its voice and plot, redeeming the individual honor while reinforcing the collective. One can see, however, that where such a shared strategic narrative does not exist or is no longer sufficiently credible, shame will be liable to silencing or to displaced forms of expression which attempt to stand in for voice. Further, while speech about shame or outrage thus depends upon a shared narrative, the very existence of such a story obviously depends in turn upon a dialogue that establishes it in the first place and then maintains it. When an ideological narrative empowering us in some of the most important areas of human existence has suffered a historical breakdown and it is shameful to speak of these things, then it is deeply puzzling to imagine how to initiate a needed collective story again.

Faulkner's writings, in whatever mode, consistently address and script such silencing and displacement of voice and, in particular, address just this interlock of mutual dependency between voice and narrative. His tragic writing represents a cultural situation in which there are but meager or dubious shared strategic narratives to deal with associated "given" sources of potential shame—death, sex, and race—and in which the problem is how to reestablish voice and narrative in a positive mutual dependency. We have just noted two approaches: the rhetoric of provocative identification, and the implicit critique of this approach. Involved in both of these approaches is a third: a formal and stylistic dramatization of the problem so as to invite a reading performance supplying narrative as it supplies voice.

CHAPTER 3

A Logic of Tragedy:
The Sound and the Fury

The tuneful voice was heard from high:
"Arise, ye more than dead."
Dryden, "A Song for St. Cecilia's Day"

The year Joseph Wood Krutch made his famous claim that tragedy is contrary to the modern temper, Faulkner published a paradoxical refutation. Krutch sought to define and decry his age by appealing to a traditional standard. *The Sound and the Fury* shows that the standard of tragedy, traditionally conceived, contains the logic of its own failure. Yet critics have typically discussed the novel as if it could be described by some comparatively stable model, apart from the debate over the possibility of tragedy.[1]

In the post-Enlightenment, *pathos* has become the term of contra-distinction to *tragedy*. According to the most widespread view, trag-edy involves suffering that results mainly from the protagonist's ac-tion, which is usually persistent, decisive—heroic. The mode of pathos, by contrast, is said to involve a relatively passive suffering, not springing from action but inflicted by circumstances. In terms of the linked root meanings of *pathos* (passion, suffering), tragedy is held to be pathos resulting from heroic action.

The stress on action, legitimized by Aristotle's poetics and ethics, was part of the general cultural defense of responsible human endeav-or from the philosophy of mechanistic determinism. For many, the horror of a universe of mere physical motion could be summed up as an oppressive passivity in which, as Matthew Arnold wrote, "there is everything to be endured, nothing to be done" (187).[2] The emphasis on the difference between tragedy and pathos—that is, between action and passivity—was thus fundamentally polemic in nature if not always in tone. By the beginning of Faulkner's career, tragedy had become *the* prestigious literary genre. *Pathos* had largely lost its neutral, descriptive connotation and was increasingly a term of denigration, especially in the form *pathetic*. Influential theorists like the New Humanists upheld a conservative position by accentuating this difference. *Tragic* had become a weapon useful for excoriating the naturalists, the "Freudians," and "the school of cruelty." Yet important writers at least since Dostoevski had reflected the modern idea of passive man while seeking to reformulate the possibilities of human action. Sometimes these possibilities were found at the very center of apparent passivity, where pathos is describable by its etymological kin, pathology.[3]

But action is not the only usual discriminator of tragedy. In Aristotle's account, the mimesis of action arouses in the audience certain passions and subjects them to catharsis. A catastrophe is instrumental in effecting this tragic relief. In pathos, by contrast, there is no final crisis, no resolution and emotional disburdening. Passion is the inconclusive fate.

The traditional conception (or kind) of tragedy we consider here focuses typically on the drastic either/or to which life may be reduced, in a tightening spiral of narrowing options. *Antigone, Hamlet, Moby-Dick,* and *The Mayor of Casterbridge,* for example, follow this pattern, as does the *Oresteia* until the last-moment reversal. Hegel's theory speaks powerfully to such cases by treating tragedy as the collision of contradictory views. In Hegel's Absolute, variances are merely differences, but when human action makes them concrete, they become contradictory oppositions, liable to tragic conflict.

Hegel aside for the moment, the idea of contradictory opposition itself points to connections between pairs of concepts that seem simply opposed—the modern temper and the heroic, tragedy and pathos. In *The Heroic Temper,* Bernard Knox authoritatively defines the hallmark of Sophocles' tragic heroes: "Their watchword is: 'he who is not with me is against me'" (21). Sophoclean tragedy dramatizes the usually unavailing attempts of advisers to persuade the intransigent heroes—Ajax, Antigone, Electra, Oedipus, Philoctetes—to abandon the self-destructive polarization of their outraged self-esteem against the world (1–44). The Sophoclean heroic outlook is the relatively rare consequence of a severe threat to personal worth that arouses the exceptional person to this uncompromisingly dichotomous attitude. Let us imagine a case, however, in which the essential quality of this temper became widespread. If dichotomy were the usual structure of consciousness, the protagonist would be surrounded by those who, at bottom, experience life in no less starkly divisive terms than does the hero on the tragic occasion. Rather than being a monitory, awe-inspiring anomaly as in Sophocles, polarization would be a constant daily potential. The result would be strikingly different from Sophoclean tragedy, though bearing the prototype's mark. The ironic product is the odd suspension of heroic temper and the "unheroism" in tone and mood of *The Sound and the Fury*.

In a traditional conception like Hegel's, tragedy advances through the revelation of oppositions to their resolution. Faulkner's novel, however, probes to an inchoate, divisive logic of tragedy operating throughout thought and experience. *The Sound and the Fury* relocates the schism of tragedy in a basically dichotomous world view. And in so doing, it discloses the potential of tragedy to become continuous with its antitype, pathos. Insofar as tragedy conventionally entails resolution, the very ubiquity of tragic schism ironically produces the repetitious, inconclusive situation of tragedy's opposite. Instead of catastrophe, there is repeated disaster.[4]

The Compsons' schismatic, incipiently tragic mental habits are strikingly—though perversely—like a two-value logic. This ordinary formal logic depends upon the Aristotelian law of identity, according to which an entity can only be what it is: A is A. Given the assumption of uniform entities, to say that a thing is simultaneously something else violates the law of noncontradiction. This is the logic of arithmetic (which Mr. Compson's language of "sum" and "problem" reflects), in which an answer is always either right or wrong. A characteristic form is the mathematical proof that depends on showing contradiction—the reductio ad absurdum. As formal logic, this binary ordering is unexceptionable. As the foundation for a wholesale system of dichotomy taken as the sole orientation to reality, such a logic becomes disastrous. Matters that call for the recognition of compound entities, gradations, and probabilities are continually reduced to the Yes or No of tragic dilemma.[5]

When polarized options are habitual, crisis becomes attrition, and passion a banal repetition. Christ was not crucified, Mr. Compson tells Quentin, but worn away by the minute clicking of time's little wheels. "If things just finished themselves," Quentin thinks at one point. "Again," he concludes, is the "saddest [word] of all" (79, 95). He yearns for decisive calamity, some unburdening conclusiveness, however terrible. He yearns, that is, for a kind of tragedy that is not his. Not surprisingly, Quentin has been the primary focus for discussing the novel's tragic dimensions. He will be so here as well.

The absence of tragic closure in the novel, then, does not stem from a view that there can be no momentous catastrophe in a modern "everyday" world. Tragic closure is absent for reasons related to the tragic process, pace Krutch, George Steiner, and others who have analyzed the death of tragedy. In Faulkner, the binary logic that in the first instance produces the tragic heroic crisis must also eventuate in devastating everydayness: tomorrow and tomorrow . . . Faulkner's title echoes the most famous protest against a life without climax. But Macbeth, by finding his resolving action, diverts his drama from the idiotic tomorrows signifying nothing. The period of Faulkner's great modern tragedies begins with a statement of the disqualification of such tragedy by its own logic. Put concisely, in the words of Quentin's false comforter, "Tragedy is second-hand" (116).

In *The Sound and the Fury,* the tragic resolution that counteracts this secondhandedness is not a function of closure but a potential of other rhetorical techniques of plot structure and voice.

I

Quentin's first memory upon waking is of his father giving him Grandfather's watch with the observation that it is "the mausoleum of all hope and desire; it's rather excruciating-ly apt that you will use it to gain the reducto absurdum of all human experience which can fit your individual needs no better than it fitted his or his father's. I give it to you not that you may remember time, but that you might forget it now and then for a moment and not spend all your breath trying to conquer it" (76). Time and time consciousness contradict human experience, as the reference to reductio ad absurdum indicates. It is, in Mr. Compson's phrase, excruciatingly apt that Quentin's interior monologue begin with this appeal to contradiction, which obsesses Quentin as much as time does. In fact, one obsession is implicit in the other. The association is made overt again when he sees watches in a

68

store window, displaying "a dozen different hours and each with the same assertive and contradictory assurance that mine had, without any hands at all. Contradicting one another" (85).

What strikes Quentin about the boys quarreling at the bridge is that their voices are "insistent and contradictory and impatient" (117). He has assimilated his father's habit of thinking in terms of conflicts between assertive, irreconcilable opposites, as in Mr. Compson's arithmetical definition of man as the "sum of his climatic experiences. . . . Man the sum of what have you. A problem in impure properties carried tediously to an unvarying nil: stalemate of dust and desire" (124). Again two things—dust and desire—contradict one another, leaving a "nil." Similarly, to prove to Quentin that Caddy's virginity was always an illusion, Mr. Compson reasons by contradiction: "Women are never virgins. Purity is a negative state and therefore contrary to nature" (116).

Quentin and his father tend to experience difference as contradiction, multiplicity as a stalemated war between "impure properties." The whole novel traces the fault lines of this mental set. A universe of antagonisms is formed, all divided and subdivided, as awareness focuses on each, into further bifurcations of A and not-A.

This universe appears in the blanket social distinction between the quality and the nonquality. The first category is further divided by Mrs. Compson's obsession with the status of Compsons versus that of Bascombs, the latter family divided into her ne'er-do-well brother Maury and her son Jason, her "salvation" and a true Bascomb. The binary set informs her belief that "there is no halfway ground that a woman is either a lady or not" (103), as well as Jason's identical idea that "once a bitch always a bitch" (180). It structures Jason's efforts to apply his commercial scheme of credits and debits to all areas of human relationships. It is resplendent in the moment when he believes his life will reach a heroic climax: "He could see the opposed forces of his destiny and his will drawing swiftly together now, toward a junction that would be irrevocable. . . . There would be just one right thing, without alternatives: he must do that" (307). In this binary universe, as in Hegel's idea of tragic collision, all *distinctions* become *divisions*. Subtly or overtly, the daily craving is Jason's lust for clearly opposed forces, the one right thing to do.

To be immersed in Benjy's perspective, which reduces everything to an unqualified opposition (Caddy and not-Caddy), is our proper introduction to the Compson experience of life. As in the novel's first scene, the mental landscape is without middle ground or nuance; there is only this side of the fence or that side of the fence. Yet Faulkner consistently evokes a luxuriant polysemous wealth. Aside from Benjy's lack of normal organic development, his mental processes differ from those of the rest of the family only in degree, not in kind of simplification. In a sense his schema is larger than life, but it shows what is in the life.

There can be capacitating strength in such a view, since it licenses an exhilarating call to arms, literal or figurative, of friends unified against a monolithic enemy. This ethos in general both attracted Faulkner and aroused his intense suspicion. Benjy's daily existence, however, most incisively illustrates that strength must be followed by impotence as the "enemy" increases and meaning becomes fragile.

Life's myriad variety through time is experienced only under a single undiscriminating rubric of the false (inferior, detrimental, unreal) repeatedly opposing that which is alone true and valuable. In other words, if all differences are opposites, then the opposition will grow very numerous indeed. In compensation, as time passes the categories are made ever more rigid and uncompromising. Thus more of life's possibilities are excluded only to reappear as an increased repetition of the negative more insistently battering at one's citadel. In proportion as the impending collapse is suspected, a sound and fury arises in protest and defense. This is the moribund stage of the process, the "loud world" (177) on which the novel concentrates. Benjy's bellow and Mrs. Compson's wail echo Quentin's outraged cry as he attacks the shadowy company of Caddy's seducers in the person of Gerald Bland.

Benjy's scream upon being driven to the left rather than to the right of the Confederate soldier statue is the novel's final instance of the exceptional fragility of meaning resulting from dichotomy, "each in its ordered place" (321). To offend against any item is to offend against all, the whole category of right. Living on such terms means being haunted by the vulnerability of the self erected upon this system and, consequently, being preoccupied with security. This apprehension flares up startlingly in Quentin's fantasy of his father's rushing to deal with Benjy's interruption of Caddy's wedding: *"Father had a V-shaped silver cuirass on his running chest"* (81–82). The one kind of heroic invulnerability, which brought the dashing Compson forebears to their power, is archaic, grotesquely helpless to deal with what follows from it, as son from father. As time discloses, impotent pathos is an inherent potential of its seeming contrary, vigorous action. It is not just around the Confederate monument but in it.

The Compsons' isolation, frequently noted, is more than a historically accurate representation of the separatism of a caste society, as are all the images of enclosure and boundaries—fences, gates, streams, doors, locked rooms, prisons. The continual bickering, vengefulness, and whining manifest the nervous strain of the besieged. Quentin's desperate fantasy of incest is in its own way a rigorous extension of the inbreeding attitude of a household that feels itself surrounded by relative nonentities.

For all these reasons, the frequent critical comment that Quentin is not heroic, like discussions that begin and end with his pathology, is both correct and not to the main point. But to see the heroic etiology of Quentin's, and his family's, unheroic condition is to begin to see what kind of work one is reading.

Walter J. Slatoff makes an explicit distinction in Faulkner's works between pathology and tragedy (193).[6] Often, however, there is a subtler implicit tendency among Faulkner's commentators to ignore or downplay the pathological element when discussing the tragic, or vice versa. The other tendency is to use both ideas but to fail to confront their problematic relationship, so that the generic term becomes a rather flaccid compliment. One of the best critics of the novel, André Bleikasten, writes at length of "Quentin's tragedy of inheritance"; yet _tragedy_ seems undeservedly honorific, because for Bleikasten "there is of course nothing heroic about Quentin," whose "story can be read as an ironic inversion of the familiar journey of the Romantic ego" (142). Bleikasten's discussion, seasoned with the words _tragic_ and _tragedy,_ considers pathology alone. He attempts to relate Quentin's weakness to the daunting consciousness of a dominating ancestral figure that prevents Mr. Compson and Quentin from fulfilling their generational roles, making both mere impotent sons of the dead Father. Yet this is a needless reading of the historical dimension of _Absalom, Absalom!_ back into _The Sound and the Fury._ There are valuable Freudian insights in Bleikasten's analysis, as in the similar approach of John Irwin.[7] In _this_ novel, however, we are presented not the debilitating awareness of an ancestral father but a structure of consciousness inherited all too faithfully from him and his like, with the decay of the family line intrinsic in it.

In his own way, Mr. Compson tries to counter his family's fixation upon victory or defeat: "Because no battle is ever won. . . . They are not even fought. The field only reveals to man his own folly and despair, and victory is an illusion of philosophers and fools." But this view still manifests an embattled life, in the form of a deadlock paralyzing action. Life is a cold war.

The factuality and calculations we associate not with the heroic but with the modern age actually reflect this cold war of the latter days of heroic action.[8] The fatal dichotomies of value are cut from the same cloth as the binary reduction of value to arithmetic. Quentin's latter recollections of the "reducto absurdum" statement show clearly that his father's admonition concerns more than the time consciousness critics have stressed. Sardonically, Quentin computes his suicide: "The displacement of water is equal to the something of something. Reducto absurdum of all human experience, and two six-pound flat-irons weigh more than one tailor's goose" (90, and see 85). In this framework, personal experience is simply another item to be counted; it is, indeed, not *personal* but a public objective fact. Mr. Compson "understands" the deadly effect on personal hope and desire of a consciousness ruled by number and the hateful siege of contraries. But fittingly, his language contradicts him. The personal human experience he sees imperiled is denatured by his own formula, "sum of climatic experiences."

II

The Compson children seek to escape from the passivity of their suffering, a condition ironically produced by the binary world view traditionally suited to heroic action. The central, insidious cause of their debility is that this same orientation threatens to alienate them from their own experience. The attempt to reclaim the personal dimension of their lives, consequently, is a deeply purposeful act, a nascent counter to passivity. For Quentin, the crucial issue is his passion.[9]

The implications of a two-value system for passion are considerable. The one-or-nothing of dichotomy is reflected in the heritage of the heroic gambler, staking all "on a single blind turn of a card" (177), as all do in their conflicting ways. Applied to relationships, this orientation can make for the single-minded loyalty Faulkner highly esteems. The tragic defect of this virtue is the narrow emotional exclusiveness, and the resulting suffering, that plagues the Compsons.

For Mrs. Compson the one-and-only who commands her devotion is Jason. Her maternal abandonment of Quentin, which he feels acutely, helps intensify his attachment to Caddy into fixation. To stake one's emotional life on the turn of one card is to become liable to suffering, but the Compson ethos goes farther in associating emotion with pain. For all the Compson children, the emotions have been given the unhealthy tinge of an ordeal or an affliction, so that for them we are justified in speaking of *passion* in the double sense of feeling and suffering. The black her mother dons when Caddy is first kissed can stand for the whole joyless association.

Mr. Compson's well-meaning argument to Quentin that pain is temporary is punctuated by Quentin's nearly stupefied repetition of "temporary." If Quentin cannot have his exclusive one, Caddy, then he desires a permanent grief over the loss, for at least grief preserves feeling. He has had to learn that feeling is suffering, but to be faced with the loss of suffering too is unthinkable.

As we saw, there is an inherent tendency in a two-value classification to treat varied negative features of life as an undifferentiated set, as if they constituted the same evil repeated through time. For Benjy, a single agony of loss recurs daily in many guises. In Quentin's more complex version, a broken leg in childhood provides him an index-pain recurring as a gasping "ah ah ah." So too, from a broader standpoint, the father tries to reassure Quentin that the dishonor of sisters recurs in life, that "tragedy is second-hand." Again the father implicitly devalues Quentin's passion by denying that it is distinctive, individual, no matter how many its analogues. Instead of being his, it is threatened with being unredeemably anonymous, not only derivative but lacking even the distinctive archetype of the Passion: "Father was teaching us that all men are just accumulations dolls stuffed with sawdust swept up from the trash heaps where all previous dolls had been thrown away the sawdust flowing from what wound in what side that not for me died not" (175–76). For the father, passion is passive: "A love or a sorrow is a bond purchased without design and . . . matures willynilly and is recalled without warning to be replaced by whatever issue the gods happen to be floating at the time" (178). The father's kind of individualism honors the personal quality of experience only in a passionless integrity: "Whether or not you consider [an act] courageous is of more importance than the act itself than any act" (176).

Similar in their experience of time, father and son diverge in their view of emotions. Mr. Compson advocates that the rational person disavow his own passion as time's minion, a weakness, an "impure property." His alcoholism is his suicidal tribute to—and Faulkner's comment on—this Stoic aim. The philosophy the father offers ends not by diminishing Quentin's pain but by threatening its significance.[10]

Quentin is faced, then, with the "reducto absurdum" of the objective absolutist approach to life and its mirror image, temporal nihilism. From these perspectives, human experience becomes mere fact, as its personal quality is erased: *my* hope, *my* desire, *your* love, and *your* loss become meaningless. The schema that began by making a decisive cut between what was on my side and what was not, concludes by enfeebling the very idea of *mine*. Each character is threatened with a radical dispossession. Benjy and Quentin, in particular, experience even their own body processes, thoughts, and actions as alienated. The personality suffers, or is threatened by, a kind of death, as when Caddy insists to Quentin that she is dead (124). The passions, which Faulkner sees as the register and index of personal value, become tainted with mortality.[11] The Compson world frustrates the individualism it espouses by a binary orientation that in effect denies basic self-esteem. Despite their aversion to anomaly, the Compsons live this fundamental contradiction. Yet they neither subside into numbness nor yield their stubborn hold on individual personal value. They continue to grasp both individualism and a self-defeating way of founding it. Although tragedy within their world is "second-hand," we as readers can see in such persistence a necessary element of tragedy.

Among the brothers Compson, this tragic persistence in vindicating the personal fosters habitual self-justification, cloisters subjectivity, and opposes whatever diminishes uniqueness. Here also their possessiveness flourishes. Each brother clutches at something exclusively his, to supply from the public world what is lacking in the private. If *my* experience is alienated, I try to reclaim something I believe mine and wrongly taken from me. This is the grain of truth underlying Jason's rationalization of his greed and thievery as "getting back his own." And Benjy and Quentin each deploys the similar fable of "his" Caddy and her symbolic substitutes as objects and embodiments of a passion he seeks to reclaim. To adopt Faulkner's later comment in the Appendix, such efforts reveal the most basic meaning of "aveng[ing] the dispossessed Compsons."

Caddy, too, for all her rebellion against the family, still dramatizes its orientation when she incites Quentin to think himself her possessor, able to dispose of her as he will, in their scenes by the branch. Indeed, her development recapitulates the family's progression along the continuum from active to passive. The young Caddy who demands obedience from brothers and servants during the period of Damuddy's death, who pushes Natalie down the ladder, fights with Quentin and dreams of being a general, giant, or king, is the same Caddy who later lies passive under the phallic knife Quentin holds to her throat and acts out a surrender to her imagined sexual "opponent": "Yes I hate him I would die for him. . . . yes Ill do anything you want me to anything yes. . . . she lifted her face then I saw she wasnt even looking at me at all I could see [her eyes'] white rim" (151, 156–57). At the same time, however, she performs what a psychologist would call a passive aggression, for she controls and "owns" Quentin by her sexual display, especially when he realizes at its climax that she imagines herself in someone else's arms.

According to the Compsons' orientation, the chosen one must be uniform, without the "impure property" represented by the young Caddy's muddy drawers. Further, her many anonymous suitors undermine the idea of possessing her exclusively or distinctively. Thus Quentin is both fascinated and nauseated by sexuality, which subverts instead of supporting his dualism. When he imagines anonymous intercourse, vital boundaries dissolve between an impure "imperious" inner realm and a vulnerable outer: "Then know that some man that all those mysterious and imperious concealed. . . . Liquid putrefaction like drowned things floating like pale rubber flabbily filled getting the odour of honeysuckle all mixed up" (128).

Symbolizing Caddy, twilight above all stands for the mixed, liminal phenomena that are ill sorted by dichotomy. Twilight evokes for Quentin a vision that his doing and suffering are mocked by inadmissible paradox: "I seemed to be lying neither asleep nor awake looking down a long corridor of gray halflight where all stable things had become shadowy paradoxical all I had done shadows all I had felt suffered taking visible form antic and perverse mocking without relevance inherent themselves with the denial of the significance they should have affirmed thinking I was I was not who was not was not who" (170). Dichotomy, not so much thought as inhabited, enervates the self. Drawn into the corridor splitting the House of Compson, we can experience, if not assent to, Quentin's conviction: better a suicide that promises, however fantastically, to transform all this.

III

We have discerned two phases in the novel's tragic process: the decline of action into passivity and the attempt at reversal. In the first, Quentin's pathos, both pathological and nonpathological, derives from a logic of tragedy which Faulkner has read back into daily life. In the second, Quentin's effort to reclaim the personal by commitment to his passion creates the passion necessary to traditionally conceived tragedy. Passion itself becomes purposeful action and transcends the condition of simply passivity.

Yet this necessary condition of traditional tragedy is not a sufficient condition. Not only is catastrophe lacking, but there is no direct recognition of suffering such as sometimes, in effect, substitutes for catastrophe (*Prometheus Bound*) or augments it. In the *Philoctetes,* for example, there is an "audience" within the play, Neoptolemus, whose final acknowledgment, rather than exploitation, of the hero's suffering is the crux of the play, releasing our emotions. But Quentin's personal experience, unacknowledged by his father, has no standing in the public factual world. The impassive eyes staring at him everywhere on his last day represent the objective "ordered certitude" that "sees injustice done" (125), like the "cruel unwinking minds" in his memory of schoolchildren who know the correct facts (88). Quentin's pain cannot be tragic in this view because, as George Eliot says of Dorothea's tragedy in *Middlemarch,* "we do not expect people to be deeply moved by what is not unusual" (144). It is made maddeningly plain to Quentin that his trouble at a sister's maturity and "dishonor" is too familiarly recurrent in life to be considered unusual. The very aberration—the really unusual form and degree—of his response is exacerbated by his desperation to break out of a vicious circle of the usual and achieve the acknowledgment that would reclaim his experience fully as his own. But the widespread repetition-bound binary outlook that fosters his pathos also prevents others from certifying that his pain is significant, that it is genuinely his.

Catharsis is thus carefully displaced from Quentin to Dilsey. And Dilsey is not so much an agent whose own suffering is witnessed as she is the novel's central sympathizing—yet in a key sense alienated—witness, its audience. The minister Shegog's Easter sermon, with its contagious refrain "I sees," evokes the one Passion that has sufficient public standing to release the congregation's passions, otherwise "banal" and inexpressible. The communally validated Passion, shut off from Quentin in Dilsey's world, combines with his own thoughts of Christ and his Passion to indicate that Quentin's death is a bid for tragic recognition. Quentin, in short, improvises his own passion, a suicidal "autogethsemane" (*Mosquitoes* 48). Its intended public impact is confirmed by his vision of himself and Caddy in hell, "the two of us amid the pointing and the horror beyond the clean flame. . . . Only you and me then amid the pointing and the horror walled by the clean flame" (116–17). If others cannot sympathize, then their impassivity will be stripped away. In this embattled conclusive suffering, a victory could be claimed for the defiant heroic temper as its passion is viewed with antipathy through the clean dividing barrier.

Quentin's suicide, an act both momentous and exclusively his, is meant as an adequate public sign of his personal experience. But others take his signal as yet another repetition of Compson disaster, their "curse." Within the novel's setting, this symbol lacks empathetic reading. That we will supply this crucial lack is Faulkner's own gamble on creating tragedy in defiance of its instability. For we can view the passion displayed within the book in a way the characters cannot, and yet the difficulty of the internal monologues necessary for this intimacy challenges our ability to witness. If by now readers can surmount this barrier, another has remained: the common two-value assumption of an unbridgeable division between tragedy and pathos.

In keeping with the key role the ideal of tragedy has played in the controversy over modernist writers like Faulkner, George Marion O'Donnell defended him as a "traditional moralist" who, like Quentin, was always "*striving toward* the condition of tragedy. He is the Quentin Compson . . . of modern fiction." Since O'Donnell's landmark 1939 essay, a dominant tendency in Faulkner criticism, represented by the invaluable work of Malcolm Cowley, Robert Penn Warren, and Cleanth Brooks, has emphasized "the conflict between traditionalism and the anti-traditional modern world in which it is immersed" (O'Donnell 299, 285). The conflict is real. In arguing for the dialectical continuity between tragedy and pathos in *The Sound and the Fury,* however, I have in effect argued that here—and I believe in Faulkner generally—the continuity between these worlds is as true and important as the change from one to the other and their conflict. Such a view accords with Faulkner's repeated assertion that certain basic human traits, types, and life patterns continue throughout history, though constantly in new forms. There is, in fact, a continuity of conflict for the inheritors of the heroic temper and its fateful logic.

IV

Faulkner's sensitivity to dichotomy is perhaps primarily a function of his complex response to the naked Yes or No of life and death. In dramatizing this and such other dualities as self and others or agent and patient, Faulkner transforms the relationship from static dichotomy into an unclosed dialectic of fusion and fission, intimate conflict, interchange, and reciprocity between opposed terms. What drives the novel, then, is a curiosity about not only the passivity that incongruously comes of vigorous action but the enabling that comes of passivity. This paradox is continuous with Faulkner's larger preoccupation: the mutual source of strength and weakness, power and fragility.

The related fact is that the dialectical interpenetration of tragedy and pathos which we have examined leads to a rhetorical crux of cathartic acknowledgment. Whereas in a standard "Aristotelian" formula for tragedy, plot resolution at the level of incident is necessary to trigger catharsis in the audience, in *The Sound and the Fury* the direction is reversed. The plot offers no resolution at the level of narrative action, so that the novel as aesthetic tragic event must be completed, if it is to be, by a successful evocation of resolving catharsis in the reader. In this significant respect, *The Sound and the Fury* is a tragedy not of plot but of voice.

Evocation of cathartic resolution by sympathetic acknowledgment is an apt description of the Easter sermon as it affects its church audience. *Evocation* is the exact term because this effect is a function of a certain kind of voice, which now demands our closer attention in continuing the analysis of the novel as unclosed tragedy opened by the author's initiatives to the reader's possible fulfillment. The examination of voice in *The Sound and the Fury* will not be fully completed until we consider it again in the next chapter within the context of *As*

78

I Lay Dying and *Sanctuary,* the other "mortuary" novels of this period. The Easter sermon, by ritually evoking a triumph over death, is an idealized but not wholly credited or credible model for these novels and for the contingent, secular transformation of pathos into tragedy in *The Sound and the Fury.* It brings both the interpenetration of genres and the rhetorical crux of cathartic acknowledgment to the foreground. In a special sense, Shegog's voice speaks in behalf of the novel; the minister also speaks both more and less than the text, however, in narrating a completed action.

On one page of the novel, the picture of a very public eye on an advertisement suddenly stares out at us (311). This remarkable device directs at the reader a blank gaze like that which follows Quentin, but because the glare of nonacknowledgment is pervasive, the image can occur, as it does, in the last section. A few pages before this graphic stare, the Easter sermon momentarily recovers a recognizing vision and simultaneously moves the novel at the level of plot away from Benjy's state of "trying to say" as he mutely watches the paradoxical unfolding of a repeated loss. The plot moves from exceptional muteness to extraordinary voice and through it to momentary communicative silence. Culminating this process, though not the plot as a whole, the Easter performance transcends the bafflement of personal desire by public language, epitomized in the boys' quarrels over their merely verbal and visual possession of the legendary fish at which they stare: "making of unreality a possibility, then a probability, then an incontrovertible fact, as people will when their desires become words" (117). The sermon, for its speaker and church audience, is a moment in which speech matches and embodies vision and passion; it is a performance directed against "blind sinner[s]" (296), in which seeing is saying and having as well. The blended vision–speech is witnessing in its fullest religious sense. The minister Shegog could say with his later counterpart in *A Fable,* "I bears witness" (180). To witness is to see and declare, to speak one's recognition: "I sees de light en I sees de word" (295). Ludicrous to the sight and at first scoffed at by the congregation, the preacher in his desire to witness and be witnessed is the type of Quentin and the other Compson children; in his success for his audience, he is the antitype who defines their failure.

Quentin experienced his suffering as an alienated voice, an "it" expressing itself in an inarticulate gasp, "ah ah ah." The preacher's voice, too, initially is an "it": " 'Brethren and sisteren,' it said again. . . . With his body he seemed to feed the voice that, succubus like, had fleshed its teeth in him. And the congregation seemed to watch with its own eyes while the voice consumed him, until he was nothing and they were nothing and there was not even a voice but instead their hearts were speaking to one another in chanting measures beyond the need for words" (294). In contrast to this use of a powerful voice to pass through both words and vocality to reach a communicative silence beyond them, Quentin's gasping voice, like Benjy's howl, is *beneath* words. It expresses the concrete reality of suffering from which objective certitudes are detached, and it bespeaks the alienated personal experience Quentin undergoes as if it were imposed from without: passion as mere passivity. As we saw, to be fully reclaimed as one's own action, passion must be witnessed, as the preacher's passion is. The preacher's voice is ultimately *beyond* words, transposed during the sermon from "it" to "I" to "we" as he achieves the symbolic public transformation for which Quentin strives.

The martyr's death testifies to the validity and power of what the victim sees and says—the word *martyr* literally means witness. In the preacher's own version of enacting the Passion, he performs a martyrdom to the voice that consumes him and makes him and his listeners individually nothing, so that as a collectivity they can speak and hear. Pointedly departing from a white man's speech, the preacher subordinates himself in language to the linguistic community for whom he witnesses and for whom he yields himself to the memorable story he repeats and reenacts. His power to act derives from his enabling passivity, his receptiveness to a capacitating state of possession by a story and a voice whose communal life he renews. To and with the congregation that at first eyed him skeptically, Shegog tells and performs the story that Quentin despairs of telling or living: the son rejected by the blind world who is recognized and vindicated at last by an all-powerful "personal Father" (*Soldiers' Pay* 319) acknowledging his son's passion. Shegog passes through a memorable enacted death to celebrate immortality in this recognition: "I died dat dem whut sees en believes shall never die" (297). His voice and his command of a communally confirmed narrative enable the minister to do symbolically what Quentin tries to do with fatal literalness.

In the novel's often sympathetic critique of a binary ordering that has difficulty acknowledging both the distinctive and the shared nature of experience and identity, the countervailing paradigm founds personhood on a distinctive experience and expression that are nevertheless not a dichotomously exclusive and excluding possession of either speaker or hearer, self or other. Thus the preacher's possession by the community's voice still distinctively displays his unusual power of yielding to it and wielding it and additionally displays his choice of it in lieu of another, white man's voice after he demonstrates his command of that one as well. What is true of the minister's voice is also true of his plot. The plot peculiar to his Easter sermon remarkably elides Jesus' resurrection and expiation of guilt and concentrates on the general Resurrection Day Quentin sardonically imagined his eyes arising to see (116), the day on which those innocent victims who have the recollection and the blood of the Lamb will be vindicated and will triumph over death. The preacher's truncated story stresses the pathetic idea of the shameful sacrifice of an innocent by proceeding without transition from the child Jesus being threatened by Roman soldiers to the spectacle of Calvary. This juxtaposition creates the sleight-of-hand impression that the child is taken from his mother's lap to his public humiliation, the "blastin, blindin sight" of being mocked by "boastin en . . . braggin" and executed with criminals (296).

For all its communal accessibility and pertinence, then, the preacher's narrative is idiosyncratic, very much his, so that in removing the ancient tale from banality he becomes both instrument and agent of a shared visionary triumph over dishonored passion and death. And what Shegog revives is not a story of guilt vicariously expunged but of mortal shame overcome.

If we understand in these terms how Shegog's performance with his congregation is the desideratum of Quentin and the Compson family, we must further conclude that the performance exhibits more than a countervailing model of the person as both distinctive and communal. It also demonstrates that a binary ordering is not by itself antithetical to this model. Certainly the preacher and his congregation nourish their mutual recognition with a renewed sense of being collectively special, rigorously set apart from blind sinners. Shegog's visionary heaven, with its Father acknowledging those who remember innocent blood spilled and closing its doors against the spillers of that blood, is the converse of Quentin's desperately visionary hell. If Benjy's dominant note is pathetic suffering, Quentin's the need for recognition, and Jason's the sadomasochistic compulsion for self-justification and revenge, Shegog's compacts all three of these, each benignly transformed by the power of a communal narrative to realize itself. Shegog's power to act, to speak, and to plot his own narrative is partly inspired by a fundamental us/them division. But here this personal power is not seen as self-frustrating; it is revitalized by the resources of a shared narrative in which "our" dishonored passion is vindicated. Shegog can make his public enactment of overcoming shameful death recognizably distinctive and can create recognition and acknowledgment precisely because there already exists a communal articulation, the Passion Story, as the backdrop against which a distinctive variant may be conceived and registered. Shegog's receptiveness to this story and its proper voice is an empowering passivity because, in fact, at another level what is passively received in story and voice is the immediately reinvigorating heroic temper, albeit stated in the accents of long-suffering and ascribing the ultimate vindicating action vicariously to another, divine agent. Without some such partisan narrative of collective self-justification, the continuing Compson habit of honor-shame dichotomy becomes a gesture lacking the syntax to give it point.

Consider Caddy, "Little Sister Death" (76), who epitomizes the mortally shameful passion to which a voice and a reply must be given. Caddy's vivid display by the branch with Quentin as sole audience, a performance proceeding from her intensely repeated words to a wordless demonstration of her racing pulse, is to sexual passion what Shegog's enacted martyrdom is to the Passion, but with the difference just noted. With her power to enact voluptuous martyrdom (*"When they touched me I died"* [149]), she shares it as a burden, scored in the memories of the brother who is her witness and commemorator. So, in their different ways, all her brothers are. But in a world whose leitmotif is "Hush!" they witness only in the silent language of their minds, which speaks to the reader but not to others. Caddy's very name is not to be spoken by the family after the debacles following her wedding; her story is beneath words, like Quentin's "it" voice or Benjy's wail, and so can never go beyond words. There is a double bind of voice and narrative. Not spoken, her inchoate story of shame and death cannot become a shared narrative. Not a shared narrative, it cannot be subsequently realized in a distinctive voicing and plot—as Quentin needs to realize it, as symbolic or literal act.

That is, Caddy's is not really a *story*. It cannot be spoken in the

Compson world because, whereas honor is mandated to speech, shame per se is subject to silence. Shame cannot become articulate unless it is articulated as shame overcome, as in Shegog's sermon. But the strategic formula "tragedy is second-hand," by self-protectively dismissing Caddy, Quentin, and the whole family as mere platitudes of dishonor, negates the possibility of speaking a shared narrative into existence. More particularly, by similarly ruling out any shared idea of victory ("Battles are never won"), the father undermines any communal story of a dishonor, or death, overcome, actually or in some millennial vision. Quentin's experience of Caddy cannot be recognized as individually distinctive; in other words he cannot give it distinctive utterance, because there is no shared narrative, much less one of honor redeemed, to serve as resource and backdrop. Because Quentin's passionate Caddy is not Benjy's or Jason's, or the father's, or the mother's, or indeed Caddy's, she is not really his, nor does he wholly belong to himself. His mind filled with fragmentary voices and narratives, Quentin attempts to get shame spoken. The unsilencing of shame would be the basic catalytic act that, like his physical act of attacking Dalton Ames, might set the needed story in motion. Yet the story itself is the antecedent required to supply the syntax and conviction to both these acts.

Quentin's declaration of incest, by accentuating shame, is not an articulated story but a violent breaking of silence, which is the condition of the creation of a shared story through dialogue. Even if it fails in such creation, however, the declaration has a second potential, oddly displaced in form though it is: to break out of the double bind of voice and narrative by main force of voice alone.

Quentin desires a power of speech comparable to Shegog's, one that would permit him, as he imagines, to shoot his voice through the floor at Herbert Head (105), the false redeemer of Caddy's shame.[12] To exercise voice as the minister does is equivalent to the most potent act, so that one attains the silence common to profound recognition, to memorable action, and to voices that carry through time and space, as in Quentin's recollection of Louis Hatcher's voice: "He never raised it, yet on a still night we have heard it from our front porch. When he called the dogs in he sounded just like the horn he carried slung on his shoulder and never used, but clearer, mellower, as though his voice were part of darkness and silence, coiling out of it, coiling into it again. WhoOoooo. WhoOoooo WhoOoooooooooooooooo" (115). Lacking such a power of vocality, Quentin tries to use the impact of the word *incest* and the act of suicide as the minister uses the impact of his own hornlike (294), amplified voice.

Here we must realize that what is at issue in the achievement of a perfected vision and voice is not knowledge but acknowledgment, not truth but the recognition of what is already in some sense known or taken to be true, as the congregation knows the Easter story and its promise of immortality. Acknowledgment is empowering for speaker and audience in a way that their knowledge alone is not. The crucial distinction between knowledge and acknowledgment aligns with that between words and voice, so that a fixation upon words, knowledge, and truth in themselves blocks the possibility of passing beyond them to the ultimate necessity. The most relevant contrast, again, is between the minister and his audience, on the one hand, and Quentin and his father, on the other. Mr. Compson, as he insists to Quentin, *knows:* "I said you dont know. You cant know and he said Yes. On the instant when we come to realize that tragedy is second-hand" (116). In keeping with this knowledge of general, secondhand experience, Mr. Compson analyzes Quentin's declaration of incest: "You wanted to sublimate a piece of natural human folly into a horror and then exorcise it with truth" (177). Mr. Compson believes, and many critics with him, that what Quentin wants is a merely verbal manipulation and control wherein Caddy's lovemaking can be transformed into fictional words and then abolished with the power of truth. Insofar as Mr. Compson describes words and truth as powerful, he speaks to the point, but his preoccupation with words, knowledge, and truth per se is exactly what keeps him from acknowledging Quentin's personal passion as Quentin's announcement of incest seeks to provoke him to do.

Quentin does not want the power of truth acting on language but the empowering recognition elicited by voice. Quentin wants to be heard beyond the words; he wants his *voice speaking* to be heard, as the horrific word *incest* could be heard and acknowledged for what such a speaking implies of the terrible magnitude and importance Quentin's passion has for him. The word *incest* is like a verbal horn to magnify Quentin's act of speaking so his experience is both particularized and made generally resonant for another. It is a substitute for the voice he does not have, one powerful enough to induce a more-than-verbal hearing and to attain the communicative silence of recognition—a recognition of *both* distinctively individual and generally shared, and acknowledgable, passion. This condition of a voice-in-duced acknowledging silence is the antithesis not only of Benjy's helpless, speechless wail but also of his father's similarly futile, "loud," knowledge-bound words, which keep sounding in Quentin's mind. Quentin consequently denies his father's dismissive explanation of the incest tale and affirms another goal for his symbolic action: "It was to isolate her out of the loud world so that it would have to flee us of necessity and then the sound of it would be as though it had never been" (177).

If in fact, as Faulkner later asserted, we are to understand that Quentin never does actually speak aloud of incest to his father but only stages their conversation on this subject in his imagination, Faulkner's point about the importance of voicing is accentuated. Quite literally, in this case, Quentin does not have the power to make his voice and passion heard by his father. His unspoken speech is a silence that displays his urgent need, and inability, to break through the silencing of shame to reach the other, transvocal silence of acknowledgment, like a voice "coiling out of" and "coiling into" silence. As I will stress shortly, however, it is just this kind of advertisement by Quentin's language that it requires speaking which helps to educe the reader's performance of a text that is "trying to say."

Addie Bundren's pronouncement that words "dont ever fit even what they are trying to say at" (As I Lay 115) has become a sort of slogan in Faulkner criticism for the noncoincidence of language with experience or reality. While it is of course accurate to interpret such a statement and consistently implied concern in Faulkner as an issue of referentiality—an issue, that is, of knowledge or truth—critics since Olga Vickery, in collectively and variously overemphasizing this aspect of language, have obscured an issue of equal or greater importance. What is at stake in Faulknerian tragedy is the devastating power, or use, of words to distract attention from and frustrate the hearing of voice and thus to drown out the silence accompanying the acknowledgment of persons and their experience, quite apart from one's ability to know them.

As Stanley Cavell has argued, the diversion of the issue of acknowledgment into a question of the knowability of others' experience is a self-protective maneuver with a substantial philosophical history and with consequences that tragic literature illuminates.[13] Acknowledgment, or recognition, entails in some measure the abandonment of the intellectual and other psychological controls Mr.

Compson relies on and some risk of a "defenseless" involvement with others. In what Cavell calls "the attempt to convert the human condition, the condition of humanity, into an intellectual difficulty" (*Claim* 493), either familiar knowledge or a lack of knowledge of others' experience can be used to escape acknowledgment and to excuse nonrecognition. In both cases, there is the self-protective deflection of interest to an ancillary issue of knowledge. Since in both cases knowledge is reductively considered the goal or essential requirement of one's interest in or involvement with others, Mr. Compson can be used to sum up both the first position, that of knowing, in *The Sound and the Fury,* and the second, that of unknowing, in *Absalom, Absalom!*: "It's just incredible. It just does not explain. Or perhaps that's it: they dont explain and we are not supposed to know. . . . we see dimly people . . . in this shadowy attenuation of time possessing now heroic proportions, performing their acts of simple passion and simple violence, impervious to time and inexplicable." In this often-cited passage, in *Absalom,* Mr. Compson goes on to describe words and reading according to the same half-lucid principle in which an awareness of a certain distinctive "otherness" potentially conducive to an act of real acknowledgment instead becomes a self-insulating puzzlement fixated on the intermediate stage of cognition and words: The people "are like a chemical formula exhumed along with . . . letters from [a] forgotten chest . . . the writing faded, almost indecipherable, yet meaningful, familiar in shape and sense, the name and presence of volatile and sentient forces; you bring them together in the proportions called for, but nothing happens; you re-read, tedious and intent, poring, making sure that you have forgotten nothing, made no miscalculations; you bring them together again and again [but] nothing happens; just the words, the symbols, the shapes themselves, shadowy inscrutable and serene, against that turgid background of a horrible and bloody mischancing of human affairs" (100–101).

For Faulkner, it is not simply or primarily that words and verbal experience are at one remove from reality (though that is a rough way of phrasing a complex relationship); it is that they are in a sense at two removes from silent recognition: first, in their tendency to distract attention from voice and, second, because voice in turn is potentially the agent for reaching "silence." Words in this respect are as removed from recognition as ordinary seeing is; ordinary vision is the certain, factual knowledge of the self-evident, the epitome of a referential certitude, which, when it is fixated on the question of general knowability, can blind recognition. *The Sound and the Fury* implies that even if it were warranted, all the certitude in the world could not produce acknowledgment and might well prevent it.

There is no question in this novel, however, of some ideal stasis of pure silence (Benjy's helpless muteness) or of pure vocal sound (Benjy's helpless howl), much less, of course, one of ignorance (Benjy's helpless mental state). In the novel's world, Benjy's wordless vocal expression produces the compassionate or irritated desire to hush him, not the communal experience inspired by an effective rhetoric like the preacher's, which is both verbal and vocal. If Benjy adumbrates the incapacitated condition of unaccommodated man, the novel dramatizes the danger entailed in words and knowledge, as necessary contributors to creating personal existence. Tragic devastation results from the depletion of the process of human accommodation which occurs when such varied human necessities as words and voice, knowledge and acknowledgment impede and frustrate one another.

And to recapitulate, the frustration of acknowledgment by knowledge derives from the sense of familiar recurrence, known, secondhand experience, which is in turn produced by an initially heroic two-place ordering of self and world. Everything changes, however, if a group ordering itself in this way possesses a communally confirmed narrative in which injured self-esteem is vindicated. Otherwise, dichotomy begets repetition, which begets knowledge and "loud" words, which block the acknowledgment necessary to persons.

To be fully witnessed—voiced inwardly or outwardly—is the novel's highest ambition. The rhetoric that solicits this reading accommodation of, and by, the novel inverts key features of tragic impasse. First, the theme of frustrated speech and shamed silencing proffers the necessary office of speaking and hearing witness to the reader alone, and the singularity of this office is one incentive to exercise it. Correspondingly, the mutual dependency of narrative and voice, which creates a double bind in the Compson world, in several ways allows each to become supportive of the other in the act of reading. Finally, as in the Easter sermon, repetition of a certain kind is transformed from burden into incentive and ally.

As different narrators fragmentarily reiterate the fundamental story to our sole hearing, the obsessive cryptic memories in a sense constantly present events as secondhand, as if the tale were too old and generally well known to require chronological recounting. Yet the retelling strongly suggests that the speaker and his implied listeners nevertheless are, and need to be, incessantly reminded of its pertinence to them. Simultaneously, each narrator's cryptic and partial retelling is always new for us because it distinctively selects, organizes, and embroiders. The rhetorical effect created, then, is that a repetition is constantly being individually repossessed through structure and language for the perception of the novel's audience, the while that the main characters themselves fail to discover in the fictional world an audience through whose acknowledgment they can reclaim their "repetitious" passions and life narratives as their own. A major contribution to this effect is the distinctiveness of the narrative voices (and collections of voices) the narrators possess and through whose agency our own speaking performance is invited.

It is *as* a succession of voices that *The Sound and the Fury* exists—or more precisely, as a succession of virtual voices scripted for actualization in reading. Critics have often tended to assume that the reader's activity largely consists in interpretive reconstruction of an inferable narrative line in *The Sound and the Fury* by rearrangement and filling in gaps. As we will see in a moment, this reading activity itself contributes to the audience's potential voicing and witnessing of the text. But surely it is a limited notion of both Faulkner's experimental achievement and the reader's flexibility to assume that the major effect of the text's obvious deemphasis of narrative is to induce readers merely to reemphasize it by blindly persisting in "processing" all novels in the same way, as essentially narrative. Novels like *The Sound and the Fury* and *As I Lay Dying,* by their distinctly styled or character-labeled sections (Darl, Cash . . .), accentuate the novel's rhetorical character not only as narrative but as a set of scripts or scores for the reader's enactment. In *The Sound and the Fury* this accentuation begins with the strikingly odd narrative voice we begin to hear (if and as we voice it) on the opening pages and the emphasis upon vocal sound, the sounding of voice, which Benjy's moaning effects.

The most fundamental form of the joint accommodation of narrative and voice is the best known and is perhaps necessary to give firmness to the first two chapters. In order to construe or create narrative coherence at the most basic sentence-by-sentence level, it is, at any rate, immensely helpful to voice the needed pauses and inflections mentally. Further, singly and through their mutual contrasts, the distinctive, aurally exciting narrative voices stimulate the auditory imagination and elicit the reader's "physical or mental" speaking and hearing so that, whatever sense the reader makes of them, they can become voices speaking. In Benjy's section, the lyricism of a simple diction recombining a few key words (like "smooth bright shapes") weaves through a richly vernacular dialogue dominated by Benjy's attendants. Quentin's section, the most varied stylistically, ranges from something like Benjy's flat reporting, through intensely realized descriptions, to the flux of sensory images and sounding language in the interior monologues and interior dialogues—all of which are stitched with Quentin's more or less involuntary recollections of others' pronouncements. In sharp contrast to Quentin's typical "Father said" is Jason's self-assertive "I says." After the extreme dialogism of the first two narrative voices, Jason's is at once the most stylistically monologic and the most publicly addressed narrative voice. This combination embodies what we might call his psychological mythology and life strategy: to rehearse his grievances against his perceived oppressors as if preparing for some ultimate judgment day of self-vindication (303, 305–6)—the psychological vestige of a religious belief like the preacher's. Before the jury in Jason's mind, his narrative voice rehearses his forensic rhetoric of caustic social repartee and stock bigotry.

The last, anonymous narrative voice, emerging from this rehearsal and the successive dichotomous orientations that underwrite repetition, begins by offering forthright sonority along with an unstraightforward, undichotomous perception: "The day dawned bleak and chill, a moving wall of gray *light* out of the northeast which, *instead of* dissolving into *moisture,* seemed to disintegrate into minute and venomous *particles, like dust* that, when Dilsey opened the door of the cabin and emerged, needled laterally into her flesh, precipitating *not so much a moisture as a substance* partaking *of the quality of* thin, *not quite* congealed *oil*" (265, my emphasis). The suggestive indefiniteness of the description seems designed to disintegrate the wall of Jason's explicitly black-white binary system the way the wall of grey light is transformed into not-quite-categorizable entities. Similarly, just as Quentin's voice, and then Jason's, comes as a certain relief from the eventual oppressiveness of its predecessor in narration, this voice begins by sounding a higher linguistic register that is welcome after Jason's unremitting middle range. Throughout this last section the narrative voice shifts flexibly and subtly from sonority to "naturalistic" report, occasionally laced with easily colloquial phrasing ("then he turned and fell to scrabbling on the littered table" [309]) but primarily allowing vernacular dialogues to carry the narrative.

Somewhat as the preacher's extraordinary voice significantly derives its point and power by its emergence from his initial manner of speaking, the final narrative voice is not so much significant in itself as it is the result of a dialogical process that has point and power as a whole.

The crafted variety of the novel's voices, taken together, educes in the appropriately performing reader a tonic capacity for those distinctive acts of saying and hearing unavailable or inefficacious because unacknowledged within the Compson world. The distinctive virtual voices of the text become the reader's own voice as well—as the nonexclusive possession of reader, narrators, and impersonating author. At the same time, the narrative and represented voices form a progression of action. Passionate voices that "happen to" or are not controlled by their speakers—Benjy's and, to a lesser but still substantial extent, Quentin's—yield to the better controlled yet obsessive monologic voice of Jason and finally to the exhibition of vocal mastery by the last narrative voice, a mastery represented to an idealized degree in the Easter sermon's sublation of passivity into power. So too, as articulated narrative emerges before us in the last two sections of the novel, it is as if the reader's prior collaboration in articulating narrative has helped to produce it. It becomes, in other words, a counterpart to the shared narrative that empowers Shegog's voice. The novel thus, as it were, step by step reconstructs a confidently acknowledged personal speaker from an all-but-incapacitated one. It not only solicits the reader's voicing, then, but also invites the reader to enact a parallel process of reclaiming a formidable voice and articulate passion as one's own action, enabled by an other's—the impersonating, scripting author's—agency. In terms of what is at stake thematically in the novel, this enactment of passion is cathartic: passion ceases to be merely an affliction upon us. It ceases also to be a dichotomous possession of anyone, something set off from others in a simple opposition.

The voicing reader's emotional engagement with the work as script, to whatever degree and in whatever mixture we sympathize with or recoil from each narrator's emotions, is complicated by the fact that the reader's own speaking-and-hearing is the instrument for voicing the narrator's passions. For instance, the passion with which we may flinch from Benjy's helplessness, dissociate ourselves from Quentin's weaknesses, or condemn Jason's pettiness and bigotry is involved dialogically with those voices of our personal repertoire which speak and audition Benjy, Quentin, and Jason. I do not mean simply that the reader possesses a certain ambivalence, for example, in both despising Jason and relishing his Thersites-like venomous zest. When we despise Jason, it is nevertheless the Jason we are performing and helping to give imaginative life; in a sense it is our voice speaking the "Jason script" that we despise. Conversely, our sympathy or empathy with a given narrator is implicated with the final oppressiveness of enacting that narrator's voice at such length as is required and so is mixed with the grateful relief we feel in turning to enact new and different voices—Quentin's after Benjy's, Jason's after Quentin's, the last narrator's after Jason's. Our combination of emotional responsiveness and enacting voice is always both distinctively ours and dialogically intertwined with other distinctive feelings and voices we assume.

By these means the novel seeks to persuade its readers to become an actively performative and recognizing audience, to enact the array of voices scored for us, to the outer or the inner ear, and in so doing most completely to acknowledge others' passions as neither mere instances of some general experience nor alien to our own. In seeking this resolution of its tragedy, the novel submits itself to its audience.

What, then, of the reader's relation to the novel's own exemplary image of beneficent repetition, desired communal acknowledgment, and cathartic completion? Can it be said that the sermon is in fact not merely the image of what is wanted by both Quentin and the novel but the thing itself, a shared cathartic denouement for readers as well as congregation? A positive answer to this question would raise two immediate objections. One is that the sermon does not have the culminating position in the novel that a completing function would require. The second is that, as we noted, Quentin has no place in this scene and its immortalizing recognition of suffering, nor does any Compson except Benjy. If Benjy experiences a releasing tranquility while hearing the potent sermon voice, it is also true that a broken flower performs the same service for him.

A third difficulty involves the rhetoric of the sermon itself. Considered as rhetoric addressed to the novel's audience, the sermon episode draws on traditionally firm sources and techniques of appeal: the Passion narrative, amply prepared for by the novel up to this point; the "unlikely hero" device, for us as for the congregation, wherein the minister's unpromising appearance and tour de force exordium serve the traditional rhetorical function of being provocative, setting up the heightened cogency arising from reversed expectations; the scene's cohering of crucial issues and aims of the novel; and its elicitation of a welcome emotional release after the tensions of confusion, pity, disgust, and hatred we have been exposed to in the successive narratives to this point—an elicitation depending on the depicted example of catharsis in a community and a sympathetic character, Dilsey, as well as on Faulkner's resonant mixture of elevated language and emotionally charged, rhythmical vernacular speech.

Some readers will, and do, respond wholly or partly to these solicitations and perhaps can maintain the sustaining memory of them through the thirty pages of the novel still to be read in all their renewed ironic frustration. For other readers, however, there must be something rather facile and troubling about this important scene which significantly qualifies or obviates the cathartic witnessing. Problems arising out of the very device of initial provocation can irremediably provoke, consciously or unconsciously. The long-standing racist epithet "monkey" used to describe the speaker (293, 294) by itself may produce this effect for many readers, whether or not they understand it as reflecting how grotesque the minister appears to the congregation. Similarly, though the preacher's vernacular when performed aloud by a competent speaker can be quite affecting, its notation in the "folk-phonetic" spelling can look condescending, especially as the supposed medium for the vocal transcendence of the verbal. Because it is an old comic solecism and aural pun in southern humor, the combination "brethren and *sisteren*" sounds a particularly discomforting false note as the first announcement of the extraordinary vernacular voice. As for the rhetorical appeal of the Passion narrative, the novel as a whole may well seem to have done as much to question the story and its untroubled cathartic application to the Compsons as to support it, or more so.[14]

The sermon episode, then, seems to be powerfully appealing to its implied author as an ideal and yet hedged with certain marks of his incredulity, and so it perforce remains to some significant degree an

image of what is wanted from Faulkner's audience and not a conclusive means of achieving it. This is to reaffirm that as a whole *The
Sound and the Fury* submits itself to the ability and willingness of
readers to complete and stabilize, by a recognition that is also catharsis, the fragmented, unstable tragedy that is not otherwise resolved.
To a remarkable extent the novel's achievement of tragedy lies in the
hands of Faulkner's audience, so that, partly by the work's own
demonstration, it is liable to the vagaries of a cultural and historical
judgment about what deserves the accolade *tragic*. In turn, completion and success are also vulnerable to the public to a degree surpass-
ing the ordinary dependency of a work on finding its readers.

The novel's scrutiny of related dialectical interpenetrations—of
passivity and action, pathos and tragedy, the individually personal
and its social acknowledgment—is keyed to an extraordinary combination of rhetorical power and rhetorical dependency on the audience. At another level of our analysis, this combination indicates
the novel's character as Faulkner's symbolic action.

V

It is well known that Faulkner's statements about *The Sound and the
Fury* consistently manifest its intensely personal nature for him. In
writing it, he claimed in an unused introduction, he wished to create
for himself a "beautiful and tragic little girl" ("Introduction" [1972]
705). Most revealing perhaps is another version of the introduction he
wrote in 1933 for a new edition to be published by Random House.
He notes that after he had "written three novels, with progressively
decreasing ease and pleasure, and reward and emolument," a door
shut between himself and his public and allowed him to make for
himself alone a book that would create lives missing from his life: "I
was trying to manufacture the sister which I did not have and the
daughter which I was to lose." He likens what he has made through
this symbolic action to an old Roman's vase, "which he loved and the
rim of which he wore slowly away with kissing it" (*Faulkner Miscellany* 159, 161).

But this absorption in an intimately possessed life must be fulfilled
at last through a shared public view, which Faulkner images as a
transition from inner to outer, as if finally his door had reopened: "I
had made myself a vase, but I suppose I knew all the time that I could

not live forever inside of it, that perhaps to have it so that I too could lie in bed and look at it would be better." The implication is that publication completes the reclaiming of what is personal by allowing the creator to participate in the public vision, with the suggestion of a heightened intimacy thereby with one's own: "I too could lie in bed and look." This implication conforms to the close relation between the artist's and the beholder's shares which Faulkner had indicated in the preceding paragraph "The writing of [the book] as it now stands taught me both how to write and how to read, and even more: It taught me what I had already read" (160–61).

In the previous chapter we noted that the escalation in outrageousness that begins with this novel and extends through the major phase creates a "hubristic" rhetoric. This process piques the audience's emulative accession of personal power and partisanship with the heroic agent, at the risk of losing the audience entirely. The door that will be closed to the young Thomas Sutpen, arousing his self-transformation into a figure of dangerous potency, is foreshadowed by the door that Faulkner imagines being shut between himself and the public. Faulkner's major phase, like Sutpen's heroic career, begins with the affront of rejection and proceeds with the constitutive risk of affronting others. The personal quality this novel captured for him by dramatizing the crisis of public acknowledgment, dovetails with Faulkner's development of a strategic self-presentation to a public. We need to broaden our focus now to include this development.

To the degree that Faulkner risks public accessibility to the experiences he represents fictionally, he can be true to his Roman vase, the idiosyncratically private aspect of experience. Yet to the same extent, he obviously risks losing his public. To put the matter more precisely, in light of what is at stake for Faulkner, he risks having a public that is his, for the public of readers who will recognize and authenticate the distinctive personal dimension will by that same token become an extension of the domain of the personal—*his* public in a strong sense. Yet there is a mutual possession as well, as indicated in the relationship of audience and speaker in the Easter sermon and the reciprocity of writing and reading through the reader's actualizing performance of the textual script by auditioning it. So that, in what Faulkner will later call a happy marriage of speaking and listening, readers can also speak in the strong sense of *their* author.

Although Faulkner declared that all his writing dealt with "myself and the world" (*Letters* 185), for him there were significant reasons for ruling out openly autobiographical writing like Thomas Wolfe's and instead experimenting with a variety of formal and technical means to enact that relationship. The lyric poetry and fantasy narratives of his early years evidently did not provide him the means to portray the tension and interpenetration between self and world, extending over time, from which his authentic sense of the personal stems. What was required was a means of delineating the social world as both external and internalized and as a personal ecology of frequently depersonalizing others, not the highly subjective natural setting that Faulkner's conventionally Romantic verses present as the stage for his stiff lyric persona. But when Faulkner turned to the resources of more or less realistic fiction to present the self in such a social milieu, the requirement for "data," for detailed specification, would constitute a barrier to autobiographical writing. For him the directly autobiographical in fiction lay too near the realm of mere fact, that reductio ad absurdum of experience. Indeed, it lay very near the particularly dangerous territory of publicly revealed private fact, in and of itself paradoxically false to the lived individual experience. Such mere data, "events," were valuable only when converted into symbolic forms that, however much larger-than-fact, could match the magnitude and dynamic character of one's felt life within an infusing social context. For instance, whatever the biographical facts about Faulkner's military flying, his youthful lies about it attempted to win acknowledgment of his personal experience, that is, to secure recognition of its distinctive inherent value, as a value others shared.

Attempting to do justice to this dimension, the young Faulkner often resorted to a set of roles he perfected: the aesthete, the aloof dandy whom some saw as the arrogant "Count No 'Count," the wounded pilot, the passive observer, the vulnerable dependent, the self-sufficient man of action, and, running through and around these personae, a revisionary enactment of his legendary great-grandfather. Joseph Blotner, David Minter, and Judith Sensibar reveal how large a part of Faulkner's early life consisted in his performance of these and other self-dramatizations, with what Ben Wasson called a "rare ability to dramatize himself interestingly" (Minter 23). The obverse side of this strategy of self-creative display was its self-protective effect. We can say of these fabrications, which extended in attenuated form beyond his youth, what Faulkner declared of his adolescent "mental life": he maintained a veneer of "surface insincerity" as a necessary means "to support intact my personal integrity" (*Early Prose and*

Poetry 114). Alternatively, if the biographical facts were not falsified or colored, the untransformed data were tucked away into that privacy that Faulkner fiercely guarded from the eyes that might see the events of his existence as banal. Better also to exaggerate protectively, as Faulkner increasingly did after his youth, the general mundaneness of his life and so preempt with this bland generality any closer look at drab facts that would demean the value of his personal experience.

What was true to the significance of that experience, he increasingly came to imply, was in his books, not in the life otherwise available to public record. That life was ultimately disposable; it was the life in which Faulkner must die. In a 1949 letter to Malcolm Cowley, Faulkner was moved to wish for a certain anonymity and oblivion to secure the preservation of his real life: "It is my ambition to be, as a private individual, abolished and voided from history, leaving it markless, no refuse save the printed books; I wish I had had enough sense to see ahead thirty years ago and, like some of the Elizabethans, not signed them. It is my aim, and every effort bent, that the sum and history of my life, which in the same sentence is my obit and epitaph too, shall be them both: He made the books and he died" (*Letters* 285). After Faulkner's years of undeserved obscurity, there is perhaps a proudly compensatory vehemence about this statement occasioned by his immediate desire to reject the *Life* (auspicious name) magazine interview Cowley had recently suggested. And Faulkner modified his tactics somewhat when in the post-Nobel years he could and did appear publicly once his literary recognition was guaranteed. But there is no contradiction between this letter and his famous desire to leave his undying mark on the doors of oblivion, to say No to death. The basic wish to do justice to the personal dimension over against the sham and shadow of the mere biographical chronicle runs continuously through the revealing introduction to *The Sound and the Fury,* through his posing, and through the self-effacement of his nonliterary life. Magnification and derogation of his biographical existence were simply different means to the end of doing justice to and securing immortality for what he felt was his most genuinely personal life, the *his-ness* of his life. And this only fiction could present with some adequacy, not only because of its resources of symbolic transformation and verbal heightening but because of its potential for winning the public acknowledgment that would complete his possession of the personal.

96

As an extension and transmutation of his early role-playing, writing became a way of displaying his prodigious command of a repertoire of personae and voices in the legitimate form of literature and at the same time implying that the reader's variously performative reciprocation to his powerful gesture was necessary to complete it.[15]

It was not only a sister and daughter Faulkner sought to create in *The Sound and the Fury* but, as he realized, the capable person who might emerge from his literary impersonating power. In an essay describing *Sartoris* as an attempt to oppose death and loss by fictionally preserving a treasured world and "reaffirm[ing] the impulses of my ego in this actual world without stability," Faulkner could ask whether "I had invented the world to which I would give life or it had invented me, giving me an illusion of greatness" (Blotner, "Essay on *Sartoris*" 122–24).

The illusion of greatness could become reality, Faulkner believed, if readers could be moved by his work. In his Foreword to *The Faulkner Reader,* Faulkner significantly implied that this achievement of "uplift[ing] man's heart" meant passing through and beyond impersonality, specifically the impersonal medium of print, in consonance with the writer's "completely selfish, completely personal" desire to achieve immortality through his writing:

> So he who, from the isolation of cold impersonal print, can engender this excitement, himself partakes of the immortality which he has engendered. Some day he will be no more, which will not matter then, because isolated and itself invulnerable in the cold print remains that which is capable of engendering still the old deathless excitement in hearts and glands whose owners and custodians are generations from even the air he breathed and anguished in; if it was capable once, he knows that it will be capable and potent still long after there remains of him only a dead and fading name. (*Essays, Speeches* 181-82)

As we already have some reason to suspect, and will later note at length, Faulkner's actual practice as a novelist makes the issue of invulnerability raised in this quotation much more complex than his flat declaration here indicates. What is clear is that Faulkner had a deep impulse to see art as a means of being both personally "capable" and invulnerable to death by turning to his advantage a protectively "impersonal" medium, print, and yet "partak[ing] of" the deathless personal "excitement" of his audience.

The need to create and preserve the personal in a non-autobiographical, "hubristic," socially grounded form helps to explain Faulkner's rather astonishing change from a limited writer of sometimes narcissistic verses into the accomplished artist of *The Sound and the Fury*. He recapitulates in this novel the change from a "lyric" persona dichotomously separated from others, as in the early poems, to a writer who knows that his door had to be opened.

From Faulkner's standpoint, apparently, the suggestions of suicide recurrent in his early writings largely express the persisting desire to slough off a lesser life and to survive only as Fame, as does Sir Galwyn in the fable *Mayday*. Somewhat as Achilles is presented the choice of either a long life without glory or a short life with immortal fame, Sir Galwyn is given the choice between being reincarnated in life or achieving fame by entering a stream in which his self and his memory will be washed away to become a memory for others: "Then you will remember nothing, not even this conversation or this choosing; and all your petty victories, your loving and hating, all the actions you have achieved will be washed from your mind to linger in these dark hurrying waters like darting small fish for those who are to come here after you to gaze upon; and this is Fame." As in Faulkner's early sketch "Nympholepsy," the waters contain a visionary girl whom the protagonist has pursued. Galwyn chooses at once watery oblivion, Fame, and the girl who is finally identified as "Little Sister Death" (83–84, 87). The imagistic similarities to Caddy here, and to Quentin's choice as a proxy for Faulkner's, are unmistakable.

It is not surprising that in an early letter praising *Moby-Dick*, Faulkner figured the novel's powerful effect in terms of Achilles' death; but Faulkner's additional trope of female memorial singers is a revealing attribution since Melville's is such a womanless text: "A death for Achilles, and the divine maidens of Patmos to mourn him, to harp whitehanded sorrow on their golden hair" (*Essays, Speeches* 198). We saw that as the focus and embodiment of passion, Caddy, with her shadowiness in the novel, represents the deathly alienation of experience for each brother, the passions that should be theirs rather than inflicted on them. Yet Caddy embodies not only this mortal threat to their self-esteem but the desired promise of a remedy. Like everything in the novel's field of symbolic forces, she carries a double valence. She is Little *Sister* Death, representing both the injury and its symbolic transformation into, respectively, a feminine comforter (for Benjy), chivalric object (for Quentin), and object of revenge (for Jason). She is passion and death given the elusive intimacy of a sister, as a sister is her brothers' own close relation but finally unpossessable.

As this trope illustrates, to defy death, it is necessary to figure it in forms amenable to at least partial transformation by feeling or action. In Caddy two forms of personalization combine: the feminizing of death and the "dialogizing" of death so that one may reply to it. The quasi domestication of death into a willful, disquieting "sister" who is a principal partner of Quentin's dialogues coheres with and complicates Quentin's simpler childhood conception of death as a "kind of private and particular friend" of his grandfather's, with whom his grandfather was "always talking and . . . was always right" (176). So too Faulkner's conception of a No to mortality figures death as a personified speaker whom one might refute or a personified silence against which a protesting voice might prevail.[16] Further, death is caught up in the interplay of speaking and listening for two different but not contradictory reasons: both because death is associated psychologically with incapacities of speech and hearing, which are for Faulkner virtually mortal failures of recognition, and because language itself is a death-stream (ambiguously female) in which one drowns but may be preserved through fame. That stream reappears in Faulkner's texts. It is, for instance, Quentin's Charles River, embodying Caddy, and the stream that murmurs, like Addie's bubbling voice from her coffin, to Darl and Cash. It is the rising tide of "female" fluidity in which Joe Christmas feels he will drown but which as blood rushing from his dying body transforms into a monument in his viewers' minds. It is the increasingly fluid prose itself.

For Faulkner, then, writing means writing oneself to death as a merely biological entity. It is, ideally, a martrydom to an impersonal medium that enables personal witnesses, imagined as female. Writing is the embracing of the female as the impersonal, as death, and as the personal, as survival. It is a raveling out into other voices, both in the virtual speech scripted in the text and, even more, in the anticipated realizing performances of readers. Writing is a relatively benign form of suicidal No through which one has a chance of becoming, as Quentin wished to be, "more than dead" (116).

It is in this general vein that the final sentences of the 1933 Introduction make Caddy a synecdoche for the personalized literary witness whose survival will make death bearable. After Faulkner describes his resolve to publish the novel—"to have it so that I too could lie in bed and look at it would be better"—he continues the association of ideas: "Surely so when that day should come when not only the ecstasy of writing would be gone, but the unreluctance and the something worth saying too. It's fine to think that you will leave something behind you when you die, but it's better to have made something you can die with. Much better the muddy bottom of a little doomed girl climbing a blooming pear tree in April to look in the window at the funeral" (161).

Implicitly, the funeral is that of the author who foresees and refutes his demise, so that although the explicit stated preference is for "something you can die with" over something to leave behind, the last image nevertheless stresses the witnessing survivor. Just as "doomed" Caddy in fact survives her deaths of depersonalization and public shame, the Caddy who witnesses Faulkner's death is the "beautiful and tragic" book itself surviving its author's rejection and disrepute to call for witnesses.

It is according to the founding principle that the individual is a theater of others that Caddy exists in her novel because, in the profoundest sense, she exists in her brothers and they in and through her (cf. Wagner and Faber). As representations of death and its symbolic transformation, Caddy and her novel portend that to say No to death is never to forget it but always to evoke the reality of the very thing to be resisted, as an overtone in a world conceived dialogically, a world of talk and sound. Faulkner's next published novel is the imagination of his desire turned into an ironic marginal condition. In this state, one is unable either to survive death or to complete it, precisely because one's death, like one's survival, vulnerably depends upon others and the stories of *their* lives.

CHAPTER 4

Voice as Hero: *As I Lay Dying*
and the Mortuary Trilogy

> Can storied urn or animated bust
> Back to its mansion call the fleeting breath?
> Can Honour's voice provoke the silent dust,
> Or Flatt'ry sooth the dull cold ear of Death?
>
> Gray, "Elegy"

> She dances now for apocryphal lovers
> To pale staring of the alive mouth of the dead.
>
> Faulkner, "A Dead Dancer"

> There's not too fine a distinction between humor and
> tragedy . . . . even tragedy is in a way walking a tightrope
> between . . . the bizarre and the terrible.
>
> *Faulkner in the University*

I

As we observed of Caddy's doubleness as sister death, symbolic transformation preserves what is transmuted so that the thing transformed is susceptible to reconversion to its former state again. But this stage too can be retransformed, and the process of transformation and reconversion is in principle an endless reemphasis: the concept sister death is a reminder of death, which then requires transformation into sister death again, and the cycle can recommence. Or in the more general Faulknerian formula, saying No to death recalls that it is death that is refuted, which spurs another No, and so on ad infinitum. The premise of this reversible transmutation is that a source of

101

danger must itself be the source of averting danger through transformation. The duplicity of sound centrally illustrates principle and
premise, as in the climactic flourish of *Flags in the Dust:* "For there is
death in the sound . . . and a glamorous fatality, like . . . a dying fall
of horns along the road to Roncevaux" (370). It is typical of
Faulkner's symbolic metamorphosis that the sound contains death in
both senses; its dying fall continues both to sound death and to "control" it by evoking immortal, heroic Roland.

This chapter will elaborate additional specific grounds for the reemphasis of symbolic transformation and reconversion oversimply
sketched here. One of the things that distinguish the first three novels
of Faulkner's major phase—*The Sound and the Fury, As I Lay Dying,*
and *Sanctuary*—is the relative rapidity of symbolic, including generic,
reemphasis. Nowhere is that rapidity so pronounced as in *As I Lay
Dying;* compared to this novel's flickering between various tonal and
generic poles of emphasis, the shifting between pathos and tragedy in
The Sound and the Fury is in slow motion.

A good place to begin to pick up this mercurial process is in the
traditional association of women with ritual vocal mourning over
death and thus, by a shifting of emphasis, with death itself. The
connection of women with death is a widespread cross-cultural association, as Maurice Bloch points out (211–30), and Faulkner's conviction of it runs deep.[1]

Works like *The Marionettes,* "Nympholepsy," and *Mayday* dramatize this association, and *Soldiers' Pay* includes a self-consciously conventional passage on the ironic intertwinings of sex and death (295).
At the same time, and inseparably, women are identified with the
ritual and artistic counters to death. We saw that, rather as Caddy is
sister death to her brothers, Faulkner conceived *The Sound and the
Fury* as both a personified Roman vase and a beautiful and tragic
sister/daughter who would survive his death. The partly sympathetic, partly wry fictional analogy in *Sartoris* is Horace Benbow's
association of his sister Narcissa with a glass vase he conceives as an
immortal Keatsian bride of quietness. (Never far from Faulkner's
mind during this period is the poet Horace's "monument more lasting than bronze.") What remains of this association in *Sanctuary* is a
cluster of tropes such as the comparison of Narcissa's appearance to
the "serene and stupid impregnability of heroic statuary" and the
novel's closing image of "dead tranquil queens in stained marble"
(253, 398). We will see that Addie Bundren is not only the focus of

comparable transformations of mortality. Addie, who imagines both her genital sexuality and a male, Anse, as a vessel shape, is the maker and reverser of these transformations.

Here are the women's voices mourning Addie's death:

> The song ends; the voices quaver away with a rich and dying fall. . . .
> Somebody in the house begins to cry. It sounds like her eyes and her voice were turned back inside her, listening; we move, shifting to the other leg, meeting one another's eye and making like they hadn't touched.
> . . . The women sing again. In the thick air it's like their voices come out of the air, flowing together and on in the sad, comforting tunes. When they cease it's like they hadn't gone away. It's like they had just disappeared into the air and when we moved we would loose them again out of the air around us, sad and comforting. (59)

The ritual voices that continue to reverberate to the listener although they have died as acoustical phenomena constitute a paradigmatic moment in *As I Lay Dying* and in Faulkner's work in general. Their dying fall prolonged, the voices continue to exist in what Don Ihde calls the broad or open focus of listening (94) because the listeners are indeed momentarily open to sensuous experience and to each other in a rare and perilous instant and because each continues to perform mentally and to hear what was just performed physically. The instant and the performance are mutually enabling; each grounds the other. Such too is the relationship between Faulkner's novel as a textual score and the act of reading it as a performance of the score. This lingering sound suggests the other modes of open-ended process with which the novel is concerned: dying, as a process that lingers beyond its physical accomplishment, and immortality, which is the cognate and sublation of this "extended" aspect of dying.

Women can serve their vocally expressive role in Faulkner precisely because, as the traditional vessels of sexual honor, they are culturally charged with muting sexual shame and thus readily become in general the bearers and icons of silence and mystery. The communal power to transubstantiate a threat to vital dignity comes from the culturally sanctioned momentary release of such a powerful cultural repression. Like Shegog, who preaches the Easter sermon, a male in the role of minister performatively accompanies and lends sanction to the release of women's voices in *As I Lay Dying*. The corresponding role proposed to us as readers, I want to suggest, is the represented structural role of women in such ritual: figures of silence and of silencing, vessels and bestowers of fragile honor, associates of death, and potentially vocal repudiators of mortality. And Faulkner's text is our pointedly ambiguous sanction and inducement.

On these and other terms the novel is a textbook of the liminal experience of being betwixt and between one state and another which is characteristic of ritual and particularly the funeral rite of passage. But here the rite is a maimed rite. This marred social rite, which accentuates rather than transforms the scandal of death, is the counterpart of the missing collective story of shame redeemed in the Compson world. The potential for reemphasis inherent in symbolic transformation is a major basis for this maiming, since, as Victor Turner notes in *The Ritual Process,* rite in general re-presents the thing to be transformed ritually; at any moment it may reappear in what Faulkner would call its bizarreness and terribleness. Although the resulting process of transmutation and reconversion is in principle endless, practically it seems exhaustible and exhausting to the mind going back and forth in the circuit of reemphasis. For Faulkner, the expansion of this circuit through extraordinary ramifications and sublative levels expresses the inexhaustibility of human effort, which he evokes to refute the closure and silence of death.

In the two novels following *The Sound and the Fury,* then, Faulkner rewrites the story of mortality. The trilogy as a whole teaches us to conceive of mortality in an extended sense, as when Addie says that Anse did not know that he was dead or Temple associates her rape with her death and funeral. Reflecting mortality's essential insult, the novels abound in violations sensational and subtle—murder, suicide, bodily corruption, rape, castration, and various psychic invasions.

The trilogy of death and death ritual is also, rhetorically, a trilogy of heroic voice. Faulkner's first novels had displayed a repertoire of styles including the heroic, in the common general sense of the term (most obviously in the Miltonic phrasing in parts of *Sartoris,* well described by Albert Guerard ["Voice" 39–42]) as well as in the particular sense in which I will use it. But as threats to the person reach an extreme thematically beginning with *The Sound and the Fury,* so voice first resonates most fully and complexly in opposition. It is as if the trilogy were a reminder of the supposed etymological derivation of *person* from *per-sona,* "through sound," or vocal sound emerging through a persona in the sense of an actor's mask. In these works, burdened with intimations of mortality, Faulkner completely finds his voice. That is, he finds not a voice but a collection of voices, personae, which produce their overall effect by playing off and accommodating one another. Fundamentally, the role of hero is not filled by Addie or any other character in the trilogy. Even in the sense of "protagonist" this function is left indeterminate at the level of plot, so the reader is left with "choices" like Quentin or Caddy, Darl or Addie, Horace or Temple. Nor is this a trilogy in search of a hero. Voice is that hero. It is a personally empowering force operating within a dialectical field of other forces that in some ways enable and reinforce and in others oppose its effect.

Behind this alliance and struggle is the most traditional notion of the heroic life, and afterlife, reflected in the root of *fame,* "to speak." To have fame is to be spoken into life—an idea that informs Gray's questioning of "Honour's voice" and Pope's skepticism in *An Essay on Man:* "What's Fame? a fancied life in others' breath." Voice seems an ideal solution to Faulkner's project of opposing death because it says No to death primordially: voice is the breath of life transformed through sound into communication, communion. Voice gives over one's breath to the keeping of the community that will survive one's death. Faulkner's early poetry is fascinated with the traditional antinomy of death and the breath of life. When the lyric persona dares to express hope directly, these lines from "Mississippi Hills: My Epitaph" represent the crux: "Though I be dead / This soil that holds me fast will find me breath" (*Helen* 156; see also the several rhymings of "death" and "breath" in this collection). Voice and breath are one; so Tull comments on one of Anse's sayings, "Never a truer breath was ever breathed" (20). It is no accident that Faulkner's characters are always panting for breath when they are profoundly threatened or that the trilogy before us repeatedly stresses difficult breathing: Quentin's suffocation by honeysuckle, or Miss Reba's, and Ruby's child's laboring for breath, or Vardaman's fear that Addie will suffocate in her coffin, or Jewel's protest that Dewey Dell's fanning keeps "the air always moving so fast on [Addie's] face that when you're tired you cant breathe it" (11). Quentin literally drowns out his mental voices, including the *"voice that breathed o'er Eden"* (81), but he nevertheless imagines his river grave as if it provided air, with a "roof of wind" (80). And the black murderer who is to be "suffocated" by hanging leads his audience in singing spirituals and laments that "dey ghy stroy de bes ba'ytone singer in nawth Mississippi" (*Sanctuary* 258). All these are the thematic precursors of the breath-taking style of *Pylon, Absalom, Absalom!* and later works, often thought of as quintessentially Faulknerian: the long polysyllabic sentences that coax the reader into a somatic enactment of the need for and recovery of breath and voice.

Although *The Sound and the Fury* is a tragedy to be resolved by soliciting the audience's acknowledging enactment, *As I Lay Dying* and the trilogy as a whole subject the rhetorical offer to a searching reexamination. The sign of this scrutiny is Addie's dedication to a certain "voicelessness," a muting of the woman's voice. The reason *As I Lay Dying* requires discussion is not that in any simple sense it can be categorized within or outside literary tragedy. Our subject is less Faulknerian tragedy as a static product, a finished achievement, than it is the process of scripting and actualizing tragic possibilities in the act of writing and reading. All of Faulkner's are contingent tragedies, and this novel both evokes a reading performance suitable to tragedy—as by seriously dramatizing issues of death and immortality and by its periodically heightened, ceremonious language—and discourages it. It thus not only anatomizes the human transformations of what is bizarre and terrible but periodically reveals these transformations to be themselves bizarre and terrible. By inviting a reading performance that experiences this idea concretely as an act and a consequence, the novel serves as a feelingly skeptical commentary on the tragic initiative of *The Sound and the Fury*. A key to that initiative is the coordinating of unclosed plot with voice.

Voice may be an opening, but the plot of life closes in a physical death. In the novel immediately before us, this death plot, with its equivalents in psychological injury, comes to the forefront as a shock that silences, as Addie's noisome body has the effect of "suffocating voice" (63). Against Faulkner's desire for a readership who will find him breath, he poses the fear expressed in the conclusive record of a life: "Here lies Horace Benbow in a fading series of small stinking spots" (*Sanctuary* 191). One way of describing the mortuary trilogy is to say that it is a dialectic of the sonorous Horatian monument and the stinking fading spots. Or one may phrase it as a dialectic founded upon the paradox of a monument erected through breath and sound, which is to say a speech committed to writing for an "audience" of modern silent readers. For Faulkner, to tempt these readers to hear the writing they see means to accentuate the accommodating sound character of language but to do so by devices that potentially interfere with what they enable.

II

In the probable source of Faulkner's title, the "Book of the Dead" of the *Odyssey,* Agamemnon complains of the unfulfilled mortuary customs that left him unreleased by culture into peaceful death:

> I, as I lay dying
> Upon the sword, raised up my hands to smite her,
> And shamelessly she turned away, and scorned
> To draw my eyelids down or close my mouth
> Though I was on the road to Hades' house.

For humans, as social and symbolic beings, there are two deaths, one physical and natural and another that traditionally occurs in funerary rites. In his own way, Dr. Peabody understands the basis for this second death, that death is "merely a function of the mind—and that of the minds of the ones who suffer the bereavement. The nihilists say it is the end; the fundamentalists, the beginning; when in reality it is no more than a single tenant or family moving out of a tenement or a town" (29).

Rituals of death in Western and many other cultures are traditionally the occasion for testing and, ideally, strengthening social solidarity and individual and communal purposiveness. In *As I Lay Dying* and its companion novels, disruptions and maimed rites threaten to defeat these aims or trivialize their attainment. Damuddy's wake is obscured by the children's squabbles over its import; Benjy's solitary "graveyard" is pitifully shabby and subjected to disrespect, his trips to the cemetery riddled with turmoil; Red's funeral is memorably travestied; Miss Reba's life of protracted mourning for Mr. Binford is beset by unintended indignities to his memory; and Addie's burial journey becomes the very definition of a calamitously defective ritual. What emerges through these and other rents in death's ceremonial shroud is a reminder of the exceptional ambivalence, conscious or otherwise, that mortality can arouse.

The living are drawn toward the deceased by affection and toward the grave by demoralization. Life's end is terrifying, yet the apparent triumph of nature, in its purposeless physicality, can threaten to unmask all human social arrangements and individual strivings as comprehensively pointless. As a product of all this, there is conflict between the will to endure, to continue the business of life, and the temptation to surrender. Handling this conflict can be one of the most urgent endeavors of symbolic transformation.

The toleration of such intense ambivalence may be difficult at best. The ambivalence itself, however, necessarily becomes an additional risk, over and above the threat of death per se, to a single-minded either/or. For this orientation there is an especially powerful impulse to flatly deny death and its associated ambivalence by repressing it privately, concealing it even from oneself, rather than to refute it publicly by the sublation of communal ritual. Since rituals mediate between what Darl thinks of as *is* and *is not,* by representing the matter to be symbolically negated, the community's ritual No to mere animal mortality depends upon the possibility of a public recognition of death and its ambivalences—the recognition that private repression would seek to escape.

But if the impulse to ignore death by private repression is strong, so is the opposite urge of ritual negation in a fictional world like Faulkner's, where community must be reckoned with. The second, social death has its full significance and power in such a communally oriented society, to a major degree informed by an honor-shame culture where one's life-sustaining self-esteem exists largely in the collective mind of the group. Mortuary rites remove mortality from the realm of nature and passivity into that of culture and action, symbolically controlling it by staging it in the costumes, gestures, and language human beings can order and manipulate. Mere physical, natural dissolution—the destruction of a nonperson—is not so much denied as refuted or repudiated by actions defining death as a cultural process. By thus choosing necessity in its own chosen forms, the community releases the deceased into a completed, a human death. The bereaved are assisted to accept a psychological "letting go" of the dead, who can then "rest in peace." Dewey Dell's distracted thoughts present the failure to achieve this resolution: "I heard that my mother is dead. I wish I had time to let her die. I wish I had time to wish I had" (78). Just as Benjy's graphic binaries illuminate the Compson outlook, Vardaman's shift between denial—boring holes in the coffin—and confused private transformation—conceiving his mother as a fish—shows in its crudity and shocking reversal of the human/bestial roles what the more highly developed strategies seek to do and what apprehension of animality inherently threatens them.

The significance of the defective rituals of death in the trilogy derives from the conflict between the two forms of negation as well as the precariousness of ritual or other symbolic transformation, which conjures up the condition to be repudiated. The defective ceremonies of negation contrast with the unmarred rituals, the Easter service in *The Sound and the Fury* and the funeral (as distinct from the burial) service for Addie. Because both successful rites are presided over by extraordinary voices raised "in chanting measures beyond the need for words," the participants, symbolically enacting death, pass out of their isolation and become as "nothing," so that the voices seem to "come out of the air." In the defective ceremonies, however, bickerings and confused words, like static, proclaim the repressive mechanism of denial and, often accompanying this, conflicting, atomistic individuals. Witness Caddy, who in her youthful ignorance cannot stop talking and arguing long enough to admit that white people can die, or the comic mourners at Red's funeral, with their verbally confused clamor for "bier." Anse epitomizes an egoism rationalized by verbal formulas that permit him to repress awareness of the scandalous degeneration of the burial journey. The psychological denial of the full reality of Addie's death and corruption, the stench and the buzzards inadmissibly accompanying them, allows the Bundrens to make their journey. At its end Addie's burial, the putative goal of their excruciating effort, is itself buried by the briefest of references—"But when we got it filled and covered" (227)—and by the shouting struggle in which they capture Darl, who has implicitly reminded them of the inadmissible throughout the journey.

The intended culminating rite of burial is maimed because Addie has by now become a flagrant corporeality, nature mocking culture, and something to be quickly hidden by the earth. At the novel's end, Addie, still without having fully completed the process of human, socially managed dying, is simply replaced by a new woman. The title of the novel dramatizes this incomplete process of cultural death.

The unfinished ritualization of death strands Addie on the margin between nature and culture, where she remains throughout the book and even at its end. It is as if from this limbo that she addresses us long after we have seen her physical demise. She has been preached and sung over, and she is costumed in her wedding dress as well in the coffin Cash has carefully tailored to her. But she is laid in backwards, her face has holes bored in it, and her decomposing body is the rankest counterrefutation of culture's effort to pull her away from nature into the communal orbit as a deceased person, not a disintegrating thing.

Agamemnon complained that his eyes were left unclosed in death. Vardaman is likewise certain that Addie's eyes are unclosed, "looking at me through the wood" of her coffin (144). The subliminal figure-in-the-carpet of the trilogy is the staring gaze of an incomplete, a socially untransformed death. In lingering, it parodies immortality. As commentators have noticed, the pervasive eye images have many associated meanings and uses. But they all connect to this unsettling sign of a death that has not been adequately negated by the communal dispensation. The last we see of Addie's natural life is in her eyes, "her eyes, the life in them, rushing suddenly upon them; the two flames glare up for a steady instant. Then they go out as though someone had leaned down and blown upon them" (32). But then as the sound of Cash sawing wood for her coffin resumes, "at each stroke her face seems to wake a little into an expression of listening and of waiting" (34). Later Darl says that in the sounds of bodily corruption "she talks in little trickling bursts of secret and murmurous bubbling," asking God to hide her "from the sight of man" so she can "lay down her life" (143, 144). Addie's is an unquiet condition in which, to use the phrasing of her slogan, one cannot "*stay* dead a long time." The theme of necessary death rites claims descent from the tragic heroism of Homer, Virgil, and the *Antigone,* where the fallen must be given proper ceremonies or else remain balefully "undead," an outrage to gods and mortals. The open eyes are shameful; they express the shame of a final mortal insult to personal worth. As in such a condition humans approach the condition of brute animals, in *As I Lay Dying* the latter in turn die like unaccommodated human beings: "The head of one mule appears [in the flood waters], its eyes wide; it looks back at us for an instant, making a sound almost human" (98). It is no accident that the new Mrs. Bundren has hard-staring popeyes and a duck shape, images that add their note of hard comedy to the tragic suggestions of the bare forked animal.

If Addie's burial journey disintegrates the last part of the death rite, her funeral ceremony demonstrates the opposite extreme wherein voices manage the ritual crossing of mortal boundaries; it is a passage we need to have before us a whole:

Whitfield begins. His voice is bigger than him. It's like they are not the same. It's like he is one, and his voice is one, swimming on two horses side by side across the ford and coming into the house, the mud-splashed one and the one that never even got wet, triumphant and sad. Somebody in the house begins to cry. It sounds like her eyes and her voice were turned back inside her, listening; we move, shifting to the other leg, meeting one another's eye and making like they hadn't touched.

Whitfield stops at last. The women sing again. In the thick air it's like their voices come out of the air, flowing together and on in the sad, comforting tunes. When they cease it's like they hadn't gone away. It's like they had just disappeared into the air and when we moved we would loose them again out of the air around us, sad and comforting. (59)

In such a perfected moment of ritual, voice announces the emergence of a person from its privacy into the public. At its most compelling, ritual voice simultaneously evokes the emergence of other persons and calls for participation in a collective expansiveness of self which opposes the threats to it. As rendered in Tull's description, the funeral is a wordless commingling of voices, a "triumphant and sad" union of persons for the moment open and audible, listening to themselves and to others. With eyes and voice turned inward, they acknowledge their own demise presaged in Addie's, and their eyes can touch one another's. The ritually permitted admission of mortality allows the privileged moment in Faulkner's world, a lowering of defenses and the instant of mutual recognition. By contrast, in usually not being mutually sought for and desired, Darl's clairvoyant ability to invade others' minds distorts such ritual reciprocity. Closer attention to the dynamics of defense and recognition in the characters' lives will further illuminate and be illuminated by ritual's recognizing moment.

Traditional tragedy often turns on the recognition of another person's identity. In Faulkner, personal recognition in itself is crucial: despite the need for defensive privacy, one must count in the life of another in order to count in one's own. The novel seriously entertains the idea that to be is to be for others. This is the burden of Darl's convoluted musings on ontology and the basis for Addie's surreal "killing" of Anse in her mind. In an important sense, one's life, death, and immortality take place in the minds of others. In order to live, in order not to die in one's life, one must receive, or compel, recognition.

Despite evident differences, Addie is like Quentin Compson in wanting acknowledgment. She believes, however, that it is not her own but others' private inwardness that presents a problem. The inaccessibility of the secreted person baffles her desire to make her mark on people by any means, cruel or kind, to compel an acknowledgment of her own proper existence. She thinks in this way of the school children she has whipped: "Now you are aware of me! Now I am something in your secret and selfish life, who have marked your blood with my own for ever and ever" (114). Ritual voice is a call for mutual recognition of human coexistence. So, in its way, is such violence, though the coexistence is hierarchical, in the mode of dominance and submission, "master" and "slave."

In the trilogy, the obstacles to recognition are severe. The person occupies a would-be psychological sanctuary, seeking protection from a punishing existence. Both self-protective opacity and aggressive intrusion are concentrated in the looks of others. It is not only Darl's probing vision that as a rule arouses uneasiness and defensive barriers. One is vulnerable through the eyes to other eyes. The paramount image of shame, death's blank gaze, proliferates into eyes that watch others. In *The Sound and the Fury,* from the moment Quentin awakes and sees the bird regarding him, he feels himself under a blank, unresponsive scrutiny, as Benbow does in the opening of *Sanctuary;* and Gowan, cringing before imagined "whispering eyes" (238), abandons Temple at Frenchman's Bend. One of the main forces in Temple's progressive collapse is her sense of being coldly watched from the moment she leaves the dance with Gowan, as she relieves herself in the woods, and up to and during her rape, which she experiences as an invasion by the old man's staring sightless eyes. Yet all this is mirrored in or mirrors her own blank gaze, the assertion of a desired sexual potency, autonomy, and invulnerability, "her eyes blankly right and left looking, cool, predatory and discreet" (198). It is as if the whole trilogy has produced the name and nature of Temple's literal assailant as an eye aggressively protruding. And at the end of *As I Lay Dying,* the new Mrs. Bundren is introduced in terms of her assaulting, silencing gaze: "with them kind of hard-looking pop eyes like she was daring ere a man to say nothing" (177). Yet in turn, the real Popeye's expressionless speech and rubber-knob eyes are only the extreme achievement of a widely shared goal that equates inscrutability with impregnability.[2] As Cora Tull looks at Eula, "when she finds me watching her, her eyes go blank" (7). The complementary moment occurs when the druggist Moseley meets Dewey Dell: "It was like she had taken some kind of a lid off her face, her eyes" (134).

Dewey Dell's desperation in her pregnancy causes her to unmask to a stranger. A profounder acknowledgment between Darl and Cash occurs at the flooded river. The torrent confronts them with the "myriad original motion" from which their lives have come and to whose undifferentiated existence death will return them. In the mesmerized imagination of that return, it is as if "the clotting which is you had dissolved" into the current that "talks up to us in a murmur become ceaseless and myriad . . . as though just beneath the surface something huge and alive waked for a moment" (110, 93).

It is this fatal collective "voice . . . waste and mournful," that the funeral service exorcises by imitating it in a benign collective form. (Darl hears its untransformed murmur again from Addie's coffin.) With this "myriad" voice in their ears, Darl and Cash have their instant of shame-free recognition: "with long probing looks, looks that plunge unimpeded through one another's eyes and into the ultimate secret place where for an instant Cash and Darl crouch flagrant and unabashed in all the old terror and the old foreboding, alert and secret and without shame" (93). Even privately and internally, "the process of coming unalone" is a vocal event of dangerously becoming open, as it is with Dewey Dell's inner speaking and listening "parts": "I listen to it saying for a long time before it can say the word and the listening part is afraid that there may not be time to say it. I feel my body, my bones and flesh beginning to part and open upon the alone, and the process of coming unalone is terrible. Lafe. Lafe. 'Lafe.' Lafe. Lafe" (41).

In the process of coming unalone in Addie's funeral service, as in Shegog's Easter sermon, there is a similar vocal opening and a truce in the war of each against all so that secreted persons can emerge to oppose by a collective self-announcement the "old foreboding" of obliteration. The force of this opposition goes beyond the strength in numbers. Other people's intrusive or blankly indifferent eyes are analogies for death, its surrogates. Thus for the secreted person to emerge to others' eyes and hearing ("meeting one another's eye and making like they hadn't touched") is in itself a symbolic counter to the ultimate threat. The menace of literal physical death overrides for a time the danger represented by others and provokes the mutual evocation of communally augmented, recognized persons, like Whitfield's voice, "bigger than" the single "mud-splashed" being and caught up in a listening directed both inwardly and outwardly. In the protective sanction of ritual, eyes that touch each other seek to close the staring gaze of death.

III

Everything in *As I Lay Dying* is permeated by the alternately clashing and supplementing strategies for managing death by either denial or refusal. These are inseparable from the various general strategies for living, projects of being. The one major strategy is that of contraction into a hidden sanctuary, "the ultimate secret place." The alternative is essentially a strategy of union with others through the jeopardy of public vulnerability, and it entails penetrable self-boundaries. The sign of the one is the aggressive or unrevealing gaze. The sign of the other is an extraordinary participation in voice. The contrast between the two is like that Peabody makes between nakedness and pride when he feels Addie's eyes shoving him from the room: "that pride, that furious desire to hide that abject nakedness which we bring here with us . . . [and] carry stubbornly and furiously with us into the earth again" (31).[3]

The Bundrens are marvelous aggregates of these distinct impulses, which at times alternate in flexible adaptation to different situations and at others poignantly or ludicrously oppose each other. Addie is the most furious, volatile mixture.

More and more consciously, she lives according to her father's motto of anticipating death—"the reason for living was to get ready to stay dead a long time" (114)—though she at last suspects that he did not understand it in the right sense. She finally attempts to weave personal violation and death throughout her life on terms in which they are under her symbolic control and so change their meaning. So at last, by an arithmetic reminiscent of Mr. Compson, she transforms the childbearing that she had experienced as violation: "I gave Anse Dewey Dell to negative Jewel. Then I gave him Vardaman to replace the child I had robbed him of. And now he has three children that are his and not mine. And then I could get ready to die" (119). In her lifelong preparation to "stay dead" in peace, Addie creates a complex chain of negatives, both of denial and of refutation.

Addie's life is like a death rite in her attempt, through such symbolic control, to satisfy her thirst for a vitalizing personal contact like that sanctioned in the community's ritual refutation of mortality and in few other instances. The prospect of her death, given in her father's motto, apparently creates in her what Philippe Ariès has called a *"passion for being, an anxiety at not sufficiently being"* (*Western Attitudes* 105). For Addie, intimacy means consubstantiality with lifeblood, and life itself, against death. This Dionysian impulse is what the genuinely erotic means to her. On the other hand, as Anse says, "She was ever a private woman" (13), one who also cherished her separateness and invulnerability as part of her opposition to death.

Pulled between these impulses, the young Addie is consequently tormented by the ubiquitous but ungraspable vitality of the early spring. She senses it in the voices of geese calling to her out of the air from the "wild darkness" at night. Since these voices are the sign not only of life but of the vulnerability entailed in open emotional dependence, they indicate at once her desire and what is for her an unfeasible condition for attaining it. It is significant that in the very moments before her death she maintains the "inscrutability" of her own voice as she summons her son: "'You, Cash,' she shouts, her voice harsh, strong, and unimpaired" (32). Thus she also senses life as frustratingly locked away in her students, as "blood strange to each other blood and strange to mine," every child "with his and her secret and selfish thought" (114). Seeking to compel the contact for which she cannot risk her innate privacy, she beats the children to mark and merge their "blood" with hers, to make "my blood and their blood flow as one stream" (116).

Unsatisfied by this displacement of voice and eroticism into violence, she then tries to quiet the call from the rife darkness by retreating into psychological denial, a domestication she still conceives as vigorous action: "And so I took Anse." Becoming pregnant with Cash shatters this false solution of denial through domesticity by reminding her that "living was terrible," not tame, and by teaching her that giving birth "was the answer to it." Gestation is, for a time, "the" answer because it puts Addie in touch with another who is part of herself, while it also places her directly into the natural process of regeneration. It gives her a "good" violation of her separateness:

"My aloneness had been violated and then made whole again by the violation." From this vantage she understands why she had been frustrated by the schoolchildren, and she scorns the poor imitation of personal connection that words afford: "We had had to use one another by words like spiders dangling by their mouths from a beam, swinging and twisting and never touching. . . . I knew that it had been, not that my aloneness had to be violated over and over each day, but that it had never been violated until Cash came" (115–16). Addie's language of violation eloquently testifies to the violent ambivalence she feels between her need for intimacy, on the one hand, and, on the other, for invulnerable privacy. She can imagine the kind of passionate union she desires only as an invasion. To her, this little death is the price that must be paid to participate in the flow of life. But after giving birth to Cash she retires to the constricted circle she quickly redraws "whole again": "time, Anse, love, what you will, outside the circle."

By fathering Darl, Anse reintroduces an uncontrollable intimacy and secrecy into Addie's life, so that she simultaneously rejects Darl and Anse and prepares to repudiate all the children Anse fathers by making him promise to bury her in Jefferson when she dies (116). By verbally empowering the inert Anse to act, she duplicates and redoubles her design of transmuting dying from passivity into her own action. Further, she symbolically cuts her ties with Anse's family line. The burial is to be her final withdrawal into separateness, yet she will require the little community of her own "blood" to effect her will. Rejecting them as a group, she wants to take her death rites into her own hands and thus, culminating a long string of negatives, finally "negative" death too.

Addie attempts to die as she has attempted to live, by imposing the repression of secrecy on an essentially antithetical public strategy of death rite. She designs a foredoomed oxymoron, private ritual.

If anyone ever possessed the heroic temper, it is Addie. No half measures long content her. Her revenge upon Anse and all the uncontrollability of intimacy he stands for aims to be uncompromisingly root-and-branch. But she is repeatedly ensnared in paradoxes of action, words, and voice as she attempts radical divisions and displacements among these terms which would give her a heroic power of symbolic action. She erases Anse by mentally destroying his name (116) and by securing his promise to bury her as she wishes, since his name and promise together make up Anse's "word" for her. The essence is privacy: "My revenge would be that he would never know I was taking revenge"; as she repeats, "He did not know that he was dead." This is an almost incredible kind of vengeance unless we realize the value and power for Addie of secrecy as such, as an instrument of personal impregnability. The cryptic quality of her own words enacts, or rather scripts for our enactment, her deeply withholding sensibility: a desired power to manipulate others in and through their public language but to remain herself just outside the reach of words. In all respects, Addie attempts secretly to "negative" Anse and in so doing to affirm herself as being beyond words: "I would be I; I would let him be the shape and echo of his word" (117).

Darl's birth not only precipitates Addie's scheme of long-term vengeance. By destroying her strategy of domestication, it also revives the wild call out of the air which still requires an answer, in the sense of both "solution" and "reply." Her answer is twofold: adultery with Whitfield and a revised conception of herself as mother. Both are conceived as "duty to the terrible blood," to "the alive"— those she considers truly alive and life itself. Rather than, as before, imagining the life principle as the airborne voice of wild creatures, she now conceives it as the divine speech of the earth, a "dark voicelessness in which the words are the deeds" (117).

Not only has Addie dichotomized actions from words (117), but now she has attempted to split action from voice as well. The reason should be clear. Addie disparages words because they betray unique personal experience. "[The word] fear was invented by someone that had never had the fear; pride, who never had the pride." Voice too must be interdicted insofar as it means an abandonment of inscrutability and autonomy. But she in fact cannot simply divide voice from action and repress it, because of the vital intimacy voice can create. Addie wants the intimate effect of vocal disclosure without the vulnerability of self-disclosure itself. In her very attempt at dichotomy, she is thus committed to a set of equivocal displacements that reveal, despite her, the essential continuity between voice and action as modes of communication. She imagines a kind of prophetic speech without words or voice that "talk[s] of God's love and His beauty and His sin." In her formulation "hearing the dark voicelessness," she conceives a pure sound without voice but with the revelatory properties of ritual voice. In a sublation like that of death rites, she imagines a negation that represents what is simultaneously refuted: "voicelessness."

Addie wants to reach the ideally communicative silence "on the other side of" voice without having to go through the medium of voice. Her sublation "voicelessness" indicates and preserves her desire by naming voice as the traditional means of fulfillment, but in a negated form. For Addie, this voiceless speech is action, since action may be both self-expressive and inscrutable. Not just any action will do, however. The specific symbolic action she chooses must duplicate the vocal communication it stands for, but in a tolerable form of intercourse. Adultery with Whitfield meets the most important criterion in that his voice is literally the extraordinary agent that sounds the keynote of ritual. In effect, her union with him, as voice displaced into action, mimes the union of spoken male and sung female voices in her funeral rite. Even more transcendently, to Addie it seems that she and the minister together "shape and coerce" the terrible blood that is God's voiceless fiat itself.

Addie's act of adultery, moreover, recreates in a form acceptable to her both the risk of self-disclosure associated with voice and the satisfactions of secrecy. Having made imagined contact with the divine life force, Addie can reconceive her motherhood, but again only in equivocal terms reflecting the tension between her contrary impulses of privacy and communion. Though the affair with Whitfield ends, Addie retains her sense of sacral continuity and timelessness: "But for me it was not over. I mean, over in the sense of beginning and ending, because to me there was no beginning nor ending to anything then. . . . My children were of me alone, of the wild blood boiling along the earth, of me and of all that lived; of none and of all." This condition, however, also passes. There is a period like sleep lasting two months, from which she is pulled by her awareness of being pregnant: "Then I found that I had Jewel. When I waked to remember to discover it, he was two months gone." In the privileged phase, the circle of self comes close to dissolving into a fluid, boundariless continuum that still, however, reveals her characteristic paradoxical tension between "mine alone" and "of none and of all." What she has attained, nevertheless, is as close as she can come to the moment in the novel when ritual voices refute death by miming the individual's dissolution into others.

Jewel's birth ends Addie's restlessness, since he is the concrete embodiment of her participation in life and with him she can now satisfy her desire for intimacy. He is, in a way that the other children were only momentarily, really "of" her alone, and of the fluid vitality for which Whitfield was merely a conduit. Voice, first transposed into the voicelessness of action, has now been stilled completely. She enters a communicative silence like that attained through ritual voice and its benign miming of undifferentiated flowing: "The wild blood boiled away and the sound of it ceased. Then there was only the milk, warm and calm and I lying calm in the slow silence, getting ready to clean my house" (118–19). The innocent description, cleaning house, belies the nature of the purging. Addie is no longer haunted by voices; she has given birth to her "salvation," and she can now rid herself of her "blood" and so put death in its place by her planned symbolic control over her burial.

For all her physical and symbolic energy, however, the capstone of Addie's design, the burial, leaves her dependent on others and consequently vulnerable to the parody of her intentions that ensues.

When life is lived under the aspect of guarding one's vulnerability to mortality, mortification becomes paramount. The fear of vulnerability in the form of emotional dependency creates ambivalence toward those one cares for. Passion thus becomes death tainted, for others must be punished for "making" us love them. Addie treats Jewel with exactly this extreme ambivalence, which also informs Jewel's treatment of his beloved horse and Anse's conception of a deity who chastises those he loves. Since one adopts toward oneself the attitude that loved ones take, this ambivalence produces in the recipient a habit of mortification, internalized small self-murders. Passion, shut out at the door of healthy emotional dependency, comes in at the window of self-induced suffering. At the minimum, mortification occurs in one's habitual arrangement or interpretation of circumstances so that God or "life" or "the way things are" can play the role of chastiser-of-the-beloved. Mortification becomes a necessity and a matter of pride, though in this novel the mortified forms are most obviously seen in the pharasaical Cora and the pseudohumble Anse: "like he would be kind of proud of whatever come up to make the moving or the setting still look hard" (73). Everything seemingly must be allied with hardship and sacrifice or at least the appearance of them. The family does things the hard way repeatedly, either actually, conceptually, or in appearance, from plunging across the flooded river when three sane options are available, to making the final collective sacrifical offering, the scapegoating of Darl.

If Addie's psychology and Darl's fatalistic tone and victimization establish the mood of tragic self-mortification by the individual or group, the mood of parodic tragedy is largely established by the sense that the Bundrens have a genius for putting themselves in the way of disaster and discomfort. Anse's "No man mislikes it more" protests too much. In this respect, the novel is a parody of the traditional notion of tragedy, that the hero's own actions lead to his suffering. Part of what the book invites us to feel is summed up by Tull: "They would risk the fire and the earth and the water and all just to eat a sack of bananas" (92).

But only part. The book's generic heterogeneity is justly a critical commonplace. Like Tull, pointing out Cora's "generic" inconsistency in trying to explain the Bundrens' river crossing by applying to it both the terms *foolish* and *hand of God* (102), the reader is urged to be as uncomfortable with applying any single fixed generic label, including parody of tragedy, to *As I Lay Dying* as with applying either *tragedy* or *pathos* singly to *The Sound and the Fury*. *As I Lay Dying* pursues the wavering line between the noble, the pathetic, and the absurd. Especially in the context of the trilogy, it shows that the wavering is not arbitrary. From the vantage of shifting perspectives and narrators' attitudes, mortification is not self-evidently discernible from heroic suffering. Anse's idea that the Deity chastises those he most favors is not far from Faulkner's statement that the tragic hero is someone whom the gods consider worthy enough to destroy (*University* 51). But this is not to say that everything dissolves into a dubious nongeneric flowing. Addie's monologue, for instance, with its vitality, cruelty, and longing, is not itself rendered farcical by the journey that travesties her design and her need for privacy and self-sufficiency.

Nevertheless, Addie's imposition of her will after death does nothing so much as supply her family with the accustomed structure of passivity and mortification that they need precisely to act in fulfillment of their own personal needs and desires. At her death, her directive for burial conforms quickly to a habituated "religious" pattern in which the sacred wishes of an absent powerful agent must be interpreted by followers. "It is sacred on me," Anse says (92). In the same way that Cora and Whitfield deftly use the claim of obedient passivity to God's will and Dewey Dell uses the putative sign that "makes" her make love with Lafe, Anse adapts Addie's design to "my word." What he could not ask or do in his own name he can in hers.

But Addie's sacred directive, though enabling in this way, is not the same as an articulated shared narrative like that *The Sound and the Fury* envisioned. The present novel, too, lacks this collective resource for acknowledging and encompassing shame and death. True to Addie's character, her directive cues the common action of the journey, beneath which is a variety of secret unvoiced purposes, so that, since the family lacks a common perspective on her burial procession, it becomes, instead of the public transformation of shame, increasingly a public display of it. The rite of voice gives way to the word. At the moment that Addie's intended deed becomes Anse's word, her action is entirely possessed by him precisely because he can disclaim initiative and responsibility for doing something. *Now* he can get them teeth.

Because a completed genuinely human death in this culture inevitably means dependency on others and on their performance of ritual, the completion of a life narrative is similarly dependent. Anse rewrites Addie's intended ending, the dependent clause that is the title, as an episode in his own life, so that again the heroic temper is left dispossessed and without a conclusion to *its* story, mired in passivity. Only Anse completely gets what he wants from the journey. And his life is based on his purposeful enactment of dependency and unjustified victimization under a transparent guise of independence. By the "wisdom" of this life strategy, "too profound or too inert for even thought," Anse lives a calculated pathos. That is his comedy for us.

With Addie, Faulkner makes more nearly explicit what was implicit in Quentin's suicide: in their perfected forms, action is the sublimation of voice and not simply the other way around. That is, Faulkner explores the conviction that to act in the fully meaningful sense is not simply to perform a deed but in this performance to achieve the recognition and passionate communion that voice potentially entails. Repeatedly for Faulkner's characters, action—nonvocal action—becomes an attractive but often inefficacious, indirect means of "trying to say." The effect of this mutual accommodation of voice to action is to make the exercise of a powerful voice—like Faulkner's literary voice—equivalent to a successful act; the vocally potent person—or writer—is a "man, or woman, of action."

IV

Addie's aspiration toward the sublation of voice, "voicelessness," instructively contrasts to a novel that is a succession of scripted or scored voices ready to be loosed "out of the air" by the reader's performance. But "ready to be loosed" is too easy-sounding a phrase; it can obscure the way in which the *virtual* voices of the novelistic script are also in and of themselves haunted by voicelessness.

As in *Sanctuary*'s opening tableau when a bird calls "meaningless and profound" (4), sound and depth are often experienced by an auditor as existing in a secreted noise where they reveal and conceal nothing, a nonperson, but not where they should exist, as in the silent man who "had that vicious depthless quality of stamped tin." This reversed impersonation also occurs at the outset of *As I Lay Dying* when Darl presents Jewel as a silent wooden Indian and Cash's boards and tools with a personified depth and resonance typographically accentuated: "Between the shadow spaces they are yellow as gold, like soft gold, bearing on their flanks in smooth undulations the marks of the adze blade. . . . I go on to the house, followed by the   Chuck.   Chuck.   Chuck.   of the adze." The total effect in the trilogy is of an environment haunted by a displaced person—in classical rhetorical terms, a prosopopoeia, but of an especially spectral kind. As Darl puts it, "It is as though the sound had been swept from his lips and up and away, speaking back to us from an immense distance of exhaustion" (148). Voices and persons, acts and bodies, have been sundered. This is one way of stating the problem to which Faulkner's rhetoric is an answer.

Making voice an act fuses what is sundered. But as we have noted, for Faulkner such fusion occurs within, and cannot end, an open dialectical process. Faulkner can vividly demonstrate the limitations of Addie's life strategy because it is so much like his. Faulkner wishes to make language not only an act. He wishes to make it a bodied act, a matter, to adapt his phrases cited earlier, of engendering excitement in hearts and glands, of making an immortal transient medium like blood or breath flow between persons: an engendering act, in short, like sex, but one always tempted to wholly self-contained "reproduction from within" (*Mosquitoes* 320). There is in such Faulknerian statements as these, as in his work, a fierce literalness that is the energy of his text's tropes and represented actions. It is a "primitiveness" about personal reproduction which earlier readers, sometimes shocked, in a sense recognized better than we do when we gentle Faulkner into epistemological subtleties and risks alone. The difference between Faulkner's strategy and Addie's comes down to this: he knows that he depends upon and cannot transcend the readers who are to be his own flesh and blood.

Contemporary criticism has appreciated the cognitive subtleties of language at the cost of forgetting that reading, even at its most "mental," is a material activity. Critics consequently find it harder to grasp or else to value subtleties of bodily activity. (Perhaps it goes without saying that I do not exclude myself here.) To take the more obvious level, it is easy to forget that for at least some readings, though not voiced aloud or murmured, there is still a more or less constant subvocalization: the regulation of breathing to perceived cues of rhythm and sound, and other minute coordinations of tongue, jaw, and throat as in speech aloud. (An older criticism knows something of this, even though in illuminating textual cues and conventions of poetic and prose rhythm and euphony, it tends to ignore the realizing acts of reading. And compare Barthes on so-called "writing aloud" with the "*grain* of the voice" [*Pleasure* 66–67].)

In such a reembodiment of voice there is a bodily making-real. This reading performance of *As I Lay Dying* experientially activates in the throat the very physicality that dies, at the fusion point of death and its means of social repudiation. It does so, that is, while enacting the novel's vocal "ritual," which helps to contain this physicality, which says No to it while dramatically acknowledging its existence. Embodied voice resistantly utters death's outrage. It works, then, at one pertinent level of what Marx calls sensuous human activity, and Burke the body's dancing of an attitude. As whole persons, embodied intelligences, we sensuously dance the dialectic of transformation.

In this and other bodily ways we may more or less completely animate tragic theme as our own activity and more fully enter into related issues and consequences. One major consequence of enacting the novel's rite is enacting the rite's maiming. To see that the novel is a para-ritualistic score and that it is purposively marred, we turn to an actual vocal performance of the text—Faulkner's. The general critical neglect of Faulkner's recorded performances seems to mirror the neglect of voicing—reader's or writer's—when "voice" is being examined. We can begin by noting that one of the few passages Faulkner chose to record is Vardaman's rush of thought on breath and suffocation.

Faulkner's recorded reading of *As I Lay Dying* makes quite clear how much the voice in this book (and the others) is "bigger than" Faulkner's slight physical voice. But there is also a pronounced physicality in the latter's high pitch and soft, breathy rush, which echo strongly in the text's vocal signature at times. Above all, Faulkner's reading has some marked qualities of ritual: it is somewhere between restrained chanting and crooning, modulating slightly toward the inflections and rhythms of actual conversational speech at appropriate times. Concordantly, what is accentuated in Faulkner's quasi-chanting, almost crooning performance is not the individual word but the continuum of voice, of sound. The ritual effect of Faulkner's recorded reading is not achieved by variations in stress so much as by variations in pitch and duration of sounds. Periodically, final words in sentences, phrases, or clauses are pronounced with a drop in pitch and held like a sustained musical note. In keeping with the idea of missing resolution, however, the final words of narrative sections are notably unemphatic and also conspicuously lacking the (by now expected) drop in pitch and sustained sound. The listener who has grown accustomed to the internal sound pattern of the section is thus left off-balance, "leaning into" the novel's next narrative section. This larger pattern of repeatedly deferred resolution is the one subtle disruption of a tone of ritual serenity (a serenity noted on the Caedmon record jacket) which subsumes all the narrative's tensions and agonies into its sonorous tranquility. It is not only ritual, then, that is suggested by Faulkner's recorded performance but the serenity that the novel's funeral ritual ideally effects by just such an act of subsuming.

The scripted cues for this kind of performance may be taken in several forms. First, the thematic coupling of ritual performance and outrageous disintegration piques our reading emulation. Second, seen from this perspective, the several departures from the conventions of ordinary verisimilitude combine to dislocate the fictional world into a stylized, liminal condition like that of ritual. As in ritual's frequent creation of a sense of "timelessness" and its concomitant slowing of action into ceremonious gesture, the narrative repeatedly treats time as if it were arrested; so we move without transition from one temporal convention to another, as when narrators refer to future events. Similarly, the narrative consistently retards the practical, fundamentally simple action of getting Addie buried. It does so by multiple narrations, episodes, and devices like the frozen moment, which Faulkner rightly calls "tableau" and "hiatus" (e.g., 9), when the visual and the aural effects are heightened in a moment as if out of time. These effects are augmented by Addie's "speaking" after death and by the preternatural suggestions of clairvoyance (not only Darl's and Lafe's, but apparently Anse's and perhaps Cash's as well in the courting of the new Mrs. Bundren). Taken as a whole, all this intimates nothing like what Gray's "Elegy" called "the short and simple annals of the poor." Instead we occupy a special condition where ordinary spatiotemporal laws that lead but to the grave are suspended by extraordinary powers of human consciousness, human passion. Since critics have often discussed these unusual stylistic features, I will simply repeat that they deserve the designation *rituallike* or *para-ritualistic* because they produce precisely the kind of disarrangement of everyday reality characteristic of ritual and because the thematic importance of ritual communication makes this the most fitting description.

From an overall perspective, this effect also subliminally sensitizes the reader to ceremonial voices, helps to define their nature as capacitation, and combines with them to suggest a specially framed reality like that of a secular ritual. By ceremonial voices I mean the periodic elevated rhetoric, the "unrealistic" narrative style that particularly Darl, Addie, Dewey Dell, and Vardaman recurrently shift into. Faulkner's recorded performance suggests, as does the ritualized quality of the novel, that it is this elevated rhetoric that sets the keynote for a somewhat stylized reading of everything, including the vernacular mimesis. Faulkner's colorful rendering of this contrasting vernacular speech and mind-voice solicits the pleasure of making it real at some interior or exterior level of our voice. But the rural vernacular, though it helps to create the novel's realistic illusion, also serves as an antiphonal contrast to help accentuate the "unrealistic" eloquence. It draws attention to the eloquence precisely as a rituallike departure—not only a deviation from the realistic mimetic convention but a scripted departure from everyday speech.

In the novel and trilogy such departures from the usual conventions of speech open the ritual moment and permit an unusual communal openness to repudiate death. Similarly, the deliberate departures from the vernacular, reinforced by the other ritual effects noted, license our auditory imagination to the more copious speech of ceremonial voices.

Readers who at some vocal level take the option for enacting Faulkner's score somewhat as he does, will pleasurably and movingly vivify the text as suggested before. They will also find themselves in interesting trouble. One reason the experience is moving is that it parallels the elevated voice, "bigger than" the individual speaker, which characterizes the represented ritual voices. Ceremonially performing the generally uniform heightened style of the narrators creates the effect that we unite them by a ritual voice encompassing them, though their lonely lives and flawed burial rite alike isolate them. Further, the shared voice that is bigger than they are is clearly that of their impersonator, Faulkner, who makes them all "speak Faulkner." He thus calls attention to his tour de force in supplying his characters the voice they need and actually do not have in their fictional world, just as imagining them supplies him with the means to exercise an accentuated literary voice. He speaks Bundren too, in every sense. And our performance in turn is the fulfilling of this potential "speaking," the realizing enactment of this virtual double voice. Ours is the embodying performance that refracts all the voices through our own characteristic accents. Perhaps stated best, the multifold voice is of none and of all. This voice involves several powerful symbolic accommodations, of characters, novelist, and reader. So, like ritual action, it contests the reminder of human incapacity in the form of unaccommodated death.

This aspect of the novel's empowering, however, is one of the potential means for creating interesting trouble. Unlike the represented ritual voice, the reader's (possible) vocal emulation is not a function of simple custom but is rhetorically piqued and so raises not only the possibility of empowering but also the accompanying potential of affront (or irritation or reading distraction). Specifically, our enactment encounters its corresponding obstacles. One of the important things that Faulkner's recording can reveal is how willful an act ritual serenity is—as willful as the persistence of human symbolic accommodations despite what the novel suggests is bizarre and terrible in them. This willfulness is felt concretely when we ourselves attempt such a performance at length.

Then we encounter the possible deterrence to a subsuming ritual serenity not only in the novel's elements of absurdity but in the very departures from realistic conventions that pique and enable our performance. One obstacle is that we will not follow the departures wholeheartedly because of the hold that the conventions of verisimilar character and speech have on us. Continuing to enact ritual serenity may be difficult if the question of "unrealistic speech" persists in bothering a given reader or reading. (These narrators are uneducated folk; Vardaman is a child; and so on. The complementary problem occurs, of course, if we try the more usual performance of the novel as realistic mimesis.) So too with the other ritual-enabling deviations from verisimilitude previously noted, including the novel's visual features such as the sketch of Addie's coffin and Cash's numbered list.[4] Additionally, visual features may be subtly distracting because, as the coffin sketch reminds us, both novel and trilogy partly associate the eye with unaccommodated death or its parallels. We may simply ignore the fact that such enabling cues for a performance of ritual serenity also potentially deter it. But if we acknowledge these obstacles and others and still feel primarily encouraged to continue our performance, then the willfulness of our enactment becomes increasingly pronounced. In the face of ambiguous discouragement, our persisting enactment (Bundren-like but more aware) may well anticipate that the novel's resolution will settle whether this exercise of audition is finally warranted. What we find is that the ending disconfirms our endeavor as successful ritual but also relies on exactly this attempted ritual exercise to fully create the effect of maimed rite.

The ritual effect remains a possibility of the book, no more and no less. It is possible from the standpoint that it may or may not be actualized or persisted in by the individual reader's participation. But it is also crucial that, on the testimony of the trilogy, it is *only* possible in a book, a novel with its own mixture of ordinary verisimilitude and fictive special effects. As *The Sound and the Fury* seeks to represent the failure of tragedy within the fictional world and yet to establish the possibility of tragedy in its audience, *As I Lay Dying* describes the failure of a mortuary ritual and rhetorically creates the grounds for an analogous secular para-ritual. The difference is that Faulkner slants the second novel against final resolution through para-ritualistic voice. That is, potential ritual moments exist, but they do not offer ultimate resolution. We (may) see, say, and hear enough to imagine what a real transfiguration of death would entail, but *As I Lay Dying* does a great deal to throw doubt on its achievement. Scandal preempts transformation.

This is true too of *Sanctuary,* as in the wonderfully glossy prose of its ending:

In the pavilion a band in the horizon blue of the army played Massenet
and Scriabin, and Berlioz like a thin coating of tortured Tschaikovsky
on a slice of stale bread, while the twilight dissolved in wet gleams. . . .
Rich and resonant the brasses crashed and died in the thick green twilight, rolling over them in rich sad waves. Temple yawned behind her
hand . . . and from beneath her smart new hat she seemed to follow
with her eyes the waves of music, to dissolve into the dying brasses,
across the pool and the opposite semicircle of trees where at sombre
intervals the dead tranquil queens in stained marble mused, and on into
the sky lying prone and vanquished in the embrace of the season of rain
and death. (398)

Death has the last word here, and its counterpart is the aurally
indifferent Temple. The references to music and the sonorous prose
of this ending constitute a knowingly quixotic gesture by the narrator
toward tempering this result. The calculated aestheticism is not that
of an achieved cathartic "rest in peace." It is a sardonic tribute to such
a serenity by a narrator whose own "thin coating" of tranquility is
like the season, "gallant and evanescent and forlorn" (398) in the face
of Temple's deathlike invulnerability.

In contrast to this sophisticated pathos, *As I Lay Dying* ends on a
flat note. In this ironic sense, plot finally has its way over voice, but
by means of a closure that mocks tragic completion. Ritual sonority
recedes in the end before the farcical everyday normalcy of the new
Mrs. Bundren, carrying her phonograph. If we sustain here the tone
that Faulkner exemplifies in his recording of earlier sections, then our
serenity has become a comedy conscious of its own bizarreness but
maintaining a straight face. The duck-shaped woman's silencing eyes
and portable phonograph, whose solacing music Cash welcomes,
sum up and travesty the problem of bestial life and death and a
potential solution the novel has presented. Cash's equable narrative
voice reminds us of the more likable features of his life strategy of
normalization, as well as its moral insensitivity to anomaly and its
overly facile resolutions: "What a shame Darl couldn't be [there] to
enjoy [the music] too. But it is better so for him. This world is not his
world; this life his life" (178). The novel's spectacle of shame lapses
into a conventional "what a shame." So mixed is the tone of this
ending that for many readers there is not even the release of laughter.
There is perhaps only an edgy smile for readers who have just heard

Darl's mad laughter and his "yes yes yes," which in effect mockingly echoes this last betrayal of Addie's and the novel's No to death.

V

It will be useful here to sum up as schematically as possible from this and previous chapters what can be concluded thus far about voice in Faulkner's major phase, particularly since in the next chapter voice will assume a secondary place in our discussion. The following characteristics overlap, but each captures a distinctive stress. Actually or potentially, voice is

an instance of performance—or acknowledging embodied enactment—which Faulknerian tragedy emphasizes as a locus of honor and shame;

an indicator of individual distinctiveness and/or a medium for activating one's larger corporate life with others;

action and a display of power;

a contributing instrument to pique the audience's emulative power;

an instrument for winning the acknowledgment necessary for vital personal life, individual or communal;

a risk involving vulnerability and dependency;

the breath of life transformed through sound and passing beyond it into a "utopian" communication, and thus transmitted to the keeping of the (reading) community;

a valuable or crucial means of mutual empowerment and opposition to death.

In sum, this is voice of course in its ideal, often ritual-associated form. *As I Lay Dying,* we saw, is a profaned rite, a profanation of the tragedy of ritual action, since the para-ritualistic voice the novel cogently solicits in some of its most striking features is bafflingly set about by competing signals.

Correspondingly, *As I Lay Dying* is the imagination of lives that— Addie and Darl being the major, complex exceptions—do not *sufficiently* need the extra-ordinary measures of fully realized ritual. So in its way is *Sanctuary*. Both novels surround these lives with a narrative rhetoric of extraordinary voice which only enters them in rare, private, furtive, or grotesque ways. Their ordinary life strategies of unconscious stoicism, denial, religious "determinism," and so on suffice for most. The other sovereign panacea is violence, especially in *Sanctuary* but also in Jewel's whole mode of being.

The upshot is that the characters who populate the two novels following *The Sound and the Fury* to a significant degree testify against the hope of that novel. They do not need their creator, William Faulkner, or they contrive without what he shows they need, or they end up judged insane. Insofar as Faulkner, in depicting these characters with craftmanship, represents and contains a fear or despair about a reading public that cannot fulfill its role as his readers, he is laying the groundwork in these novels for the greater authorial control over tragic closure which he attempts in *Light in August*.

CHAPTER 5

Rest in Peace: The Promise
and End of *Light in August*

> that peace which is the promise and the end of the Church. The
> mind and the heart purged then, if it is ever to be . . . by the
> stern and formal fury of the morning service.
>
> *Light in August*

> I hope some psychological good will come out of my novels,
> that they will give the reader what the Greeks call catharsis.
>
> Faulkner, interview (1947)

As I Lay Dying as both parable and rhetorical appeal developed the
implication of *The Sound and the Fury* that Faulkner's attainment of
literary tragedy is not a hermetic act. As Faulkner implicitly conceives its form, tragedy shares with the ritual defiance of death a
dependence upon the performance of those to whom the initiating
agent necessarily bequeaths the completion of the enterprise. *The
Sound and the Fury* and *As I Lay Dying* are by turns hopeful for and
dubious of the reader's realizing performance. Since the display of
personal artistic power in Faulkner's pyrotechnics of style and form
also implicitly acknowledges a chancy dependence on his readers, it is
equally, though more subtly, a display of receptivity and vulnerability in a world where, Faulkner insists, such a display comes hard
indeed.

Light in August is a new departure. It is a reconsideration pursuing
these themes and implicit rhetorical negotiations of his writing in
search of a different conclusion. Briefly put, in *Light in August*
Faulkner entertains anew the possibility of a tragedy of plot as well as

131

one of voice. Here catharsis turns out to be not only an implication of scripted voice to be realized mentally or aloud in reading but the product of a represented action that is resolved. It is this combination that distinguishes it from *Sanctuary,* which has a resolved tragic action, though, as we noted, accompanied by an ironic scripting of vocal catharsis.

The first sign that *Light in August* is different is that Faulkner's voice, though obviously still distinctive, also obviously calls less attention to itself here than in *The Sound and the Fury* and *As I Lay Dying.* The sequence of scripted voices, which in these novels represent characters *as* voices to be performed, gives way to conventional narrative. The implicit issue of whether the reader will at some level voice the material becomes, like the associated theme of silencing and speech, relatively less salient and crucial than it was before.

On the other hand, the first three chapters make the question of plot resolution quite salient. By the end of this section, the simplest expectations of a conventionally sequential plot aroused by the first chapter, devoted to Lena Grove, have been denied by Faulkner's abrupt switches to new characters whose stories begin and then hang suspended with little obvious connection between them. Once this section broaches the issue of plot, however, this pattern of arousal and denial of expectations gradually diminishes, beginning with Chapter 5, when we settle into the Joe Christmas story for several chapters. As the changes in perspective and focus become less abrupt, so we become habituated to the interweaving narratives, until at last the tragic plot of Christmas resolves. Further, in Christmas's story we do get, for the first time in Faulkner, the representation of a whole human life from beginning to end.

In these ways and others, *Light* concedes much to readers in the sense that it satisfies many more expectations of conventional narrative than did the two preceding experimental novels. Habitualized, these conventions seem to enact themselves and not to require our action. Things seem to have been done for us. But precisely in this vein, Faulkner reclaims the author's right to complete his own work. Compared to the previous novels, this text attempts to balance plot and voice; it implies that the artist's and performing reader's shares in creating literary tragedy are evenly reconciled with each other. In this attempted balancing, however, the issues of performance retain center stage. Although this novel, unlike the others we are considering, does not prominently array a sequence of scripted voices, it does marshal narrative strategies informed by theatrical tropes.

Light in August stresses the peace associated with a symbolic repudiation of death and the strategies—at once individual, cultural, and rhetorical—for attaining this state. In these terms, we have been recapitulating two rhetorical strategies for cathartically achieving the peace accompanying the No to death. In the one case, this end is achieved by an incompleted plot and by the reader's fulfilling the textual script through vocal enactment; here the author is vulnerable to the reader's possible nonperformance. In the other case, a finished plot conduces to cathartic peace, and it is allied with the idea of self-sufficient invulnerability. Not only does *Light in August* seek the effect of cathartic peace by combining completed plot with solicited voice, but it dramatizes and deploys a third strategy: a sustained imperviousness or tranquility, or both, that *obviates* the need for either form of catharsis. In this novel, the characters' strategies of plotted action and voice are designed either to produce for themselves a tranquility arrived at through catharsis or to maintain an imperviousness or serenity making catharsis through tragic plot or voice gratuitous. If the latter aim recalls the represented world of *As I Lay Dying*, *Light in August* stands out in the extensiveness and complexity with which Faulkner treats nontragic strategies and sensibilities and makes them contribute to a tragic effect. Hightower and Christmas in comparable dramatistic ways attempt both strategies, while Lena Grove maintains an extraordinary noncathartic serenity. The strategic, theatrical plots these characters live are enactments of different cultural possibilities. I wish here to understand how the novel deploys these and similar strategic devices to create its distinctive tragic effect—or, more simply, to grasp the implications of the novel's being at once horrific and serene.

Therefore, while I will frequently treat voice here, plot will be much more closely attended, not because voice is unimportant but because the new importance Faulkner gives completed plot requires that we examine it in order to profile the novel's distinctive effect. As we saw with Quentin and Addie, issues of speaking and hearing are the same as issues of action and response: the temptation to entire self-sufficiency versus the reality that what one person initiates another must complete. Again, the same is true for issues of plot and the reader's vocal performance. In *Light in August*, relatively speaking,

Faulkner stresses the "action" side of this dialectic, in terms of plotted action and characterization.

At the most general level, *Light in August* further develops the interdependency of voice and shared narrative, particularly a narrative of shame redeemed. This novel presents readers a relatively articulated narrative and evenly balances plot and scripted voice; correspondingly it models the Christmas narrative on the culturally shared Christian story of shame overcome. The trajectory of Faulkner's writings to this point makes it logical that, however uneasily, he should now attempt to reach some firmer accommodation with this story, whose potentials he outlined in Shegog's Easter sermon. By dramatizing white Calvinism as a violent variant of the Christian story of promised immortality, Faulkner taps its resources of narrative coherence, closure, and passionate resonance. Simultaneously he suggests that in important ways its cultural resources are depleted. Christmas is a shameful cultural anomaly who both enacts the abstract pattern of the Calvinist drama's all-too-coherent narrative and imposing voices, and acts to distance himself from narrative and voice. Hightower performs a similar double action, except that he tries to preempt rather than to avoid the cultural drama. These dual actions represent and effect Faulkner's enabling of voice and narrative by his own arm's-length employment, and overriding, of the Christian narrative.

In the end, even with the novel's doubly closed plot and an accompanying vocal solicitation to closure, *Light in August* still leaves the effect of cathartic completion dependent on a third, entailed element, the characterization of Joe Christmas, whose violent sexuality puts the novel's closure at risk. In a novel whose style and structure do not particularly hazard outraging the reader, Faulkner's instinct for the rhetoric of risking affront surfaces here to put assured peace in jeopardy.

I

The passage in which Hightower overhears "Protestant music" evokes the promise and end of peace implicitly held out to us throughout the novel: "that peace which is the promise and the end of the Church. The mind and the heart purged then, if it is ever to be . . . by the stern and formal fury of the morning service. . . . The

organ strains come rich and . . . sonorous, with that quality of ab-
jectness and sublimation, as if the freed voices themselves were assuming the shapes and attitudes of crucifixions, ecstatic. . . . Yet
even then the music has still a quality . . . without passion so much
as immolation." Thus the congregation's voices plead for "not love,
not life, forbidding it to others," but "in sonorous tones death as
though death were the boon," because "ecstasy, they cannot seem to
bear: their escape from it is in violence, in drinking and fighting and
praying; catastrophe too, the violence identical and apparently inescapable" (670–71). To begin with, this epitome of the dynamics and
subversion of securing peace tells us that catharsis results from a plot
of sacrificial violence or its sublimated ritual substitute, communal
sonorous voices. Cathartic peace accompanies catastrophe, in the
strict literary sense of a conclusiveness, a denouement, which follows
in turn upon catastrophe in the sense of disaster.

Some, like Christmas, Hightower, and, at one point, Byron Bunch,
most obviously seek such peace through a purging violence, either
direct or vicarious. This is what the crowd avid for an "emotional
barbecue" (612) of vicarious violence fundamentally desires. Violence
yields the serenity that both Joe Christmas and Byron Bunch temporarily experience as the aftermath of being physically beaten (560,
724). At a profounder level, this is the peace that Joe realizes was all he
wanted after he has killed Joanna and physically and verbally assaulted
the black congregation. It is above all the supernal condition, "of itself
alone serene, of itself alone triumphant" (743), that the spectators
perceive in Christmas as he dies by terrible violence.

Even more than before, then, Faulkner describes a world in which
the peace of consummation is sought through the pursuit of violence
or the hazardous vulnerability we have seen entailed in ritualistic
voice. According to this more or less traditional tragic psychology,
emotion is purified of suffering by raising agony or vulnerability to a
culminating extreme—"*crucifixion of themselves and one another*" (671).
Yet in the remarkable description of the "Protestant music," the
public sublation of violence by and into vocal ritual has not, in fact,
transpired. The process is stalled at an intermediate stage that both
lays bare and subverts its workings. Pledged to heightening peaceful
life and passion in opposition to death, the ritual process aborts itself
by smuggling in immolation as the only serenity that can be trusted
to be a final resolution, "as though death were the boon." Death, as
the promise of peacefulness, subverts the ritual transformation di-

rected against death. As in *As I Lay Dying,* we are presented with a maimed rite. It is led by those "who have ever loved death better than peace" (612) because they profoundly conflate the two. And the dialectical reversal epitomized by the "Protestant music" embraces Christmas and Hightower, both of whom, entangled in privatized, maimed para-rituals, become the image of the death they oppose.

As before, the possibility of literary tragedy depends for Faulkner upon representing certain lives that desire an inherently tragic structure, one that would lift them through tragedy from a subtragic malaise. Comparably yet distinctly, the novel is dedicated to completing the process aborted in the religious ritual.

Lena's peace, in contrast, cannot be called cathartic, since it results from no catharsis she has undergone. It is as though Faulkner had set allegorized bliss comically on its feet to walk through the tragic world. Lena Grove images the ambulatory promise and end of the catharsis others must undergo, drifting into and out of their lives or flowing by them. In her, Faulkner imagines a comic sustained invulnerability and serenity, one that is neither malignly impersonal nor achieved in death. Unusually, Lena's sexuality is not death tainted, which is to say that it is not, in either the ordinary or the more technical sense of an honor-shame code, shameful. Although—or better, because—she is highly decorous in her own way, she entirely convinces herself that she is a pregnant lady traveling. She is to a high degree insulated from the code of honor and shame as it is embodied in the community of outraged women like Mrs. Armstid, while she depends upon—that is, potently draws out—its best impulses, even from the furious Mrs. Armstid. Like another Don Quixote, she is so persuaded by her own performance of her role that she represents a self-esteem impervious to the tendency of the code at its worst to reduce individuals merely to their appearance in the community's eyes. She has the peace that accompanies this invulnerability to the potentially withering public eye. On the crucial matter of sexuality, she is tranquilly practical and matter-of-fact, so that she thinks little of the scandal she presents to the public eye while she walks the roads in an advanced state of pregnancy.

By the same token she is a foil to the very project of artistic immortality. In its invulnerability to outrage, her performance of self-assurance coincides with her condition of fertility. Her untroubled sexuality maintains a serenity like that of one already immortal, invulnerably observing life's pleasurable spectacle as she travels, and it achieves, without thought of it, the common immortality of a posterity, "the good stock peopling . . . the good earth" (699). Faulkner's revealing novelistic joke is to put on the road not exactly a Don Quixote figure but a damsel who is singularly undistressed, yet whose vulnerable physical condition arouses quixotic feelings in certain others, Byron especially. To sum up the set of attitudes that the novel evinces toward both quixoticism and Lena's arousal of it, we could do worse than cite Faulkner's comment on Quentin Compson and Gavin Stevens: "That's a constant sad and funny picture. . . . It is the knight that goes out to defend somebody who don't want to be defended and don't need it. But it's a very fine quality in human nature. I hope it will always endure. It is comical and a little sad" (*University* 141). Nor, with her aplomb of the immortals, does Lena require the help of William Faulkner's art. Figuratively speaking, she is the negation of the woman's ritual role offered to the reader in *As I Lay Dying*.

The obvious fact that Lena functions tranquilly by reducing life to its simplest terms helps us to isolate the less-obvious general feature of simplification within the other life strategies designed to establish peace. All mysterious complexity, being uncontrollable by the self, can be mentally sorted with death as the epitome of an uncontrollable threat to personal power and esteem. Epistemological and personal simplification means reestablishing control, at the heart of which is the power to cope with agitation at mortality. Hightower reacts against his complex, distant father and, conjointly, the fascinated horror of death symbolized by the father's multipatched army coat, the blue patch suggesting a slain Yankee. Hightower compensatorily imagines his grandfather as a "heroic, simple, warm" figure. Consequently, the grandfather's wartime involvement in death holds "no horror" (752), and in identifying himself with the grandfather's own death, Hightower can imagine that he has, as it were, predeceased himself and survived. Less baroque controlling forms of simplification are sought by Byron Bunch through a routine-filled life and by the orphanage dietitian, whose life "seemed straight and simple as a corridor" (492) once she recalls that Doc Hines can help her get rid of the child Joe. The corridor image also describes Percy Grimm's transformation by his military role: "He could now see his life opening before him, uncomplex and inescapable as a barren corridor" (732).

In an important respect, however, the widespread bias toward simplification is itself complex compared to Joe Christmas's desired pattern of life, which is not a corridor so much as "one street, with imperceptible corners and changes of scene" (563). For Joe's "religious hatred" (534) rebels against the cultural master plot of white Calvinism, which provides most simplifying resources for the desired communal peace. But the fact that he early absorbs from his cultural environment a pattern of expectations and behavior abstracted from the southern Calvinist model renders him all too susceptible to reabsorption by it. Readers have long understood that a secret complicity exists between Joe and his tormentors, but here I wish to understand both the tragic nature of his rebellion and the breadth of this complicity as these key into, first, the general cultural ordering of life and death; second, Hightower's more particular strategy nested within this ordering; and ultimately, the peace that is the novel's promise and end. To do so, I must pause for a while on the principles governing the irenic simplification at work in the fictional world and, in a different way, in the master plot of the novel: linearity and punctuality.[1] The linear simplification of reality is the culturally dominant, potentially tragic No to death corresponding to Joe Christmas's cathartic plot. Corresponding roughly to Lena's serenity is a culturally recessive nonlinear and nontragic No to death which Faulkner plays against the dominant form.

II

The principles of strategic simplification, linearity and punctuality, introduce considerations that Faulkner criticism usually treats under the rubric of time versus timelessness. Yet the rubric, pace Faulkner's own usage, for our purposes is imprecise and rather misleading. We would do better to think of different concepts of time, each with its own entailed concepts of narrative, of dramatistic person, and of strategies of immortality. The advantage of the perspective I will adopt is that it focuses the coherence among these and allows us to examine them together for their contribution to the remarkable effects of this novel.

Though the concept of linearity has now entered the popular stock of ideas, it is, or should be, subject to caveats—which apply also to the honor-shame concept and the oral/written distinction—about the limitations of such broad schemas in describing cultures without regard to their specific functioning and to other cultural elements that modify or transform them. Since it is exactly such functioning and inmixing of cultural modeling and Faulkner's craftsmanship which concern us here, we need a perspective on linearity which will point up its opposite number of punctuality with enough precision.

Plot, Aristotle asserted, is the soul of tragedy. The concept of tragedy is thus enfolded in the linear modeling of reality. Walter Ong has argued that Aristotle, by his stress on plot, reflected the rise of a writing culture, since he praises the compressed beginning-middle-end of dramatic tragedy as superior to the more extensive, meandering work, preeminently Homer's *Iliad,* which Ong believes to be characteristic of oral culture. Hightower at one point sums up the traditionally tragic perception of irrevocable consequences, wherein an action unfolds into a passion, agent into patient: " 'Man performs, engenders, so much more than he can or should have to bear. That's how he finds that he can bear anything. That's it. That's what is so terrible" (620). If tragic art, including Homer's, is generally linear in the sense that it depends upon the fresh recognition that action can breed an irreversible sequence of disastrous consequences, Aristotle implies in effect that the advantage of a tight, closed dramatic structure is that it formally accentuates this realization in a way that oral epics do not (Ong, *Orality* 141–44).

The traditional Aristotelian ideal of tragedy is thus even more strongly oriented toward inevitable consequence and so is a paramount Western artifact, in that the cultural chart of the West is heavily marked by the selectively linear organization of experience as sequential connections and differences, continuity or change, and the "from-to" structure of a vector: cause-effect, delay, rising tension, climax, resolution.

Two contrastable but equally linear temporal models are those of degeneration and progress, the descending or ascending lines on which one's existence is presumably plotted. These may be combined into a third, also familiar subcategory of cyclic recurrence: growth and decay, collapse followed by rejuvenation. Both in general and in commentary on *Light in August,* the cyclic is often usefully contrasted to the linear, but for our present purposes, as in elementary geometry, the cyclic is better understood for the most part as a form of linearity, not something contrasted to it.[2] (Note that Joe's street travels in a circle [650].)

So self-evident, so seemingly natural is this sociocultural orientation to the vector that it may at first be difficult to imagine the schema of what Clifford Geertz has called punctuality. In this cultural ordering, the point instead of the line, "at" rather than "from-to," forms the more salient life-world.[3] The nonlinear, or punctual, symbolic order does exist, it seems—more relatively and recessively in contemporary Western cultures and most unambiguously and dominantly perhaps in Bali. It is the sense of life summoned up by the Indians in Faulkner's great story "Red Leaves," who serenely intone, "Tomorrow is just another name for today" and "Man must die. . . . Let him; there is still the Man" (*Collected Stories* 337, 323), even while Faulkner surrounds them with the evidences of decay, corruption, and deviation which contradict their cultural management of reality.

It is not, of course, as if Faulkner's Jefferson were located just off the coast of Bali, despite such Eastern, specifically Hindu, allusions as "avatars," "suttee," "Juggernaut," and "eastern idol" in this novel, which criticism has discussed for their thematic implications. My recourse here to what may at first seem to be farfetched non-Western analogies is heuristic, a pragmatic use of a purer instance of a cultural arrangement of life to throw into relief otherwise elusive systematic connections in this novel's represented world and rhetoric.[4] What we see preeminently in the Balinese assimilation of Hinduism, as Geertz describes it, is a *this*-worldly theatrical enactment of a No to death by serene persons, performing in consonance with a nonlinear picture of reality. The more diffuse strategic counterpart to such performance in *Light in August,* again, is not as clearly highlighted by the other-worldly, nondramatistic connotations that tend to prevail in Western concepts of "timelessness." Although in the Christian version the timeless may momentarily reveal itself, say, in a moment in Eliot's rose garden, fundamentally, the realm of the timeless is a destination to be attained at the *end* of a drama played out before the eyes of God and existing independently of the enactment. In punctualism, time is immobilized *through* an enactment of an ever-present here-and-now. Similarly, the common critical invocation of the timelessness of archetype or myth obscures the character of this enactment as, precisely, a narrative and dramatistic reality.

In the linear simplifying model of reality, in its "progressive" modern form, repetition is a burden. It connotes undesirable stasis and a lack of individual distinctiveness that damages self-esteem, as I noted in discussing *The Sound and the Fury,* where I simply assumed a linear predisposition in analyzing the effects of dichotomy. But in a point-oriented ordering, repetition is the staff of life. It vindicates and reinforces one's identity, since in this construction of existence, distinctiveness tends to be seen as mere deviation from the formal pattern of behavior and being that ineluctably *is* and has always been. Genre is reality. To replicate that authoritative form is to do well and to be well, but the ideal is to replicate without acknowledging a past compared to a present in any way, even as "tradition." What is aimed at, then, is like a simple coincidence of points, an absolute simultaneity of form and event, genre and instance, not the consciousness of a line, a connection, stretching (or broken) between them. Correspondingly, in both life strategy and narrative or dramatic strategy, there is a relative "absence of climax": "Social [and artistic] activities do not build, or are not permitted to build, toward definitive consummation" (Geertz 403). Or, to return to Faulkner for something close to the punctual experience of existence: "a flat pattern . . . since all that had ever been was the same as all that was to be, since tomorrow to-be and had-been would be the same" (606). From this perspective, as Faulkner once put it, there is no such thing as "was" (*Lion* 255). Moment and pattern are copresent, immortal in an eternal Now.

Since every punctual moment is "an unperishing present," it is "discrete, self-sufficient unto itself" (Geertz 379, 403). The stimulating essay by Geertz which I have been largely drawing upon cogently analyzes the close fit between categories of time, person, and immortality. Geertz demonstrates how the punctual schema downplays direct and indirect evidence of time's passage in order to suppress recognition of the perishability of individuals. Thus instead of identifying persons with the individual characteristics that will disappear with death, punctualism identifies persons with a set of formal, ideal features theatrically performed. These features—"metaphysical" generic names, titles, and the rituals and ceremonious actions realizing them—constitute what is genuinely real. They are in principle immortal as, putatively, they meticulously recur in everyday life.

Both linear and punctual life strategies may be seen dramatistically, but in punctualism theatricality per se is played up. Daily life is designed to construct for everyone an immortal role enacted on an eternal stage. As the players daily *are* these ideal roles, they are supposed to manifest the inalienable serenity appropriate to beings who, in complete contrast to Macbeth's poor player who struts and frets his hour on the stage, will always be on stage in an endless play. And for the same reason that this life play appears to Western eyes relatively plotless, "as directionless as a pageant" (Geertz 403), it also dampens the elicitation of catharsis. The tranquility to which, in the linear schema, the artfully plotted heightening of painful emotions leads, is in a punctual strategy possessed as the characteristic of an eternal unchanging present.

This, then, is a schema of earthly immortality in constantly enacted serenity. Yet this cultural strategy against mortality, though in one sense it preserves the person, involves what seems from a linear perspective a depersonalization of the individual, just as nonlinear time seems detemporalized, timeless. The distinctive (but perishable) individual, in our sense of the term, disappears in order to be preserved. In contrast, within the dominant Western orientation, the Christian religion offers a linear strategy of immortality and tranquility. In a religious cognate of the Aristotelian drama leading to resolution and catharsis, the traditional Christian master plot features distinctively individual pilgrims who, before their divine audience, journey from sin (in Calvinism and other "Augustinian" versions, an inherited, "original," sin) to a denouement of peaceful salvation or painful damnation for the immortal soul in an unearthly realm.

With this sketch of two different irenic strategies, two different death-opposing conceptions of the personal and the impersonal, we now return to the novel.

III

There are some significant general resemblances between Faulkner's art and a punctual phenomenology. Like the aesthetic cultural strategy Geertz describes, Faulkner's writings are fascinated with what is "impersonally" and tranquilly immortal, in opposition to what is fretfully perishable in human life, and with the thousand devices used to retard or immobilize mortality-saturated time. This is the side of Faulkner that, in the 1953 essay quoted earlier, spoke of readers as being the *custodians* of hearts and glands, as if the latter were unperishing constants. But in Faulkner the linear orientation, with its different and sometimes competing dream of unending peace on the other side of climactic action, suffering, or extraordinary voice, is never absent. The strong plot linearity of *Light in August* makes this novel's punctualism especially vivid by contrast.

In *Light in August,* the punctual orientation appears in two principal ways. One, an "impure" form, is within the linear tradition: as in Hightower's recurrent vision, the momentary epiphany of the eternal "Now" which is built up to and passes. From our preceding review, it would hardly seem correct to class this moment as punctuality, since it is so clearly the product of a miniature plot of rising and falling tension. But it is best to see it as a mixed or approximate form for two reasons. First, such moments recur throughout the novel— for Hightower, they are in fact predictable—and so in their very frequency suggest that an experiential domain of peaceful ever-now may be tantalizingly close, bordering on its linear antithesis. This suggestion would be faint or dubious, however, except that it is strongly reinforced by the second way in which punctuality makes itself felt, one in which it appears as simply *there,* without buildup.

In *Light in August* a primarily linear world is accompanied by the luminous nimbus or ghost image of a punctual, immobilized time that periodically becomes superimposed and dominant. The novel thus unfolds by a curiously beautiful, or disturbing, syncopation. Faulkner takes stylistic pains in the first chapter to tune his readers into this border region of perceptual flux, crisscrossed by two different phenomenologies. The character and the perceptions of tranquil Lena Grove provide a powerful instrument to introduce us into this flux, as in the elaborate dramatizing of the wagon as a phenomenon of sight and sound, of which this is a small portion: "It seems to hang suspended . . . forever and forever, so infinitesimal is its progress, like a shabby bead upon the mild red string of road. So much is this so that in the watching of it the eye loses it as sight and sense drowsily merge and blend . . . with all the peaceful and monotonous changes between darkness and day, like already measured thread being re-wound onto a spool. So that at last, as though out of some trivial and unimportant region beyond even distance, the sound of it seems to come slow and terrific and without meaning, as though it were a ghost travelling a half mile ahead of its own shape" (404). Sound, the "progress" it here indicates, and the "mild" line of road all become irrealized, without being truly eliminated, in a tranquil hypnotic visual inertia of "forever and forever."

Even Lena's feet are as "inert" as her shoes (407), and the opening pages marvelously capture an entire atmosphere, at once hers and her environment's, of an inertial point yielding, "slow and terrific" (404), to movement. Linearity is, as it were, emerging from punctualism and sliding repeatedly back into stasis. Lena converts the burden of her quest into an adventure in reperception, a delighted discovery of linearity with seemingly inexhaustible pleasures. Lena's astonishment at a from-to perspective is a source of endless satisfaction to her: how a body gets around, from Alabama to Mississippi, to Jefferson, to Tennessee. The "forgotten bead from a broken string" (402) which was her home of Doane's Mill becomes the bead on the mild red string of road, which is in turn but one of the "identical and anonymous and deliberate wagons" carrying her in "a long monotonous succession of peaceful and undeviating changes" (403). This atmosphere is stylistically scripted for our performative auditioning in the minimal linearity created by such devices as a succession of simple sentence formulas and primitive "then" connectives: "Then one day her father said . . ."; "Then some of the machinery . . ."; "The sister-in-law told the brother. Then he remarked . . ." (402–3). Emerging through this at times is a stronger linearity, also stylistically scripted for the reader's enactment, in the contrasted forms of the irreversible decay of human works and the returning cycles of the natural order: "staring, motionless wheels rising from . . . rubble . . . with a quality profoundly astonishing . . . beneath the long quiet rains of autumn and the galloping fury of vernal equinoxes" (402).

There follows upon this scene the shocking intrusion of linearity, an incomprehensible vector impinging on a one-dimensional sensibility: "Once a day a mixed train fled shrieking through. . . . [B]y ordinary it appeared . . . with apparitionlike suddenness and wailing like a banshee, athwart and past that little less-than-village like a forgotten bead" (402).

Lena's inchoate experience of from-to reperception sensitizes her, and us, to the process of this perception itself because it is partly defamiliarized. This defamiliarization is especially evident in the passage in which she paradoxically pictures herself within the framework of both a physical location and the continuity of her perception. In the one case she is no longer moving with the wagon, and in the other she is, but the linear and nonlinear sensations of self are presented as pleasingly blended (404). In keeping with her emergent phenomenology, Lena lives out, shapes for herself, the most rudimentary of plots, with the simple linearity of following a road in search of an ever-moving goal and with the minimal expectancy and doubt necessary to keep her and her plot going in its mild string of from-to episodes.

By suggesting an alternate, nonlinear dramatic and narrative arrangement of life, the effect we are examining both issues from and goes considerably beyond the "frozen moments" and the effect of simultaneity so often noted in Faulkner.[5] The most famous of these images in this novel epitomizes the punctual component of his characters' living of space and time: "avatars, like something moving forever and without progress across an urn" in an eternal "hot still pinewiney silence" (404). More pervasive than the urn metaphor, however, is the imagery of theater by which Faulkner dramatizes the "theatering of evil as [well as] good" (547) according to the linear and the punctual models.

From the time of his early persona-like drawings of flattened figures and his play *The Marionettes,* Faulkner remained fascinated by a form of art dominant, for example, in the shadow-puppet plays of Indonesia but recessive in the West. In this art, which in Bali contributes to the general aesthetic of life we noted, one-dimensional puppets by their very type-character and constant reappearance, to say nothing of their frequently divine status, refute vulnerability and death. In figures like the marble faun, Marietta, and Pierrot (in his several appearances in Faulkner's apprentice work), Faulkner could portray his theme of death-in-life or an inability to come fully to life and yet at the same time indulge a fascination with partial self-projections who could never suffer annihilation because of the very fact that they did come short of fully human life. (Concomitantly, death is constantly invoked in *The Marionettes,* yet in such extravagantly "aesthetic" terms—as in Marietta's last speech—that it becomes something alien to actual flesh and blood.) Since to die, one first must have lived, insofar as one falls short of life, one also cannot to that degree die—this is the "psychologic" that Faulkner, by the time he wrote *Light in August,* could portray with critical empathy in Gail Hightower, whose death-in-life strategy supplements that of vicariously predeceasing and surviving himself.

Also by the time of *Light in August,* Faulkner has perfected the means of adapting to the conventions of literary realism certain features of the art used for a long time in the West only to amuse children. Faulkner wishes to draw upon a serious effect he elsewhere describes well: "remembering, still recapitulant, not amazed or if amazed, the tireless timeless amazement of the child watching tireless and timeless the repetitive Punch and Judy booth" (*Knight's Gambit* 242). Lena Grove both tells and enacts her story in this way, with the "patient and transparent recapitulation of a lying child" (417). And in his more energetic way Hightower recapitulates the story of his grandfather's death with childlike glee and exuberance and stresses that its actors were "boys. . . . Here is that fine shape of eternal youth and virginal desire which makes heroes" (756). When the novel's tone changes to somber, the implication of a shadow play adds its increment to the aura of punctual phenomenology which the novel sustains by several means: "But the shadow of [the pistol] and of [Joanna's] arm and hand on the wall did not waver at all, the shadow of both monstrous, the cocked hammer monstrous, back-hooked and viciously poised like the arched head of a snake. . . . He was watching the shadowed pistol on the wall; he was watching when the cocked shadow of the hammer flicked away" (607; cf. 679).

Although Faulkner implies that the stylized, masklike features and gestures are his characters' shared means of *facing* life and death, they nevertheless simultaneously create the effect of personae, or like Hightower's servant, "with a face both irascible and calm: the mask of a black tragedy between scenes" (751), they suggest that the persona simply is the actor, the total person.

By the hyperbole of a few recurrent epithets, we are encouraged at one level to perceive Joe Christmas as a mask fixed in the sneer borrowed from the criminal Max Confrey and composing a simple mosaic of set expressions—lonely, contemptuous; to imagine Lena Grove as always serene and inward-lighted; to think of generic rural folk spitting and talking with "the timeless unhaste and indirection of [their] kind" (406); and (in a wonderful seriocomic contrast with the latter) to think of one of these folk, Mrs. Armstid, as if forever banging furiously about. Recall too Percy Grimm's platoon and the crowds who execute a kind of slow dance around them: "And [the platoon] now wore uniforms. It was their faces . . . grave, austere, detached, looking with blank, bleak eyes at the slow throngs who . . . drifted before them, slowing, staring, so that they would be ringed with faces rapt and empty and immobile as the faces of cows" (737). These and such other devices as the characters' typological names hint at the eternal presence of type-characters, as if they had always been there, "having apparently materialised out of thin air, motionless, with that diamondsurfaced tranquility" (559), or vanishing abruptly back into it to reappear later.

It is in this spirit of an assumed immortal *thereness* of people with a few set expressions to wear that Faulkner disregards a convention of the "well-made" novel by having three new characters materialize abruptly in the last section of the novel to act as significant narrators and actors: Gavin Stevens, Percy Grimm, and the itinerant furniture salesman. Now, if one assumes a simply self-contained, wholly linear plot (as Ong argues it is easy to do in a print culture, with its bound books), to introduce important characters as the plot approaches its end can indeed seem aberrant. But to recall Hightower's servant, what if one wants to write not only linked linear scenes in a "black tragedy" plot but also to evoke a constant "between scenes" realm in which the mask, the faces, can be calm without ceasing to be irascible? If the writer is using a number of techniques to insinuate that another, subordinate narrative code circulates between and around the dominant linear linkages, then the gambit of introducing new characters makes sense. For in this other, punctual narrative code, the effect to be produced is that among a few set personae there simply *is* an endless climaxless story, and what may appear to be an approaching end is but an illusion and practical convenience. The sense conveyed is that, in an ever-present story of Yoknapatawpha, exactly where one picks up and leaves off the tale is a matter of less than decisive moment. Faulkner accentuates this loose-jointedness by the furniture salesman's relaxed narration of the last section.

Similarly, each of the three new characters either narrates or is depicted in ways that buffer the appalling death of Christmas with overtones of an encompassing shadow play or puppet theater. Faulkner reinforces this effect by introducing the conceit of the Player who moves the figures on a chess board. For example, in a story told and then recapitulated to a visiting professor, Stevens describes Mrs. Hines as "like an effigy with a mechanical voice being hauled about on a cart by that fellow Bunch and made to speak" (729; cf. 671–72). To similar effect, Faulkner, always ready to risk excess, mounts Percy Grimm ludicrously upon a bicycle to chase Christmas; describes the bicycle as moving "with the delicate swiftness of an apparition, the implacable undeviation of Juggernaut or Fate"; and says of Grimm, "Above the blunt, cold rake of the automatic his face had that serene, unearthly luminousness of angels in church windows" (739, 741). This treatment is at once like child's play, with Grimm mentally awarding points to Christmas during the chase, and as grim as the pursuer's typological name.

On the largest scale of point-on-point superposition, almost seven chapters of what is inadequately termed "flashback" are imposed

147

upon a moment in which Joe Christmas is poised between passivity and activity as he moves toward Joanna's house and her death, with the thought that he is going to "do something" and something is going to happen to him. And when the narrative present action resumes, the "calm paradox" between the punctual and linear perspectives and assumptions is nicely suggested in Joe's further thought: "He believed with calm paradox that he was the volitionless servant of the fatality in which he believed that he did not believe. He was saying to himself *I had to do it* already in the past tense" (605). It is in keeping with this telescoping of linear development and climax into a coincidence of moments that a narrative present tense materializes recurrently throughout the novel with rather unobtrusive abruptness to take over the business of recounting the story from the conventional narrative past tense. In the context of the pattern we have been tracing, the technique further contributes to the impression that a nonlinear temporal code and life-world constantly shadows the predominant cultural narration of a linear world.

As we would expect, Faulkner's sensitivity to sound and voices powerfully enhances the array of punctualist devices. Particularly effective here is the flat tone typical of both sympathetic and unsympathetic characters. In Chapter 4, for example, Faulkner misses no opportunity to remind us of Byron's "flat, inflectionless, countrybred singsong" (471–72), contrasting it to the distant background of church singing and giving its homely stylization to the story of Joe Christmas which Byron feels compelled to tell Hightower. And the overheard changeless sound of insects accentuates the effect. A social decorum of the calmly indifferent tone ranges from Armstid and Winterbottom's unhasty bargaining over a farm tool to Mrs. Hines's restrained pathos as, with the help of Byron's uninflected singsong, she narrates the terrible story of Joe's conception and birth. In pages whose stylistic rhetoric have had little critical attention, Faulkner brilliantly scripts Mrs. Hines's slow-motion paratactic voice as he describes it here: "She speaks in the same dead, level tone: the two voices in monotonous strophe and antistrophe: two bodiless voices recounting dreamily something performed in a region without dimension by people without blood" (677).

The combined effect of these and similar vocal and nonvocal devices is that of the chorus intoning here in strophe and antistrophe. The chorus intimates that a dreamy unchangefulness shadows the novel's tragic plot. At one level its inalienable calm reinforces the promise of the plot's end, the cathartic peace that will arise from resolution. In contrast, at another level its tranquil ever-present covertly denies that the plot need take place at all to attain peace—it disclaims the linear apparatus of catharsis, disclaims Aristotelian tragedy. This double-layered intimation resembles the sense of combined necessity and gratuitousness with which Byron contemplates Hightower's earlier history of persecution and final acceptance by the community: "As though, Byron thought, the entire affair had been a lot of people performing a play and that now and at last they had all played out the parts which had been allotted them and now they could live quietly with one another" (451). On the one hand, the whole incident was unnecessary pain, *just* a play, absurdly incongruous and gratuitous. On the other, it was apparently somehow necessary for these people so to act, according to a dramatic plot written for them, prescribing a troubled sequence in order to reach a quiet life.

Joe Christmas's passing realization of intense tranquility emerges from such a sequence, along with a comparable sense of its amazing incommensurability with the simple aim of peace: " 'That was all I wanted,' he thinks, in a quiet and slow amazement. 'That was all, for thirty years. That didn't seem to be a whole lot to ask in thirty years' " (644). The novel's suggestion of immortal figures acting in an unperishing present with "monotonous" stylization subtly works to persuade us that a punctualist calm indeed should not be too much to ask for, from the perspective of either a marionette show or a shadow play. But the novel's special tragic poignancy is that this experiential conviction, while remaining a conviction, also constitutes a demand on life that is in fact all too frequently excessive. "Peace is not that often" (612).

The dreamy inertia of punctual time counterpoints the novel's momentum of traditionally tragic linearity, the series of irrevocable consequences of action—as Joe thinks "quietly" toward the last, "what I have already done and cannot ever undo" (650). It is not untypical of tragedies that, while creating a machine of felt necessity, they also introduce an agonizing element of temporal contingency: had the messenger only come forward sooner, had Romeo only arrived at the tomb a few moments later, at Juliet's awakening, and so on. But *Light in August* amplifies this effect extraordinarily. The plotted tragedy that in fact occurs is all the more affecting because around its edges we glimpse a whole world, an entire cultural personal-temporal script, of alternative perceptions and behavior.

As the "Protestant music" epitomizes, tragedy is a potential of the community's codification of reality, with its surreptitious desire for cathartic peace through violence. Joe Christmas and his prosecutors, who are also his secret sharers in this desire—Doc Hines, McEachern, Joanna Burden, Percy Grimm—actualize this potential. Given the pervasiveness of this desire within the cultural script, it is necessary, "fated," that some such combination of victims and victimizers should occur. But although the tragic sequence is an outgrowth of a cultural script, for Faulkner it is notable that the script itself is not without alternative. It is a play that people play; another play, another script, could be played, and another novel could be written. That alternative, I have argued, haunts the actual novel. It periodically lights up the dominant cultural script with a luminous stillness, a lambent suspension, that helps to remind us of other cultural, and human, possibilities and to make the scripted frenzy seem either ruefully or absurdly gratuitous, or both at once.

This sense of both necessity and gratuitousness is essential to the tragedy of *Light in August*.

IV

We have discerned the general means, with their broad cultural resonance, by which *Light in August* seeks to produce its effect: interlacing alternative irenic strategies of cathartic peace and inviolable serenity. The first occurs as the temporal unfolding of persons in and through their violent performances, the second by the coincidence of times and persons, as if in one point. We saw, in other words, that these strategies for plotting time and action implied the simplifying performances of person as well. By a finer focus on the workings of theatrical simplification, especially the first strategy, we can now examine the creation of tragic persons, Hightower and Christmas, and the voice-related issues of action. These are performative issues of initiative and completion and, more specifically, the ascriptions of role and motive that this set of issues involves. Hightower, in order to repudiate death and find peace, wants to allot dramatic parts so that finally he can play all the roles—the hero, the hero's immortalizing poet, and the audience—and so collapse initiation and completion of performance into one tranquil self-sufficiency. Christmas, more unconsciously devoted to the same general goal as Hightower, wants in contrast to strip away imputed symbolic depth, which others consistently ascribe to his action, as one means of redefining his action as simply his own initiative. Our analysis will conclude by turning to the role the novel's plot and voice seek to ascribe to its readers.

First Hightower, the would-be alloter of roles. At one point, Hightower chides Byron, "What a dramatist you would have made" (687). This remark is not inappropriate to Byron, but that it suits Hightower himself much better becomes obvious when he later accuses himself of being a "showman . . . a charlatan preaching worse than heresy, in utter disregard of that whose very stage he preempted" (760). And as Faulkner combines both a punctual and a linear narrative strategy, as well as the devices of voice and plot, so does Hightower in preempting the Christian stage. Hightower, unlike Christmas, is not surprised that he essentially wants peace; it is his conscious aim. We discover as the novel progresses that Hightower has set out to compose his life as a script to produce serenity, first by entering the church as a shelter, then by using the two different implicit dramatic models.

In the pulpit his "wild rapt eager voice" (446) evokes and recapitulates a moment of death defiance—his private myth of his grandfather's cavalry raid on Jefferson. Hightower wants his vision to be more than an exciting reliving of what *once* had happened; he wants to *be* his grandfather at the point of his death and to immortalize that moment (and thus Hightower) through a perpetual celebration of it in a few depersonalized, formalistic terms: the galloping horses, the shadowy figures against the burning sky, the shotgun blast in the dark: "I have been a single instant of darkness in which a horse galloped and a gun crashed" (762). This shadow play is, by design, an infinite prolongation of "as I fell dying," "as though the seed which his grandfather had transmitted to him had been on the horse too that night and had been killed too and time had stopped there and then for the seed and nothing had happened in time since, not even him" (445). A beginning and an end, a seed and a death, telescope into each other in the recapitulatory *"Now, soon"* that is Hightower's private incantation. But, in contrast to the minister Shegog's revitalization of communal ritual in *The Sound and the Fury* through a vocal stylization at once individual and communal, Hightower's preaching, as he recognizes at last, preempts the communal ritual. It is not a rhetoric enlivening commonly held stories but an extreme, private form of the honor-code rhetoric of defiance, daring the audience to make a place on the Christian stage for the bravado of Hightower's grandfather, onetime invader of church revivals (748). It is, in other words, one vein of the Faulknerian "hubristic" rhetoric we have noted, in a magnified form. As Hightower exaggerates it, it is doomed to defeat—in Hightower's eyes, in fact, a convention-flouting, desirable "defeat and glory" (444) just like his grandfather's.

Like so much of Jefferson's ethos, Hightower's mythology is an amalgam of an honor code and certain Christian assumptions. At one level, not only does Hightower, as one of Faulkner's lesser-self dramatizations, ritualistically challenge the community to share his idiosyncratic master story, but he celebrates and emulates a No to death askew from the Christian drama of immortality. As Hightower emphasizes, his grandfather tops off his daring cavalry raid by being shot while stealing chickens from a henhouse. What Hightower admires is the immortal vitality he sees expressed in such an individualistic, boyish nose-thumbing at both death and convention: the "eternal youth . . . which makes heroes. . . . Any soldier can be killed . . . by a weapon approved by the arbiters and rulemakers of warfare. . . . But not with a shotgun, a fowling piece, in a henhouse" (756, 758). At a little lower layer, the grandfather's fabled death does follow in its quite "pagan" way the logic of the religious paradigm imbued in Hightower. The grandfather serves imaginatively as Hightower's proxy in action and suffering, and in the minister's private religion has died a vicarious death for him.

As for the linear aspect of Hightower's double-pronged strategy, Hightower perceives finally that preempting the church's stage by substituting cavalry for Calvary itself amounted to a subconscious plot. In effect, Hightower has scripted a plot of tragedy for himself, not one that would produce a catharsis of suffering but a plot that would permanently immunize him against further suffering. By scheming for his own martyrdom at the hands of the townspeople, he has, as he puts it, "bought immunity" (627), "making it appear that he resigned his pulpit for a martyr's reasons . . . with that patient and voluptuous ego of the martyr . . . until . . . he lifted the mask with voluptuous and triumphant glee: *Ah. That's done now. . . . That's bought and paid for now*" (761). This public display is a means of finally being free of the public eye. Much of Hightower's tragedy is that he has created for himself this pseudotragedy, this *act* of passivity and shame. By this means he tries to buy off—to redeem—the greater passivity and shame that is death and, concomitantly, to give himself a calm imperviousness to further shame, like Lena Grove's.

Not the least of his tragedy is the unforeseen consequence of his wife's suicide. According to a reasoning he shares with Addie Bundren, the shame that is self-chosen is immunizing and constitutes the secret assertion of a regal self-enclosure in autonomy: *Honi soit qui mal y pense*. But Hightower's realization of his implication in his wife's "despair and shame" (762) constitutes a shame he has not chosen, one forced on him in the sense that it is an unforeseen entailment, shattering his illusion of safe autonomy: "If I am the instrument of her despair and death, then I am in turn instrument of someone outside myself" (762). With acknowledgment of his wife, however limited, Hightower's way is open to a certain self-recognition, a more piercing awareness of his life as death.

Hightower's living martyrdom must be sustained by the oxymoron of private ritual, conducted behind the yard sign "which he calls his monument" (440) in his now lonely nightly vision: "They have thundered past now and crashed silently on. . . . The street lamp at the corner flickers and glares, so that the bitten shadows of the unwinded maples seem to toss faintly upon the August darkness. From a distance, . . . he can hear the sonorous waves of massed voices from the church: a sound at once austere and rich, abject and proud, swelling and falling . . . like a harmonic tide" (453). To Hightower's perception, the sonorous voices help to furnish his real monument. Like the "choirs of martial seraphim" (444) he once associated with his grandfather's death, the distant church voices are levied upon by Hightower's imagination to supply the immortalizing elegy for the slain hero, the grandfather who is above all himself. Hightower is at once, then, the grandfather-hero and the grandson-poet who celebrates him. He is a vulnerable Achilles, who proleptically experiences his immortalization and state of invulnerability in an imaginative re-creation, and a Homer, who immortalizes himself by immortalizing Achilles. And he is the audience, mentally performing the nonacoustical but audible heroic sounds and hearing "the echo of the phantom hooves still crashing soundlessly" (453). By identification with his grandfather, Hightower has contrived to be around to enjoy his own enacted and celebrated immortality, as he stages it with the help of public props.

It has been often noted that, however barren and vain in form, the "something of honor and pride, of life" (442) which Hightower nourishes imaginatively does finally help him to act constructively in the public world when he assists in delivering Lena Grove's baby and feels a resurgence of vitality and reinvolvement with others. For Hightower, then, his excessive commitment to his vision is both a foolish, tragic indulgence in his self-composed pseudotragedy and a means of maintaining the "blending of pride and hope and vanity and fear, that strength to cling to either defeat or victory, which is the I-Am, and the relinquishment of which is usually death" (690). Faulkner is too wise and, in his distinctive way, too tragic a writer to pretend to know the exact boundaries between pride and vanity, hope and fear, in the human resistance to death.

Conversely, even Hightower's most conventionally tragic moment, while he is suffering a cathartic self-knowledge through acknowledgment of his wife, retains a tonal complexity. Faulkner uses Hightower's development of this awareness to recount for the first time how Hightower's obsession grew from childhood and continues as an element of dotty immaturity in him. Surely, too, we may be allowed to suspect that Hightower's final "autogethsemane" of self-recrimination, in which he is covered with a bloodlike sweat, manifests to some degree his continuing impulse toward voluptuous martyrdom. Thus, if we expect all tragic figures to maintain a certain uniform, unmixed grandeur of the "I-Am," we are liable either to overlook qualities in Hightower that Faulkner does not overlook or else to reject him as a tragic figure.

It has been one theme of these chapters that Faulkner and many of his characters, Hightower preeminently, also evidence this very desire to find or ascribe a heroic simplicity and simple heroic stature. As Faulkner depicts it, their search for such a quality mirrors a certain expectation in Faulkner's audience and offers a rueful critique of its strengths and limits. A related passage on ascribing motivation partly catches the tone of this critique in *Light in August:* "Man knows so little about his fellows. In his eyes all men or women act upon what he believes would motivate him if he were mad enough to do what that other man or woman is doing" (433).

V

Defining action by such a projection of motivation upon it founds Joe Christmas's tragedy. The childhood toothpaste episode, in which the orphanage dietitian ascribes motives to Joe that only mirror her fear and guilt, is the representative anecdote of a minor act with far-reaching consequences and projections rippling out endlessly from each other. Such attributions of motive, whether applied to define one's own actions or those of others, simplify in one sense and complicate in another, as they seek to disentangle what is done from what is suffered. We have seen enough evidence to recognize the broad, diverse applicability of Joe's foreboding awareness that action and passivity can coalesce: "*Something is going to happen to me. I am going to do something*" (475). It remains to understand how this particularly applies to him, in what Minter has called "Joe's secret affiliation with the world that pursues and mutilates him" (132). If Hightower's is a self-composed tragic pseudotragedy, Joe Christmas, in resisting his world, collaborates with it to compose his version of tragic drama.

In several regards, we confront here a tragedy of strategic simplification. Christmas pursues an abstract pattern of repetitive behavior, the sketchiest of strategic life narratives: deviant action—violent punishment suffered—momentary peaceful release. With his fixed mask, he is like a skeletal persona without a full-fleshed story, an abstract to be filled by tragedy. To be Joe Christmas is to have a story imputed to oneself, as Max Confrey mockingly ascribes to him the role of Romeo. Christmas is an unwilling yet ready-made candidate for recruitment by others as a supporting player in their more concrete life dramas, which fill out his purposely simple, abstract pattern. He is figuratively as well as literally an orphan. The orphanage dietitian, Doc Hines, McEachern, Joanna Burden, Percy Grimm, and the community in general all try to adopt, and adapt, Joe to their explanatory fictions. All their fictions are informed by the underlying logic of actions-by-proxy epitomized in the Christian drama by original sin and vicarious purifying sacrifice. Joe's social status as an illegitimate orphan of ambiguous racial origin who is putatively black corresponds to their Calvinistic versions of original sin, or the curse of predestined damnation. His status is as it were the seed of their plot, the anticipation of their cathartic design.

Doc Hines's mania provides the most straightforward case. In his eyes, for his grandson Joe even to exist is for him to be guilty of a

wrongful act (actually performed by his biological parents) compounded of "bitchery" and "miscegenation." That is, the *status* of
being illegitimate and (supposedly) black is treated as if it were an *act*
the child has performed and for which he must suffer. To be is to
be guilty of a deed and its consequences. Though the Calvinist
McEachern does not especially share Hines's particular obsessions
with misogyny and racism, it is in light of the same general logic that
he ascribes to the innocuous actions of the child Joe the weightiest
religious implications. The same is true for Joanna Burden and the
inherited myth of black curse and redemption which she applies to Joe
and their relationship. Although these religious fixations are not at-
tributed to the dietitian, her excessive imputation of sinister motives to
the child Joe fits the pattern in a parallel Faulkner underscores by
likening her vein of cunning insanity to Doc Hines's madness (493).

The Sound and the Fury implied the logical progression of action
into unwelcome passivity. *Light in August* describes a world where a
passive condition, a mere state of being, is tantamount to a malign
action. However the child Joe is categorized—by race, miscegenation, illegitimacy, Calvinist predestiny—he *is* an offense.

The powerful opening of Chapter 6, which presents Joe's orphanage "enclosed by a ten foot steel-and-wire fence like a penitenti-
ary or a zoo," its windows streaked with soot "like black tears"
(487), makes plain that Joe is born into penal captivity. Joe is singled
out for punishment above all by the constant pressure of Doc Hines's
fanatical eyes watching him and waiting for the unfolding of the
anticipated plot. From the first, one law is imprinted upon Joe: guilty
action is presumed, punishment is inevitable. The assumption that
punishment is a fact of life is assimilable to the idea of action-by-
proxy, since Joe is being punished no matter what *he* has actually
done. Not to be immediately punished when he knows he has acted
wrongly, then, is extremely disturbing, for it doubly implies that
what he himself does makes no difference. Thus Joe is disturbed
when the dietitian does not punish him for eating the toothpaste, and
when the adolescent Joe returns home late after having avoided sexual
intercourse with the black girl he accepts as perfectly reasonable the
fact that he is punished anyway (516).

To state the matter another way, there is a presupposed issue of
action prior to that of freedom or determinism (that old critical war-
horse of discussions about the tragic status of Joe Christmas). That
prior issue, fundamentally, is the community's necessary furnishing

to its individual members the means to act at all. This is not the "freedom from," in other words, but the "freedom to," the enablement to act, to endure, to *exist* in one's situation. Joe's initially given cultural situation, the punitive situation defined by the orphanage, he takes to be the law of life, and he seeks, as we all must, to borrow from his culture the available equipment to encompass his situation. For Joe—and again here he is not alone—the tools of the culture are turned against it in such a way that problem and life-strategic solution are versions of each other.

Since punishment is a given, Joe's characteristic tendency is to act so as to deserve it, to make it not some vicarious projection upon him but something his own action has caused. He will act in his own right, to erase the absurdity of vicarious action that others impute to his mere condition of being and to substitute for it his own deed. And the subsequent punishment will be, similarly, *his* punishment; it will be, indeed, *his* action. He will then exist, though within the pattern's circle, within the realm of freedom, as he thinks, "the savage and lonely street which he had chosen of his own will" (589), the "thirty years that I have lived to make me what I chose to be" (594). He announces that he is a white man among blacks and is beaten. He announces he is black among whites and is beaten. He wears a facial expression that tempts his fellow workers to beat him; he gratuitously insults a black man among a group of blacks; he engages in schemes and criminality that invite punishment; and so on. His bootlegging in Jefferson similarly asks for trouble, since, although he is himself a model of tough silence, he takes as his partner the soul of indiscretion, Lucas Burch.

The very fervor with which Christmas pursues a masochistic life strategy of transforming passivity indicates the depth of his horror at passivity in general. For him, the spectacle of what Hightower calls "the Passive and Anonymous" (744) is suffused with death and carries a contagion from which he tries to protect himself by contempt, violence, or their ritualistic counterpart. Offered a sexual initiation along with other boys, the young Joe strikes at the black girl who passively awaits him, "prone, abject," and in whose eyes he sees "two glints like reflections of dead stars" (514). Joe shares, but more intensely, the emotion of the boys when they learn about menstruation: "It moved them: the temporary and abject helplessness of that which tantalised and frustrated desire; the smooth and superior shape in which volition dwelled doomed to be at stated and inescapable intervals victims of periodical filth" (535). Joe is deeply disturbed that such processes victimize and defile the autonomous, free power that he seeks and that females seem to possess as desirable objects who can say no to desire.

When Joe kills a sheep and bathes his hands in its blood, this is a para-ritualistic act of immunizing displaced violence against the menstrual "deathcolored" (538) fluid of sexual vulnerability. That which marks vulnerability can immunize, that which pollutes can purify, that which is cursed can redeem. Understanding this, we understand not only what is fairly explicit, why Joe is a fascinating challenge for Joanna, but also what has puzzled many readers as well as Joe himself: why she too fascinates him, so that he stays with her long after he decides he should leave. As Joe in his presumed blackness does for her, Joanna embodies the curse that is a potential blessing and so must be either transformed or destroyed. Joanna Burden reintroduces for Joe the fascinating chain of issues and behavior that he had thought to be under his control. Her double nature, like Caddy's in *The Sound and the Fury,* is expressed as an invulnerable strength and integrity untouched by Joe's raping her, combined with an extreme display of sexual passivity and self-degradation in her "nymphomaniacal" stage of "not alone . . . sin but . . . filth" (589). Overall, it is this combination that binds him to her.

At first, however, her invulnerability alone holds Joe's interest, initially as an unexpected frustration and challenge to him. Later, when he cannot overcome it, her impregnable will is a source of what can only be called comfort, which permits him, presumably for the first time since his romance with Bobbie Allen, to lower his guard and experience the significant measure of openness and intimacy manifested in their quiet talk (581–87). Here Joanna reenlivens for Christmas the potential for a healthy dependency that he had first experienced with the one strong nurturing person he had encountered in the orphanage, the older girl Alice, whom he had even allowed to "mother him a little" (499) and who disappears abruptly from his life as a heroic figure: "He seemed to see her then, grown heroic at the instant of vanishment beyond the clashedto gates, fading without diminution of size into something nameless and splendid, like a sunset" (500).[6]

But when such a powerful female volition as Joanna's is again shown to be susceptible to extremely "abject" passivity and degradation—as Joanna melodramatically follows her inherited script of corruption-and-redemption-with-a-black-man—Joe is again disturbed and mesmerized. The female "shape in which volition dwelled" wills what the narrative voice later calls a "suttee of volition's surrender" (737). This is compounded finally by Joanna's menopause, which resurrects in a new form the biological "victimization" of menstruation. The last refinement is that her increasingly insistent religious motivation resurrects McEachern's voice in Joe's mind. Christmas can no more simply leave her than he could cope with the crux represented by menstruation by running away.

To appropriate as his own action what Joe perceives as the natural order of existence, he wishes to simplify it in all its phases. He will then be his own, not "God's chosen own because He once cursed him" (586). He wants to make wrongful behavior a simple case of his wrongdoing, not a portentous act before the watchful eyes of God. (For images of the watchful eye, see, e.g., 516 and 736). The meanings sexuality has for Joe match too well with the sexual nexus of the cultural script, so that he responds with horrified fascination and at last rebellion as Joanna Burden seeks to entangle him in her increasingly extreme symbolic action—"as if she had invented the whole thing deliberately, for the purpose of playing it out like a play" with Joe in the key supporting role of "Negro! Negro!" (590), instrument first of climactic defilement and then of purification according to her controlling cathartic plot. Christmas wants punishment, too, to be a simple affair, an enforced submission to a superior power, not a scene in a large drama of retribution or redemptive sacrifice—"the punishment which, deserved or not, just or unjust, was impersonal" (522). Through this kind of impersonality, Christmas seeks the personal, his own stripped-down, self-instigated version of what he has assimilated as the natural order of things.

He accepts McEachern's punishment as a given as long as the older man is physically superior, but Christmas rejects the religion and the prayer McEachern uses to justify the punishment, with "that monotonous voice as of someone talking in a dream . . . arguing with a Presence" (512). McEachern's remembered "*monotonous dogmatic voice which . . . will never cease*" (568) is in fact reincarnated in Joanna Burden's voice when she begins to "pray over" Joe and asks him to join her in repentance. When Joanna says of her request, "It's not I who ask it," she voices much more than she knows (607). For Joe, her voice, like McEachern's, transmogrifies into a visual image of death. Joe's memory of lying in bed with "his hands crossed on his

breast like a tomb effigy" (512), McEachern's "phantom" knee-
prints on the rug, projects itself onto the floor where Joanna has
recently knelt: "And it would seem to him that he could distinguish
the prints of knees and he would jerk his eyes away as if it were death
that they had looked at" (605). Again, for Joe to resist such reappropriation of his life pattern by the Calvinist voice and drama from
which he has basically abstracted it is for him to resist death.

Joe is another of Faulkner's characters haunted by voices who use
action, at last self-defeatingly, as the substitute for and sublation of
voice. Fleeing the vocal, he recalls it in irrevocable action.

Conversely, true to Hightower's insight into the religious sublimation of violence, when Joe refuses to participate in Joanna's penitential
ceremony, her transition to direct violence is presented as the easiest,
most natural of occurrences, as she aims a pistol at him. After killing
Joanna when her pistol misfires, Joe goes to the black church to
attempt once more to deliver himself from that drama and its voice
by his assault on the congregation and his blasphemy from the pulpit.
This purgative act too of course requires that he operate on the very
stage and presume the very Presence he defies. Like Hightower's
attempted preemption, Joe's attempted avoidance of this cultural
drama becomes its sometimes garbled but in the end painfully accurate translation. It is at this level of symbolic projection of the white
Calvinist drama upon Christmas—and not in the scattered, purposely twisted "parallels" with which Faulkner teases his readers to
be alert to the projection—that the novel's tragic irony of Joe as a
"Christ-figure" appears most significantly.

Joe's violent eruption in murder, assault, and blasphemy and his
exhaustion and hunger in his flight from capture produce a peace that
intersects with the punctual experience of tranquility (643–44). In the
linear life pattern known to him, however, Joe has no master narrative or set of habits to sustain this occasionally glimpsed condition
in some adapted form. So, once more discovering the day of the
week, mounting the wagon to Mottstown, and walking the street
until he is captured, he returns to the circling street, the linear circuit
he has always followed and claimed as his own: he enters "again, the
street which ran for thirty years" (649–50). By his action, he proceeds
to the phase of punishment and final cathartic peace in violent death.
Because he resists the Calvinist reappropriation of his life pattern by
abstracting the cultural plot, this appropriation is exactly what happens. He becomes again an abstract anomaly waiting to be con-

scripted, as the corruptingly sexual black man, in a drama of salvation and damnation. Percy Grimm, who castrates him so that Christmas will leave white women alone in hell, is one more variation on Joe's white victim and victimizer, Joanna Burden. Seemingly we have returned to the fate of Addie Bundren in *As I Lay Dying,* where with death one's ending is composed by the various stories of others.

But in manifesting a narrative that is communally shared, *Light in August* imagines a step beyond the point that the previous novel reached. Quentin Compson sought exactly that symbolic resonance for his life and death that Christmas seeks to avoid. Addie Bundren indeed made her death a spectacle for others, but of an unintended kind. Though Christmas fails to strip his life of evocative depth, his provocative action still obtains for him the final violence and serenity he wishes: "He crouched behind that overturned table and let them shoot him to death, with that loaded and unfired pistol in his hand" (731).

Joe's death meets both his needs and, in a sense, those of the community, represented in the anonymous onlookers. The exceptional violence of his mutilation and the exceptional serenity he manifests in death together constitute the "perfection" of a common desire, the meeting ground between their master plot and his pattern of action. He makes actual in one moment of climax and completion the dramatic narrative ordinarily diffuse in their lives. Thus on the basis of what white southern Calvinism teaches them to recognize and him to experience, he enters their minds as an immortalized figure in his own right. But by that very token he is transcendent, set apart from them as a standard they despair of attaining. They are not, then, in the full sense witnesses—participant "martyrs," to recall the witnessing congregation Faulkner depicted with limited conviction in *The Sound and the Fury.* Joe's onlookers are spectators. They only observe and forever remember a peace that passes not only understanding but, more important, their sharing. Faulkner's usual sign of participation, communal voices that go beyond words into communicative silence, is ironically negated by the siren that reaches a crescendo of violent sound and then passes beyond it:

> For a long moment he looked up at them with peaceful and unfathomable and unbearable eyes. Then his face, body, all, seemed to collapse, to fall in upon itself, and from out the slashed garments about his hips and loins the pent black blood seemed to rush like a released breath. It

seemed to rush out of his pale body like the rush of sparks from a rising rocket; upon that black blast the man seemed to rise soaring into their memories forever and ever. They are not to lose it, in whatever peaceful valleys, beside whatever placid and reassuring streams of old age, in the mirroring faces of whatever children they will contemplate old disasters and newer hopes. It will be there, musing, quiet . . . not particularly threatful, but of itself alone serene, of itself alone triumphant. Again . . . the scream of the siren mounted toward its unbelievable crescendo, passing out of the realm of hearing. (742–43)

Although Joe's catharsis, "alone serene, of itself alone triumphant," is what the spectators desire, not what they have, its memory will always awe them. So Joe's final "attainment" is not the private, incommunicable event that Hightower's final vision is. Faulkner describes Joe's death as if it were a public monument rising in the minds of the small community of observers, and it stands out against the transitory column of yellow smoke over Joanna's death and the equally ironic monument that occupies Hightower's front yard. Joe's monument is the group's shared memory of having seen someone else achieve the covert communal ideal of eternal impervious peace in death.

Joe's monumental dying as the serene, psychologically unmoved mover of others transforms an extreme of shameful vulnerability, sexual mutilation, into its opposite. This scene is the partial fictional parallel to Faulkner's idea of a No to death through writing that is invulnerable and eternally moving. It is partial because Faulkner's readers are more fortunate than Joe's spectators within the fictional world. The latter have no counterpart to the vocally powerful Easter sermon of *The Sound and the Fury* and so are moved only by viewing a valued experience they cannot share. Faulkner, however, not only scores an eloquent cathartic voice for his readers but frames a structure that amplifies it. Generally, as we have noted, the subtext of tranquil nonlinearity increases the poignancy of the catharsis as well as encourages the reader's desire for its *requiescat in pace*. After the long proliferation of alternating subplots, the buildup of tension, the chase, and the brutal killing, Joe's extraordinarily peaceful release in death is, for the sympathetic reader, astonishing, welcome, and subliminally well prepared for by the pattern of his life.

Both in the impact of Joe's death on his observers and in what the impact lacks in the way of a vocal communication to them, we are further sensitized to what Faulkner's voice provides his audience as we read the description. Faulkner's sonorous, prophetic celebration of Joe's immortalization in the minds of others thus climaxes the process. And Faulkner takes care to confirm and draw out the effect with a further arousal of tension in Hightower's final appearance, and then a denouement.[7]

By placing Hightower's last scene after Joe's rather than before it, Faulkner confirms that within the novel's world only death brings a cathartic peace. Correspondingly, he thus raises the reader's emotional irresolution again, but to a much slighter degree than before, and then, with a new shift in narrative and scene, releases us into the final chapter and Lena's departure. Here, the depiction of Byron as a comically Keatsian bold lover suspended in pursuit of Lena, who is on her travels, leaves the novel's action open only in a lighthearted sense that by contrast affirms the closure of Joe Christmas's tragedy. The ending affirms more: the containment of tragedy, as if Faulkner, having closed a tragic action, makes doubly sure of this closure by comic buffers. The image of the furniture-dealer narrator cozily bantering in bed with his wife and audience, amusingly distances into comedy the serious reconciliation of author and audience Faulkner has sought. If this framing device and the narrator's tale cannot make Lena's preternatural calm available to us, it does allow us the relaxation of amusement at her characteristic feeling and the rudimentary excuse for a continuing plot Lena stands comically contemplating, as Faulkner's tragic plot, without haste, is attenuated to its doubled close.

VI

In reasserting his privilege as an author to give his work more self-sufficiency by closing a tragic plot, then, Faulkner simultaneously offers his readers a privileged position as well. It is epitomized in our advantage over the spectators of Joe's death, by virtue of cathartic voice. In context, the rendition of Christmas's death implies that only in death or in Faulkner's art is a widely desired cathartic serenity possible for most. At this level, Faulkner's art presents itself implicitly as the benign substitute for violence and death, which, in contrast to the church voices, does not disastrously relapse into these realities it works to transform. Kartiganer and others have argued that Faulkner, like modernism in general, holds to a strong discontinuity between art and life. It seems more convincing to me to say, rather, that Faulkner implies that his art can remedy the deficiencies of an existence that lacks his art. And it also seems to me more credible to say that Faulkner's "modernism" is reflected in his mixed feelings—with changeable proportions of satisfaction, doubt, and rebelliousness—about the artist's dependency upon the living, actual audience, both contemporary and future. Faulkner's command of a tragic art that bridges from traditional societies to the modern world rests partly upon the convergence between this "modernist" ambivalence and the mixed condition of the traditional honor-code hero, as we examined it in an earlier chapter. That figure too is pulled between a proud self-sufficiency on the one hand and on the other his performative dependency upon a community with the power to confer on him the very status of immortalized hero. After the hopeful initiative of tragic achievement offered to the reader in *The Sound and the Fury* and after the doubt of *As I Lay Dying, Light in August* most confidently affirms that the author's and the reader's shares in tragic creativity are reconcilable. *Absalom, Absalom!* in its turn will reexamine the grounds for this reconciliation, this "happy marriage of speaking and hearing."

The greater role that plot "self-sufficiency" plays in *Light in August* underwrites the novel's rendition of pathologies of powerful vocal self-sufficiency in two complementary autocratic forms. One is solipsistic rant: Hightower preaching in the pulpit or reading Tennyson's putatively empty sonority, "like listening in a cathedral to a eunuch chanting in a language which he does not even need to not understand" (634); or McEachern bombastically praying at Joe's bedside; or Doc Hines self-hypnotically fulminating of "bitchery and abomination." The related form is voice reduced to a would-be impersonality, to "writing."

I have been suggesting that for Faulkner, as for traditional "oral peoples," according to Walter Ong, "generally language is a mode of action and not simply a countersign of thought. . . . Oral peoples commonly . . . consider words to have great power." Yet we have seen that Faulkner also evidences the marks of what Ong calls "typographic culture," which in Faulkner's work contests the oral, for as Ong goes on: "Deeply typographic folk forget to think of words as primarily oral, as events, and hence as necessarily powered: for them, words tend rather to be assimilated to things, 'out there' on a flat surface. Such 'things' are not . . . actions, but are in a radical sense dead, though subject to dynamic resurrection" (*Orality* 32–33; see also 81).

Although there is danger of overgeneralization in Ong's approach, his remarks do help freshen our sense of what is at stake in Faulkner's 1953 essay celebrating the immortalizing power of "cold impersonal print" and thereby to conclude by placing *Light in August* within its informing context of symbolic action. We can compare to this essay a passage in *Light in August* describing McEachern's manner of speaking to the boy Joe, where voice resembles writing: "His voice was not unkind. It was not human, personal, at all. It was just cold, implacable, like written or printed words" (508–9). By this metaphorical designation of "writing," Faulkner in this novel makes explicit the connection between writing and the temptation to impersonal power. More overtly than in Faulkner's previous major works, *Light in August* explores a strong ambivalence about the attractions and dangers of the potent "cold print"—or some analogue clustered about it in Faulkner's characteristic set of associations. Not only vulnerability but invulnerability has its ratio of risk and reward.

Faulkner early depicted the writer as a hapless figure driven to write for an audience—often specified as female—indifferent or hostile to his creation, while the writer was concerned with his ego.[8] When, however, Faulkner considered the writer's product, writing, it was seen as having compensatorily encapsulated and made serenely invulnerable the writer's urgencies, so that now their "isolation" was splendid. In his novels Faulkner explores how various inferior analogues of writing, as thus conceived, operate, impassively affecting others, sometimes in morally objectionable ways. Faulkner's works conduct a long argument with themselves about the isolated impersonality, invulnerability, and power to affront others which writing and its analogues in certain kinds of voice and demeanor can possess.

This is an argument that, taken as a whole, variously reflects upon the life-conducive or deathly potentials of a would-be invulnerable potency and autonomy in given circumstances and embodiments. For all the doubts and exceptions Faulkner expresses, the major recurrent theme in this argument is his implication that only real writing—Faulkner's writing—is able to do what the inferior analogues to writing attempt and fall short of, often tragically. As we noted, all such symbolic action against death in some fashion mimes or incorporates death, but only writing—real writing, and not its analogues—can escape it, if readers will do their part. Such appears to be Faulkner's firm hope, if not his firm belief.

A case in point, Joe Christmas makes himself into the image of the writinglike voice of a psychologically unmoved mover of others. By this displaced miming of voice, he tries to render himself invulnerable to its speaker, McEachern, and the religiosity he represents. Yet, in contrast to this reduction of himself to one "writing" persona, the collection of voices Joe hears on the evening of Joanna Burden's slaying evokes a more complex person fundamentally and constitutively implicated with others: "myriad sounds . . . —voices, murmurs, whispers: of trees, darkness, earth; people: his own voice; *other voices* evocative of names and times and places—which he had been conscious of all his life without knowing it, *which were his life*" (my italics). Then as Joe momentarily despairs of the success of his revolt against McEachern's religiosity, voice metamorphoses back into "writing" and the death associated with being conscious of an inadmissible, inimical belief: "*God perhaps and me not knowing that too* He could see it like a printed sentence, fullborn and already dead *God loves me too*" (476). The potential flattening of an oral-aural reading into a merely visual, death-associated reading (one implicit issue for the audience of *As I Lay Dying*) appears in *Light in August* as a character's perceptual experience of a "printed sentence" of impersonality and death.

Within the broad range of its significance, the light in August of the title indicates both the premonitory chill of death and the dangerous mimesis of mortality, like Joe's, that seeks to control it. Thus Joanna Burden at one point speaks to Joe "in a tone . . . detached, impersonal. . . . But it was as though she were not listening to her own voice, did not intend for the words to have any actual meaning: that final upflare of stubborn and dying summer upon which autumn, the dawning of halfdeath, had come unawares" (595).

By exploiting such potentials of voice for moral and symbolic reversal, *Absalom, Absalom!* probes the confidence of *Light in August*. *Absalom, Absalom!* has something of the relation to its predecessor that *As I Lay Dying* bears to *The Sound and the Fury*. But there is the significant difference that *Absalom, Absalom!* reconsiders its predecessor to establish fresh grounds for tragedy. The peace that *Light in August* offered through catharsis and sustained tranquility transforms into Sutpen's self-simplification and strategic iron calm, growing out of revulsion at Lena's sort of reproduction; and into the disquiet of his witness Quentin Compson, who repeats "Nevermore of peace."

Looked at from a rhetorical standpoint, *Absalom, Absalom!* explores the possibility of readers who will not or do not play the role of reader presumed by *Light in August*. The latter not only is, arguably, Faulkner's most horrifically violent novel in "content" but rhetorically contains and transmutes that violence into a kind of immunization by means of the devices we have examined. To argue that the novel offers an inoculation whose inferior analogues are the ritual blood in which Joe Christmas dips his hands and the permanent immunity Hightower believes he has bought is not to settle the question of how the offer will be taken. Readers realize *Light in August* as a disburdening catharsis and immunization not only by being sufficiently alert to Faulkner's blending of plot and voice with the painful material the book evokes but by weighing this artistic rendering sufficiently in their balance of value. Sufficiently alert and sufficiently weighing—but at one level of Faulkner's concern, the question of reading Faulkner tragically, reading him into immortality, is also the question of what will suffice in a particular circumstance for particular actual readers. How will the artistic transformation of the events depicted be weighed against the mental and physical violence thus represented? What is offered as a catharsis and inoculation may be taken or received as a poison, and the novel carries within it the knowledge that immunization of every kind is hazardous, analogous to the mortal affronts the audience-narrators of *Absalom, Absalom!* must encompass.

The represented narrators of *Absalom, Absalom!* are like certain imagined recalcitrant, injured, or otherwise "unpersuaded" readers of *Light in August,* an audience for whom a received and completed narrative of long-past violence and death is and remains problematic. *Absalom, Absalom!* gives them a story they cannot walk away from, as a reader may close a book; it gives them an affront they feel they must help to perform themselves. They compose both the affront, in part, and the handling of it, since they must recreate it in order to elaborate an answer to it. By virtue of this very fact, rather than simply failing to respond to symbolic transformation, they engage in it.

One audience dominates the opening narrative of *Absalom, Absalom!:* the woman outraged by a role into which a man has implicitly cast her. From the vantage of an actual reader, suggested by Rosa

Coldfield, *Light in August* looks different from what we have seen, and we are helped to focus on a rhetorical gambit with significant implications for the closure of this novel. For the reader persuaded by the rhetoric of *Light in August* is not someone who would balk at Joe Christmas's rape of Joanna Burden and at his generally disturbed, sometimes violent sexuality to such an extent that he or she would thereafter find it impossible to sympathize sufficiently with Joe and thus to be absorbed in the catharsis of his death and its rhetorical rendering.[9] Encouraging further resistance to Joe as tragic figure may well be the affront of Faulkner's associated depiction of Joanna's lurid sexual behavior during her "nymphomaniacal" stage (including her eyes glowing in the dark). This affront may be only partly tempered but not alleviated by understanding Joanna's sexual surreality as an element of her melodramatic cultural script, corruption-with-a-black-man. Similarly, however obviously Doc Hines is shown to be insane, his rantings about bitchery and abomination, in this context, may serve to deepen this affront and recall it to mind. Even if such a reader were to experience a conscious or unconscious "punitive" relief at the castration of Joe, this kind of relief would be likely to strongly qualify or block the entire sequential experience of engendered catharsis we examined above. Compounded with such relief might well be a negative reaction to the comic serenity conveyed by Lena Grove, taken to confirm objectionable sexual stereotyping.

Without slighting this potential reading engagement with the novel, we are prompted by our general critical purpose to consider the fact of this potential affront further, in relation to the rhetoric of Faulkner's symbolic action. Faulkner's typical hazarding of affront keeps the novel from casting a general spell of autonomously achieved adequacy to the issues it raises—a spell that would be contrary to the very nature of action as socially implicated. Along with its attempted balancing of the writer's and reader's powers of completion, the novel manifests a "sexual vulnerability" of its own—a vulnerability to certain reader reactions to sexual matters that the novel's themes in fact portray as deeply troublesome. The potential outrageousness keeps the novel from concluding a pact of achieved catharsis, as if the work had delivered a tragic effect guaranteed for all, in all frames of mind, as if one could *buy* immunity, as if achievement of some measure of immunity did not carry any inherent risk. The element of risk, the live possibility of an untransformed outrage at Joe Christmas which can disrupt the tragic effect, keeps the novel open.

And that impulse to push some element of his fiction until it threatens to be outrageous paradoxically rescues this novel and helps to save Faulkner's best writing in the major phase from the finish and apparent self-sufficiency of "writing" and books. It saves his writing from being "writing" by implicitly seeking in some fashion to make its effects contingent on the live auditioning of living readers.

The death and apotheosis of Christmas is a symbolic composite of sexual vulnerability and potency, in the now-familiar basic Faulknerian tropes imaging his aspiration to engender deathlessness in his flesh-and-blood readers in generations to come. It is all there in the images of blood rushing from loins like a "released breath" to be transformed in the audience into an apotheosis of serene immortality.

CHAPTER 6

The House of *Absalom, Absalom!*:
Voices, Daughters, and
the Question of Catharsis

creatures . . . brutely evacuated into a world without hope or purpose for them, who would in turn spawn with brutish and vicious prolixity.

Absalom, Absalom!

We build our houses, block by block, in pain
For our children to pull down, then build them up again.

Vision in Spring

William Faulkner, Sole Owner and Proprietor
Yoknapatawpha map legend, *Absalom, Absalom!*

Everyone knows that according to Quentin's narrative in *Absalom, Absalom!* "Sutpen's trouble was innocence" (220). For all the attention this statement has had, it remains to be understood how extensively these words sum up the development of Faulknerian tragedy in this novel. Because *Absalom, Absalom!* perfects Faulkner's treatment of issues he variously entertained before, this is a good place to review their relationships as we anticipate their development.

The starkest traditional form of the pathetic situation, distinguished from tragic action, involves victimizing an innocent. Innocence emphasizes that the calamity suffered is not of the character's own doing. In *Absalom,* by making the innocent an enactor of innocence and thus reworking the innocence of pathos into tragic action, Faulkner again transmutes the stuff of a simple generic contrast into a dialectical interchange. *The Sound and the Fury,* it will be recalled, implied that initially tragic action declined to pathos. *Absalom* reverses the arrow of initial transformation and shows us this moment of reversal. It shows the full range of a tragic logic, from the first premise to its consequences over time. Tragedy occurs in Quentin's version of Sutpen's tale, we can say preliminarily, because innocence is not simply a given condition, as in pathos, but becomes an action. Tragedy here results from Sutpen's heroically constituting effort to redeem an outraging of his "given" boyhood innocence.

As Sutpen's strategic action taken against this affront, his innocence performatively maintains a "childlike heroic simplicity" (246). Innocence so enacted means that Sutpen purges assimilated ineffective voices by commiting himself to an impervious heroic voice.

From the perspective of *The Sound and the Fury,* it is remarkably appropriate that Quentin imagines Sutpen's reversal of pathos by a powerful voice and corresponding action. Sutpen speaks with the power Quentin desired in the earlier novel. But this is the fateful power of displayed invulnerability, not that of communal openness. More generally, whereas earlier characters comparably struggle against heterogeneous "impurity" to transform a given, passive condition into their own action, they stage their figurative dramas largely in their minds, and Faulkner thereby underscores the point that the individual is a theater of others. Still, the scope of these characters' symbolically conceived setting and performance goes far beyond the scale of the actual staging they create or inhabit. For all the much larger scale of Sutpen's Hundred, however, in Sutpen's conception his theater also outstrips it and, we will see, includes an immense audience who give purpose to his acts. In accord with tragedy traditionally understood, *Absalom, Absalom!* gives this theater an actual historical grandeur that corresponds more directly than before to the symbolic size of the action. And in an obvious sense, the plot representation of this action closes with the destruction of Sutpen and his white family, a destruction implicit in his inceptive action. Also clear, however, is the continuing existence of his black descendent Jim Bond as well as the members of Sutpen's symbolic genealogy, including Quentin, who recognizes that Sutpen made them all. In and through their performative action, the Sutpen plot remains open.

To preview this much of Sutpen's enacted innocence is already to give pride of place to one version of Sutpen, Quentin's. Though there are good reasons for doing this, Sutpen's magnitude as a legendary hero of literary tragedy also stems from Faulkner's deploying multiple stories that call Sutpen and his family into being on a grand scale because the Sutpens simultaneously represent the deep problems and troublesome solutions of a specific ongoing cultural shaping of human beings. These problems and strategies converge in the creative commerce of voices. The proprietors of the narrative voices are simultaneously fascinated and frustrated by Sutpen's imperviousness and purist self-enclosure, which—as the preceeding discussions help us understand—grow out of their culture itself as its empowerment, temptation, and nemesis. As the narrators fill out what is unspoken or unspeakable in the other narrators' stories of Sutpen, with their voices they keep him heroically alive despite the fact that he in effect established his heroism as the antithesis of such vocal reciprocity. They as much create as discover him and his legend's magnitude and power. Vocal reciprocity, as we will have further occasion to elaborate, as much defines their culture as does Sutpen's rejection of it.

"Be Sutpen's Hundred" goes to the heart of the matter. Sutpen represents the collapse of cultural dialogue into monologue, the unhearing fiat rather than the interchange of constitutive vocal power. He especially tempts Quentin, surfeited with voices. In fact Quentin conceives him in such a way as to heighten the very temptation and caution against it. At another level, Sutpen with his eventual indebtedness to other voices is the enabling monological temptation within Faulkner's writing, critiqued by "dialogism" and critiquing it in turn.

In brief, the monological fiat designated in Sutpen is, in the long run, not only tragically self-destructive but dependent on the dialogical practice it excludes, as Sutpen's immortality is sustained by others' mutually completing stories. But the dialogical speakers are themselves constantly attracted to and repeatedly produce quasi-monological speech, and associated purgative actions, to deal with the pathos of others that has been absorbed in the openness of speaking and hearing.

The preceding paragraph sums up as well one important version of the dialectic between invulnerable autonomy and vulnerable performance in the preceding novels. But whereas, for example, in *As I Lay Dying* Addie's attempt at an independent "voicelessness" was undone

by her actual dependence on others' actions, *Absalom, Absalom!* sharply accentuates voice itself, with all its conflicted accommodations and
dependencies. Here we recall the dynamic of dangerous empowering
first examined in Chapter 2. The potential outrageousness of monologue is played against and articulated within the dialogical rhetoric
of the novel. It contributes its tonic provocation to the work's rhetorical power and risk.

So far, these anticipatory comments on *Absalom, Absalom!* as tragedy have concentrated on catharsis, spoken voice, and immortality.
(Another key concept, the daughter, has yet to appear, but its place
has been marked by the idea of assimilation and thus a potential
"impurity," which the daughter, like Caddy Compson, represents to
the patrilineal purity of the House.) The concept that has so far
dominated criticism of *Absalom,* on the other hand, and has greatly
helped to secure for it the immortality it can claim, is knowledge.
Since I propose that the question of knowledge is a subset, an in-
cluded issue, of the terms I have offered, it will help to glance at the
founding critical statements.

Cleanth Brooks wrote that *Absalom, Absalom!* concerns the "nature
of historical truth and . . . the problem of how we can 'know' the
past. . . . [The novel] is a persuasive commentary upon the thesis
that much of 'history' is really a kind of imaginative construction"
(309, 311–12). Brooks's highly modified New Critical cognitive perspective on *Absalom, Absalom!* has passed on a significant legacy to
Faulkner criticism. His first book on Faulkner in 1963 effectively
completed the reclamation of Faulkner from derogation and neglect.
In the earlier phase of this recognition George Marion O'Donnell
(1939) had emphasized Faulkner's importance and propriety by describing his work as a coherent "myth" reaching toward tragedy, and
a few years later Malcolm Cowley, introducing his famous Viking
edition, had similarly appealed to the honorific connotations of
Faulkner as creator of myth. After Faulkner was honored with the
Nobel Prize in 1950 and increasingly became a subject for academic
teaching and criticism, a cognitive framework was constructed
around author and oeuvre to facilitate their reclamation. Hyatt Waggoner, for example, in 1959 declared that *Absalom, Absalom!* "gets its
chief effect as a novel from our sense that we are participating in its
search for the truth" (169). This statement repeated the central idea
given prominence in Harvey Breit's 1951 Introduction to the Modern

Library edition: "The [novel's] system of [stylistic and structural] obstacles is precisely the means by which one ultimately learns the truth" (x). *Absalom, Absalom!* remains housed in this cognitive frame.

Ars longa is a commonplace because we usually take for granted the secular and religious institutions of learning which have made it true over the centuries. But the fit between this novel and its academic means of preservation is, as is not infrequently the case, both odd and revealing. There is obviously no quarreling with the idea that *Absalom, Absalom!* concerns knowledge, and the critical conception of the novel as epistemology has yielded valuable results. But without denying the novel's epistemological element, a rhetorical criticism interested in symbolic action and reading performance readily discovers the cues to reconceiving these questions and raising others.

An immediate incentive is the novel's sardonic attitude toward the academy that temporarily houses Quentin and Shreve, where "the best of ratiocination" is described as "a good deal like Sutpen's morality and Miss Coldfield's demonizing." Fortunately, this "logic and morality" is located in the university, where it does "the least amount of harm" (280; cf. 258). As has often been observed, Sutpen's morality, like his "design," and the demonizing per se of Rosa's discourse are excessively abstract; they pay scant attention to the exigencies of particular situations, occasions, and persons. Walter Ong has pointed out the distortion that comes of projecting the academically abstract ideal of a print culture onto people more oriented to orality. He notes that such people think much less abstractly, in the respect that they stress the situational, operational, and interpersonal, but that their intelligence in these matters can seem stupidity when they are tested by situationless academic questions, which uncritically assume that all proper thinking seeks to manipulate disembodied ideas. In terms of the contrast between the situational and the desituated, the print-culture, academic ideal is logic, since a logical "syllogism is self-contained: its conclusions are derived from its premises only" (*Orality* 53). Though Sutpen springs from and inhabits a still highly oral culture, his thought and action, "logic and morality," are syllogistic in this respect, and the counterpart of this attempt at closed system is his attempt to keep his House pure of such racial heterogeneity and interpersonal, situational variability as Charles Bon represents. A logic of tragedy is a tragedy of logic as well.

Faulkner's sarcastic link between academic ratiocination and this logic of "innocence" might well dispose critics quite ratiocinatively to seek to compensate for the limits of the academic "search for truth" model for this novel. At least since the publication of Olga Vickery's study, it has been demonstrated often that the narrators' efforts at knowledge are "unreliable" because Rosa, Mr. Compson, Shreve, and Quentin manifest various individual interests implicated in their depiction of the Sutpens. Given the legitimate academic aspiration to achieve abstract knowledge, these interests can be too easily disparaged as mere "bias" and limitation of knowing, when the situationless ideal of knowledge is tacitly taken as the universal norm. Or the interests can appear to be merely eccentrically individualistic, whereas in reality they exist within a cultural process that is both specific and widely relevant.

Because rhetorical study, though clearly an academic endeavor, classically explores the speaker's means of dealing with specific occasions, it reflects its origins in orally grounded culture. In this orientation, knowing or arriving at the truth may well be important, but the emphasis is on what knowledge is for and whom it concerns, specifically within one's situation of action. In considering these matters I will be particularly interested in the novel's extraordinary stylistic embellishment and sonorous elaboration.

Absalom, Absalom! contrasts the narrative's ornate volubility to the historical characters' typical taciturnity and reserve and so continues Faulkner's preoccupation with silence and speech. It returns to the related issue of unaccommodated mortal existence advanced in *As I Lay Dying,* where, we noted, the basic convention and analogy for the novel's departure from ordinary verisimilitude was ceremonial communal voice. But the departure was also made at once possible and frustratable by, among other things, heightening certain features of the print medium, of the printed book.

The primary narrative and rhetorical conventions of *Absalom,* however, are neither those of ritual nor those of an inscriptive, a print, culture. The invoked conventions are those of a transcriptive, largely oral, manuscript culture, where speech is rather freely transcribed and conjectural embellishment fulfills dialogical and transcriptive conventions. In order to appreciate the tragic correlations of these conventions in this novel, we will treat two other, thematic grounds of embellishment, answering to two kinds of silence, which make elaboration less free because more tragically constrained. If Sutpen's descendant Jim Bond represents self-containment carried to its rigorous conclusion, the first silence suppresses and displaces the outcry of such an unaccommodated man. The second silence embodies the necessary reticence of "serious persons" in an honor-shame code. The elaborations that speak to these silences or effectively accomplish them and that round out the statements of others as in dialogical response create *Absalom*'s vocal richness. After reverting to the classical consideration of the tragic effect on an audience, I will trace the related issues of assimilation and catharsis by concentrating on two key figures and vocal actions, which a more adequate grasp of voice and action should allow us to see, and hear, freshly. One is the daughter and her opening of the self-enclosed House by transmitting Bon's scripted voice. The other is Quentin and his attempt to deal with his burdensome commonwealth of voices, partly by strategically imagining Sutpen's strategy. These steps will permit us explicitly to develop the rhetorical implications for reading enactment of *Absalom, Absalom!*

I

The height of tragic pathos for Aristotle is the killing of kindred, and catharsis here in turn depends upon the protagonist's ignorance of whom he has killed and his subsequent discovery of his victim's identity. The hero's ignorance of his victim's identity keeps the audience from seeing his act as merely evil, something we would not knowingly do. It thus arouses our fear that we might fall into a similar hamartia, error, and the hero's belated enlightenment and his sorrow at his deed similarly arouse our pity. It is pity at knowledge that, instead of being useful, is merely painful: knowledge as grief, remorse, shame at having struck fatally at one's own House.

So we may gloss and extend somewhat, along familiar lines, Aristotle's suggestive, cryptic account. Though we would have to enter, as we will not, into a thicket of competing glosses to investigate exactly how catharsis of pity and fear actually occurs once such emotions are raised, for Aristotle, in the "best tragedy"[1] the protagonist's initial ignorance and later knowledge of kinship with his victim is instrumental to arousing pity and fear and securing catharsis. Crucial to the rhetorical effect of the protagonist's ignorance is the potential of reliable knowledge founded on a clear-cut, momentous dichotomy about which one may, in principle, be clear: the victim is either kindred or not, and a supposed stranger killed at the crossroads can be shown to be the father of one's House—or not. In Aristotle's traditional society, this dichotomy perhaps made even more of a difference, and the horror and *miasma* (pollution) of a deadly mistake about it was more fearful, though perhaps not more pitiable, than for a modern audience. In a way corresponding to the necessary conditions for catharsis and paralleling this experience in the represented action, the polluting agent can become decisively known, as Oedipus is, and the House be purged by casting out this now-illicit insider.

For Faulkner in *Absalom,* tragedy means the killing of someone whose kinship is ambiguous, where the distinction between kin and stranger is not clear-cut, but even so, in a significant sense the killer and his deputy know whom they are killing: this troublingly ambiguous son/brother/alien who is both within and outside the House. We must ask, initially on Aristotelian grounds: after this knowledge, what catharsis?

Yet the killing itself was intended as catharsis. Catharsis, in the sense of purging an already existing perceived pollution, clearly motivated Doc Hines in *Light in August* to help instigate the murder of his illegitimate grandson Joe Christmas, whom Hines sees as the product of his daughter's "bitchery" and the "abomination" of supposed miscegenation. But as it is represented, this action is probably too attenuated *as* a family killing for this aspect to figure very much in most readers' experience of that novel. In *Absalom,* however, the symbols representing a catharsis of the House by knowingly slaying kindred loom large. Wash, whose very name states his function, purposely kills Sutpen, his patriarchal father figure though coeval, as well as his own granddaughter and her newborn daughter, and sets fire to his house to wipe his family from the earth, along with their debasing involvement with the Sutpens of the world. Near the end, Clytemnestra, Sutpen's illegitimate black daughter and one of his proxies in the novel, knowingly burns Sutpen's old mansion along with herself and her white half brother Henry, as Rosa returns for him. Charles Bon's murder by his apparent half brother Henry, Sutpen's proxy, because Bon threatens incestuous and ethnic pollution of the family line, epitomizes knowing purgation of ambiguous kindred through act or symbol.

As several allusions to Agamemnon and Clytemnestra suggest, then, Faulkner's major fulcrum of action for producing a tragic effect has more in common with the knowing killings of the *Oresteia* and *Iphigenia in Aulis* than with the Aristotelian pattern of ignorant kill-

177

ing, belated knowledge, and catharsis, perfected in *Oedipus*. Further, this effect has even more to do with Faulkner's rewriting of such classical tragedy and its economy of the pure House, the unmixed people, within a modern world struggling with the reality of human heterogeneity and mixed voices. Faulkner's modern baroque tragedy also claims in its mixed heritage *King Lear,* which presents a father destroyed by his multiplicity of offspring, who frustrate his relation to his one true loving child. Faulkner once said that *Absalom, Absalom!* is about a man who "wanted sons and got sons who destroyed him" (*University* 73); it is a description that suggests a similarity with the Gloucester subplot of *Lear,* but the simple contrast between this statement and Lear's destruction by his daughters is more apparent than real. When Lear poignantly, terribly calls upon bystanders to howl at the death of Cordelia, it is an incongruous echo of the time he effectively silenced her into saying "Nothing" and becoming herself unspeakable by his bad-faith command "Speak," which she, more finely respecting her own honor as well as his, could not obey. This interlock of outcry and speech, of the howled and the unspeakable, has much to do with *Absalom*'s dynamics, beginning with the outcry over a dead, rejected son evoked by the title but not spoken by the father. To allow that outcry and its cognates to sound is to subvert the father's pure House, and from the beginning the novel assigns this subversive amplification to the daughter.

Quentin hears the first such mediated "cry aloud" (14) beneath the outraged voice of our first characterized narrator, Rosa Coldfield. Rosa is rejected and abandoned first by her father when, in an act of purist detachment from the world's imperfection, he nails himself into his attic to oppose the Civil War. Rosa in turn effectively rejects him by writing poems glorifying the southern war heroes, including one who had been the "ogre" of her childhood, Thomas Sutpen. It is in her narrating voice that this second rejecting father figure, and imagined lover, Sutpen, still resides awaiting his own catharsis from her.

The voice of the outraged woman not only dominates the novel's beginning, but its mode of congested outpouring stylistically sets the pattern for the rest of the novel's variations. As a keynote within the novel's interpenetrating voices, it thus always speaks in the other narrative styles. It is explicitly remarked when Shreve and Quentin most strongly feel themselves part of a universal brotherhood, as the

sons of outraged women, when they imagine a young Charles Bon
inundated by his mother's voice:

> a kind of busted water pipe of incomprehensible fury and fierce yearn-
> ing and vindictiveness and jealous rage . . . part of childhood which all
> mothers of children had received in turn from their mothers and from
> their mothers in turn. . . . [H]ence no man had a father, no one personal
> [place of origin], but all mother faces which ever bred swooping down
> at those almost calculable moments out of some obscure ancient general
> affronting and outraging which the actual living articulate meat had not
> even suffered but merely inherited; all boy flesh that walked and
> breathed stemming from that one ambiguous eluded dark fatherhead
> and so brothered perennial and ubiquitous everywhere under the sun—
> (298–99)

The voice that transmits a symbolic kinship of vicarious outrage and
suffering is distinctively a voice of daughters who become mothers
speaking to sons and daughters and who in expressing this pathos
pass on to them the "ambiguous eluded dark fatherhead." In doing
so, from the father's perspective, the daughters tangle and knot a
pure, straightforward patrilineage.

Though each sex in fact is shown to possess contrary impulses, the
novel designates the vocal transmission of outrage as the office of
daughters and mothers and the vocal suppression of outrage at affront
as that of the primary "fatherhead," Sutpen. Both impulses for handling outrage contend in the novel's double-voiced rhetoric, so that
engaged, performatively hearing readers enter into the personally
formative handling of a pathos that their "actual living articulate
meat had not even suffered but merely inherited."

It is not only in their transmission of outraged suffering that
daughters oppose the father's design. It is also in their status as
daughters. What Charles Bon is in one version—a rejected son with
black blood who threatens to marry his sister if he is not recognized
by his father—his sister Judith approximates simply by virtue of
indubitably being a daughter: that is, a threshold, transitory phenomenon that constitutes a vulnerable point in the pure transmission
of a patrilineal House over generations. As Lynda Boose notes, "To
[the patrilineal] institution that fears loss, the daughter's presence by
definition constitutes a threat to its maintenance of closed boundaries.

She is always the transitory member of the group and is thus . . . a 'liminal' or threshold person within cultural space . . . whose very presence asserts a breach in the genealogical fence of family enclosure. In multiple ways, she signifies all that the father desires and simultaneously cannot have. She exists only to be lost—or, as Polonius recognizes about Ophelia, 'I have a daughter—have her while she is mine.'"

On the threshold, she is also central, since Judith's sexual capacity for reproduction is the symbolic center that was to be preserved from Bon's formidably ambiguous intrusion in the House: incestuous union with an alien group. Symbolically, she works to undo this preservation by conveying Bon's scripted voice, his "dead tongue speaking" (129), to a stranger and by taking in Bon's child. Yet with Bon and Sutpen dead and Henry gone, she loses her traditional transitory role in the family and becomes the permanent keeper, though also the at least temporary opener, of the House. Clytemnestra, as an illegitimate black daughter possessing an even greater liminality, in her turn after Judith's death possesses the House. Clytemnestra symbolically reverses Judith's work, thus acting as the daughter to Judith as father *and* as the reinstatement of Sutpen as father, as agent of catharsis and its victim.

This tragedy of the unrecognized, marginal son who must be purged is also a novel of two rejected daughters, Rosa and Milly Jones's child; another, Clytemnestra, devoted to catharsis; and a fourth, Judith, who in effect questions the logic of catharsis.

Sutpen is undone by daughters as well as sons.[2] At the most literal level, one such daughter is the child of Milly Jones, since in scorning this child Sutpen brings about his murder by Wash. But all four of his literal or symbolic daughters help to confound the project of the pure and continuing House. In this novel, one can have either purity or continuation but not both together.

II

In *Absalom,* to repeat, catharsis is represented as knowingly slaying one's kindred to eliminate the family's involvement with some sullying, impalpable intrusion. Just as Bon must be stopped at the gate when he returns to marry Judith, just as Clytemnestra and Judith stop Rosa when she seeks to view Bon's body, the outsider is to be kept out, stopped at the door of the house or the inner sanctum. The novel presents a series of such forbiddings at the threshold, actual or symbolic, as in Quentin's imagined self-forbidding at Judith's door. If this forbidding fails, then the House must destroy itself wholly or in part in order to purify itself, as in effect Henry destroys it when he kills the intimate alien Bon. But this last self-destructive step, the novel suggests, must always be taken, since the outside threat is never simply outside. It is already inside the House, as Bon's body and his sonship are, as a shadowy marginality that cannot be evicted without self-destruction. Correspondingly, Bon may be seen as committing suicide by proxy through goading Henry to kill him, in order (among other things) to destroy two Sutpens. The first is the Sutpen Bon has internalized as the validator of his existence. The second is the Sutpen whose dynastic plan Bon thus imperils by making Sutpen's son Henry a guilty pariah. So in her very existence the daughter as central outsider is a living embodiment of the self-defeat of the father's design of an exclusive self-reproduction.

For Quentin is not alone in being a "commonwealth" (12) of personal multiplicity. The novel defines personal existence as tacit reciprocation, mediation, and proxy, as Bon and Henry are said to use Judith as a medium in which each male "strove to preserve . . . what each conceived the other to believe him to be" (120)—a complex minuet that includes the mutually expected roles both play in Bon's death. The recurrent dream is a reciprocation of recognition supporting one's necessary sense of self-worth. It is such a relationship that Bon wishes with Sutpen and that Wash thinks he has in a reciprocity of noblesse oblige he has profoundly internalized, until he inadvertently hears how much his granddaughter, and therefore he, is scorned by the god who is Wash's own "apotheosis" (282).

But the equally recurrent opposing desire is for a freestanding personality—simple, direct in its executions of will and in its fate, and above all unentangled. In Mr. Compson's attempt to create his own kind of Greek tragedy, this is what he wishes to think existed in Sutpen's heroic age: people "simpler and therefore, integer for integer, larger, more heroic . . . not dwarfed and involved but distinct, uncomplex . . . loving once or dying once instead of being diffused and scattered creatures drawn blindly limb from limb from a grab bag and assembled" (89). (Note how the image of creatures "drawn . . . limb from limb," by suggesting the cliché "torn limb from limb," implies that the creation of persons from a mixed "grab bag" is simultaneously a painful death by dismemberment of a putative simple "integer.") Yet in Mr. Compson's own version of her story, Judith Sutpen's sense of lives frustratingly entangled, in her famous image of the loom, belies and undoes Mr. Compson's nostalgic tragic design. So do the novel's indications that people in all times can love and die more than once and suffer what Bon calls his "spirit's posthumeity" (317) long before physical death. Even death is not clear-cut in this book of ghosts who haunt ghosts: like Rosa, dressed in mourning for herself, people die yet linger on to speak to and through others.

Who better than Mr. Compson's Judith would know of the enmeshing of lives? She is presented as a crossroad of mediated relationships: Rosa loves Bon by proxy of Judith, and Henry and Bon use her a proxy for their own mutual love. Yet seen as Mr. Compson's creation, Judith as fiction parallels the daughter as patriarchal family member. Both fictive and literal daughters contradict and embody the self-defeat of the father-creator's implicit design of realizing the integrity of an integer.

On this double level, too, Judith is her father's daughter. Her chagrin at entanglement evidently reflects Mr. Compson's and Sutpen's deep wish to disentangle persons, if only by describing historical personages who are like the self-monument standing on a bare plain that Quentin's Sutpen sees in his inaugurating heroic vision. The difference between the father's version of heroic identity and Quentin's is that Mr. Compson sees it as a superpersonal given condition of a lost age, with the central heroic masked figure moving to a whispered chorus of "*Sutpen. Sutpen. Sutpen.*" (32), whereas Quentin sees it as the result of a personal, active process. All these heroic visions clearly double for a catharsis that seeks to purify one's individual or collective identity of ambiguous involvements with and assimilations of what should be kept out—which is also to deliver it from multiple loving and multiple dying. The affront of all affronts is to be intruded upon by and involved with an outsider like Sutpen himself. "The affront," Mr. Compson explains, "was born of the town's realization that he was getting it involved with himself" (43). Quentin similarly believes that Rosa's narrative about Sutpen posits a God determined to purge this outsider who has so enmeshed himself in the lives of the proper southern community that the community fabric must be destroyed. It is "why God let us lose the War: that only through the blood of our men and the tears of our women could

He stay this demon and efface his name and lineage from the earth" (11).

In Rosa's own ritual catharsis, Sutpen's existence for her evidences the *"miasmal mass"* at the foundation of the factual world from which she says the human *"prisoner soul"* rises and escapes and which it *"relicts"* by its power to reduce this massiveness to a *"fragile evanescent . . . sphere"* (143). The huge cloud of dust that accompanies Rosa and Quentin to the Sutpen house makes palpable her, and the novel's, imagination of invasive pollution, "permeant dust" (362). It begins to build on the opening pages, which insist on the dust motes that gather while Rosa's voice surges and vanishes in Quentin's hearing "into and then out of the long intervals like a stream, a trickle running from patch to patch of dried sand" (8). Her narrative, like her last two visits to the Sutpen mansion, seeks to expunge Sutpen as a sovereign ghost evoked by her voice, "as if it were [her] voice which he haunted where a more fortunate [ghost] would have had a house" (8). But her "fragile evanescent" narrative voice does not successfully reduce and "relict" Sutpen as a miasma; instead it reevokes and invests him with more massive size. So braided into Rosa's present existence is her inverted priesthood to this demon cult that it is difficult to believe she wants to succeed completely.

The dying Ellen long before planted the seed of Rosa's last visits to the mansion by commanding her to protect Ellen's children. But Rosa feels helpless to do so, since for her their only real threat, their father Sutpen, has already been absorbed within them, especially Judith, and Rosa cannot protect them from themselves (22–30). So too Rosa the in-law relative, the orphaned aunt too young for her role, is not neatly a family outsider with no claim to admission. She must repeatedly be admitted up to a point only to be *"stopped dead"* (139), until at length, persisting, in a last attempt to enter the House and remove Henry from it, she precipitates its catharsis at the hands of her finally victorious (or is it at last conquered?) intimate foe, Clytemnestra/Sutpen—Clytemnestra the marginal member of the House who is its last gatekeeper, deputy, and purifier-by-destruction.

But of course the novel's whole demonstration that personal enmeshing and incalculable influences spread far beyond the actor's intentions makes words like *finally* and *at last, conquered* and *victorious* but provisional resting places or wishes for a simple identity and completed tragic action. Rosa, despite her desire for purging, knows this: *"That was all. Or rather, not all, since there is no all, no finish; it not the blow we suffer from but the tedious repercussive anticlimax of it"* (150).

Everything tends toward one point: the daughter in patriarchy, and in this novel, is the counterpart of voice, as a transitory, potentially assimilative phenomenon that is also central to the reproduction of being. This relationship highlights the key feature of voice in this novel. We can further substantiate it and follow its implications by equipping ourselves to examine more closely Judith's telling questioning of catharsis. To rephrase the initial encompassing question: After such knowing catharsis as we have traced, what catharsis for an audience?

The principal represented audience and sometime narrator, Quentin, ends the novel panting, physically expressing his thought "Nevermore of peace." Quentin has spent his life hearing the living "garrulous outraged baffled ghosts" (9) who populate his community. Just as Rosa's voice is a house haunted by Sutpen, Quentin is a "barracks" haunted by his assimilated "back-looking ghosts," a "hall echoing with sonorous defeated names" (12) he had sought to control or to exorcise, first by sullen silence and then by giving their voices a hearing as his voice. As Brooks and others have pointed out, Quentin does comparatively little actual narration, and he usually lets others speak for him even when he narrates. His narrative is so full of "Father said" and "Grandfather said" that Shreve mimics Quentin's habit. Perhaps by thus trying both to speak and to mute his responsibility for what he says, Quentin seeks to evacuate it without becoming caught up in it. With Shreve as more than willing collaborator, Quentin conjures up his ghosts and reenacts their destruction in permutations and combinations. Nothing can relieve him, however, of the sonorous shades who suffocate him.

What he comes consciously to grasp partway through his effort is that Shreve and he *"are both Father. Or maybe Father and I are both Shreve, maybe it took Father and me both to make Shreve or Shreve and me both to make Father or maybe Thomas Sutpen to make all of us"* (261–62). But in this all-male achronological genealogy, he yet expresses as an exclusive *or* relationships that have been shown to be an *and*. His effort continues, in pity and fear of what he conjures up with Shreve, "the two of them back to back as though at the last ditch, saying No to Quentin's Mississippi shade" (280).

Each member of the literal and symbolic Sutpen genealogy is a "shade whom they . . . existed in" (316) and who exists in them. No more than in *The Sound and the Fury* can Quentin elude his shadow. For Quentin as for Rosa, to speak is to keep reevoking the very shade—one's shadow, one's intimate other, one's death as an unencumbered individual—to be negated by the speaking. In the images of dust and trickling water which open the novel, voice is like the stream that clears a path in the dust as it continually disappears into it and reappears out of it. It cleanses, but it accumulates its own detritus. One's own voice is the House of assimilated others, and to purge it would mean the No of total silence. It would be to lapse back into the silence Quentin maintains for much of the book, which he only breaks at length by speaking in a "voice level, curious, a little dreamy yet still with that overtone of sullen bemusement, of smoldering outrage" (218). His voice manifests the constant conflict between the equally incomplete cathartic, regulating strategies of silence and of voice.

At the last, Shreve taunts him about this incompletion: "'You've got one nigger left. One nigger Sutpen left. . . . You still hear him at night sometimes. Don't you?' 'Yes,' Quentin said." And Shreve goes on to his concluding prophecy that the descendants of this miscegenation will "conquer the western hemisphere" (378) and to imply that Quentin must hate the South as the breeding ground of such potent mixing. This claim prompts Quentin's excessive protest, his closing No.

Following Quentin's and Shreve's extraordinary "marriage of speaking and hearing" (316), this closing dialogue about reproductive mixing and the sense of continuing oppression it manifests in both characters offer the delayed crystallization of insight typical of the novel. That is, Quentin and Shreve too, though less consciously than the people they have conjured up and exist in, have been knowingly engaged in an attempted catharsis of ambiguous assimilated others— others produced in either biological generation or performative narration. In their marriage of mutually enacted voice, Quentin and Shreve have reproduced in and through each other more vividly realized versions of the shades who had more obscurely haunted them before—Quentin, because of a lifetime, and Shreve, because of a semester of listening to "old tales and talking" (303). The speaking and hearing of this conjuration both serves the desire for catharsis and creates an accompanying, escalating need for purging away what they are reproducing. In Hightower's words, each "performs, engenders, . . . more than he . . . should have to bear." One means of reducing the oppressive power of the evoked figures is Shreve's periodic parody and "protective coloring of levity" (280). The more extensive means, emphasized by both comparison and contrast to the cold "tomblike" room (345) of their academic surroundings, uses all available analytic and empathetic knowledge of the ghost-Sutpens to purge them as mysteriously motivated presences. Quentin and Shreve clearly and plausibly define the Sutpens' motives and imaginatively reenact the story as thus explained. They have radically reduced the captivating power of mystery and mysterious personages per se. However, although at one point Bon and Henry, Quentin and Shreve, are said to be acting as one shared identity, the narrators' effort, spectacular and moving as it is, has failed of catharsis. And Faulkner emphasizes this failure.

Jim Bond, the mixed Sutpen descendant whose howl Quentin still hears, summons up the inexhaustibility of assimilation, shades, and their voices. The wordless anguish he cries is what the other voicings talk about, and around, in language, "that meager and fragile thread by which the little surface corners and edges of men's secret and solitary lives may be joined for an instant now and then before sinking back into the darkness where the spirit cried for the first time and was not heard and will cry for the last time and will not be heard then either" (251). This anguish sounds for the first time in the wordless outcry the exclamatory title edges around by wording it. It sounds for the second time in Rosa's "cry aloud," audible within her speech and its echoes throughout the novel, and for the "last" in the sheer outcry right at the edge of Quentin's final protest.

The double nature of this outcry is that of the novel's catharsis as well. In the respect that it is an expression, a pressing out of suffering, it is a necessary catharsis. But not only is the expressed anguish irremediable and an inescapable influence on others. One of its principal causes is the constantly attempted purification of individual and collective ("white") identity by destroying its "impure" assimilation of others. The cry of near inhumanity therefore indicates a catharsis whose complete success would destroy human identity itself. *Absalom, Absalom!* need not mention Quentin's pending suicide. This novel comprehends a suicidal urgency on a scale that *The Sound and the Fury* did not imagine—though its foundation is discernible there in the Compsons' wholesale campaign against impurity. That suicidal impulse is fortunately, though painfully, opposed in *Absalom*. It is time to examine this side of the coin: *"the raging and incredulous recounting (which enables man to bear with living)"* (161).

III

Stephen Booth describes the critical fervor to define tragedy, above all other genres, as a reaction against the very indefiniteness of things and the inadequacy of our epistemological categories, which tragedy unbearably dramatizes to us. As good as it is, Booth's own theory of tragedy as indefinition has not gone far enough. For at least some of those tragedies to which his theory, and my answer to it, applies, the more unbearable available awareness is not what he calls indefinition and epistemological uncertainty in themselves. It is what these intimate to us about themselves: that such limited cultural furnishings as our mutually loaned categories are all that separate human beings from the incapacity, thus the unviability as a species, of genuinely unaccommodated humankind.

It is, moreover, the open display of irremediable suffering that threatens us especially acutely by confessing a helplessness at which our cultural accommodations falter. It is the howl that Lear, feeling shorn of all supports, evokes on the heath and at the sight of the dead Cordelia which reminds us of how close are kings to mad wretches, princely Charles Bons to wretched Jim Bonds, the reciprocating furnishing of humanity and its failure. This outcry has an additional impact in *Absalom, Absalom!* The impulse to purge dialogical assimilation and reciprocation strikes at the very basis of human being in culture. The outcry that testifies to and witnesses against this impulse discloses a tragedy of unaccommodated existence.

This howl evoked in *Lear* and *Absalom,* or the imagination of that horror, impels creative countermeasures—including both tragic art and the theory of it. These weave out from the intractable simple cry an elaboration of fragile threads, making a complexity less obdurate, more endurable to contemplate by its reach into sharable intelligibility and collaborative action: stories, explanations of cause and effect, tracings of philosophical, theological, aesthetic, political, moral, critical implications. Much of this amplification may be immensely difficult and troubling, but it is at least more bearable. And in being bearable, it can be capacitating. This, in brief, is much of the stuff of culture itself, so that cultural accommodation in part reverberates from an unendurable human annihilation, to create humanity.

Absalom, Absalom! memorably expresses that impulse to creative elaboration at the cultural loom by making the major represented action one of collaborative embellishment, revision, and reweaving. The remarkable corresponding style now often thought of as essentially Faulknerian in fact first appears here and in *Pylon,* which Faulkner wrote in the midst of composing *Absalom.* At the heart of both this creative elaboration and its answerable style is a simple intractable agony about which there is in an important sense nothing to say or do. In one version of how the wound is sustained, there is the aging Sutpen's outrageous proposal to a young, worshipful Rosa that they trial breed together to see if she will produce the son the House needs. All Rosa's volubility elaborates and embellishes this moment. In another version, there is Henry's equally blunt, devastating announcement to Judith:

> *Now you cant marry* [Bon].
> *Why cant I marry him?*
> *Because he's dead.*
> *Dead?*
> *Yes. I killed him.* (172)

The elaboration that proceeds from this moment we will take up shortly. And there is, most memorably, the stark conversation Quentin has with Henry, after hundreds of pages have led up to this much-delayed scene. It will be noted that the one line not repeated in the near palindrome of their exchange is the line that leads from the home, the House, to death:

> *And you are—?*
> *Henry Sutpen.*
> *And you have been here—?*
> *Four years.*
> *And you came home—?*
> *To die. Yes.*
> *To die?*
> *Yes. To die.*
> *And you have been here—?*

The House of *Absalom, Absalom!*

Four years.
And you are—?
Henry Sutpen. (373)

That's it in its starkest statement. It is all the more stark because the interchange itself, with blueprintlike clarity, presents the impulse to fashion at least a minimal elaboration and embellishment about and around the stark "And you are . . . to die." One sign of the need for this stunned verbal accommodation is that the place of traditional accommodation, the home, has not interposed itself where it should be to circumvent the brutish transit from existence to death. Rather, home is in this context associated with death; home leads to it and not away from it. There is nothing else to say and do: "And you are . . . to die." And because of that fact, there is everything to say and to do. There is the whole complexly amplified novel as the prima facie evidence that this is so.

The novel is both the expression and the transformation of a sheer cry aloud. It is a prolonged outcry audible in prose whose intensity is unprecedented in Faulkner's career. It is also, like Rosa's narration, the articulate transformation of outcry. The novel fuses outcry and articulation so they by turns bring each other into the foreground, as the stark exchanges emerge like a vocal blueprint from the circumlocutory architecture. The novel subliminally conveys a spectral outcry at human unaccommodation. The novel simultaneously transforms that subverbal voice so that it can, possibly, be endured. The very strenuousness of the rhetorical transformation affirms the strength to endure the in itself unendurable outcry by creative sublation. It further testifies to the volume of the agony that requires such strenuous measures both to give it mediated verbal expression and to transmute it into something other than sheer outcry.

Even the three stark statements just instanced (Sutpen's offer in fact being only indirectly rendered for us in Shreve's sarcastic paraphrase) and even Jim Bond's wail are deflections about and around the central calamitous attempt at catharsis of the Sutpen House. Three climactic occasions lead up to and away from this attempt, but Henry's shooting of Bon is never rendered directly. In a novel that makes sound and voice or their lack a constantly noted feature of life, this silence resonates. The sound of that shot along with the outcry or outcries that accompanied the fatal wound constitutes a phenomenon that disappears into the repercussive anticlimaxes Rosa laments. Two of the most obvious of these are Henry's harsh announcement to Judith that he has shot Bon, and Wash's bawling out the news of Bon's death to Rosa in the street. This auditory phenomenon of death disappears also into its chronological anticipations. Primary among these is the single ever-sounding opening shot of the Civil War which Bon's letter describes in order to render his sense of living in a roaring time vacuum. In parallel with the nonappearance of Rosa's actual "cry aloud" when she receives her "mortal affront" (177) from Sutpen, the death outcry (especially Bon's, but also Henry's, or both) disappears into its antecedents, successors, and transforming repetitions. This suppression and transformation of sound is the necessary reaction to a constant fraternal war within a House divided. So, indeed, is the elaborate indirection of Bon's letter itself.

The narrative silences an unbearable mortal outcry but makes it bearable through transformative amplification. This hybrid device incorporates, yet as a whole is the antithesis of the merely nonexistent father's cry at the son's death. (To that vacancy, the title constantly points.) What we are now ready to see is how Judith's treatment of Bon's two bodies, his literal one and his letter, definitively performs a similar combination of suppression and transforming elaboration.

Bon's letter is introduced as his "dead tongue speaking." It is both body and voice. The letter, which emphasizes its physicality as black stove polish written on elegant white paper, is a symbolic gesture imaging and itself embellishing what it talks about. Its subject is his body, persisting in the midst of conclusive evidence of its fragile mortality, "*a body which, even after four years* [of war], *with a sort of dismal and incorruptible fidelity which is incredibly admirable to me . . . ignores even the presence and threat of a torn arm or leg as though through some secretly incurred and infallible promise and conviction of immortality*" (131). Since Bon sends this letter to Judith to announce his return although he knows that Henry will probably kill him, the letter, too, acts upon as well as expresses the conviction of a sort of immortality, indeed acknowledging what its first sentence states: "*You will notice how I insult neither of us by claiming this to be a voice from the defeated even, let alone from the dead*" (129). This is the voice and symbolic faithful body, the conjoint self-creating and revealing instrument of an honor-shame culture, which Judith wishes to transmit to a stranger.

In effect, she transmits the instrument as if it were both Bon as a still-living envoy of herself and a daughter to whom she, as her father's daughter, is father. She treats it as a speakable daughter perhaps destined for the "marriage of speaking and hearing" that Quentin and Shreve attain. The figure of the loom deepens these implications by bespeaking the father.

Judith's transmission of Bon's letter at once follows from, confronts, and transforms her image of lives and purposes entangled on a loom chaotically mixing individual designs:

> like five of six people all trying to make a rug on the same loom only each one wants to weave his own pattern into the rug; and it cant matter, you know that, or the Ones that set up the loom would have arranged things a little better, and it must matter because you keep on trying or having to keep on trying and then all of a sudden it's all over and all you have left is a block of stone with scratches on it provided there was someone to remember to have the marble scratched and set up or had time to, and it rains on it and the sun shines on it and after a while they dont even remember the name and what the scratches were trying to tell, and it doesnt matter. (127)

Further, Judith emphasizes that the letter is something physically transitory ("a scrap of paper . . . passing from one hand to another, one mind to another") and that in this ephemerality it is able to "make a mark" on others: "while the block of stone cant be *is* because it never can become *was* because it cant ever die or perish."

Two impulses struggle here. On the one hand the desire to make a mark reflects Judith's statement that normally "you make so little impression" because of the intermixing of designs upon the loom. This reflects in turn her father's similar desire to make his mark by establishing his monumental House, his "design," free from outside entanglement. It thus manifests the cathartic urge and the patriarchal House.

Although Judith is evidently ignorant of Bon's mixed birth, she turns the very source of threatened bodily pollution of the House, Bon's black and white body, into the object of consecration, not to be profaned even by Rosa's eyes. Bon's body, however, is to be made symbolically available in turn by proxy of his black on white letter, in a mediation of "passing on" which demands that it both be transitory and signify transitoriness. That is, it becomes in this respect too a stand-in for the daughter, an aspect reinforced by Bon's own often-remarked "androgynous" characteristics (e.g., 317). Judith acts toward the body first in the traditional forbidding father's role, to protect the daughter from profanation, and then acts toward the embodying letter in the father's transmitting role in the marriage ceremony, transferring the daughter to another House.

But this envoy of herself which Judith transmits in itself represents the undoing of the House, and in contrast to the act of knowing catharsis or fatherly control of transmittal, she hands it via the known female hands of Quentin's grandmother into the unknown, and unknown involvement.[3]

Correspondingly, Judith rejects as an image of immortality a monumental stone like those Sutpen had ordered for himself and Ellen; since the marble itself futilely endures, but the graven family name is forgotten. For Judith, the means of making a mark is by entering into transition and ephemerality, as if one were identifying with that which gets put out, or sent from, the House in catharsis—or marriage. Moreover, just as the daughter traditionally loses the name of the patrilineal House, the letter from Bon is without salutation or signature; from the first it proclaims the loss and forgetting of family names. It is not even Judith's writing, but Bon's; but a stranger who would receive it might well know nothing of either. It is thus a sign of connection with others and across generations, but one that must be taken up and acknowledged by another. Especially since its first sentence announces it as a voice, it may well be spoken in another's voice. Indeed, it was *as* another voice that Judith sent it out in the first place.

A significant part of its power to mark is that the letter displays in its fragile transitiveness how much the option to receive it or how to receive it rests with the stranger-reader. Even to its "spidery script" (129), it constitutes an appeal to implicit recognition of how meager, and thus how much to be protected, are the threads of human connection. Nothing is forced on the reader. "Keep it . . . or destroy it," Judith says. But a great deal is consequently made available by a power of displayed vulnerability which controverts Sutpen's power of displayed imperviousness.

Thus the second, implicative desire within Judith's gesture of transmission counters and transforms the first impulse of a cathartic disentanglement. The second impulse also indirectly transforms the image of the loom and confronts it without erasing its force, its evocation of frustration at heterogeneous connections and designs. The image is transformed because the letter's transmittal is an overture to acknowledged involvement, to the inevitable metamorphosis of design it entails, and to the immortality of living precisely as and in this transforming otherness. Living only, in fact, the way Sutpen, despite his desire, ends up in Rosa's voice and its transmittal to Quentin.

Because of the very unpredictability noted, a further genealogical reversal is in principle foreseeable from the fact that, in however ambivalent and daughterly a way, Judith is father to the daughter and the voice that are her letter. A major basis of the letter's appeal, its physical fragility, is its obvious and considerable limitation, an ever-present potential for self-destruction according to its own design for making its mark. It is reasonable to surmise, in fact, that it has been preserved because the solicitous hands of a known patrilineal family have kept it instead of transmitting it to a stranger. And if it survives beyond the father's and son's hands now holding it, beyond the family line that keeps it, it will most likely be thanks to an extension of this process. It will be because it has been passed on—as it is in this novel—as a voice sustained by an articulated narrative and put between the covers of a book, in the long run preserved by an institution like the academy, where the best of ratiocination is curiously like Sutpen's logic and morality. And this, in the continuations of "fathers" and "daughters," is not the last word either.

As the vulnerable and transitory entity in the structure of the patrilineal House, the daughter and not the son is the equivalent of an alternative immortality. It is an immortality through transformation into unforeseeable forms, rather than through recurrence of a simple, freestanding identity and the catharsis that attempts to guarantee it. Bon's embodying letter is an important transitive part of Judith, of her House, and of its undoing. As such, at least in the purity of its own rhetorical design, it will not transmit a House from one generation to the next in purity from strangers. It will instead be liable to haunt and exist in the voices of unknown others, with their constitutive heterogeneity. On the one hand, we have Shreve's taunting prophecy about the conquest that Jim Bond's inextinguishable voice portends. This is of a piece with Shreve's disgust at the miasmal involvement of men and women: "that massy five-foot-thick maggot-cheesy solidarity which overlays the earth" (312). On the other, we have Judith's transmission of Bon's letter. These represent two competing but dialectically implicated attitudes toward the future of a mixed House, voice, and species, which is to say, toward Bon's death.

Bon's death, the central knowing attempt at purgation of the House, exists in reading as a narratively suppressed and elaborated outcry. Neither suppression nor elaboration can finally purge it. Similarly, it cannot be purged by knowledge. The meaning of Bon's death is convincingly explained, the motives of the historical actors are plausibly conjectured and imaginatively relived in a marriage of speaking and hearing between Quentin and Shreve which is surreal in perfecting reciprocal cognitive experience. One could not ask for an agreed-upon understanding more thorough than this. Yet as we saw, it clearly leaves them dissatisfied at the close, Shreve aggressively sarcastic toward his erstwhile marriage partner in analytic and empathetic knowledge and Quentin still speaking his No against another version of his Mississippi shade, "the South."

The issue is not, by itself, a "more perfect" knowledge about the Sutpens and the killing of Bon, nor is it the questioning of authoritative knowledge. What is in question is catharsis: catharsis for an audience in the face of a knowing attempted catharsis, as well as attempted catharsis through analytic and experiential knowledge— none of which, for the Sutpens or their narrators, has worked. This failure is fortunate, since the novel maintains that the ghosts of our assimilated others are in our voices, and a world of sound speaks them back to us. To silence them is to jeopardize our human accommodation, our human being.

IV

As *Absalom*'s elaborations compensatorily thicken the fragile weaving of language to silence and transform a mortal outcry at unaccommodation, the novel entices and exhausts the reader's voice from the first. Even before it sets the formidable example of representing voice as theme, or marshals all its oral analogues, the novel's stylistic sonority and rhythms and its initial representation of a bizarre oral narrative situation invites and piques readers to emulate, probably to murmur, its voices. For the reader who accepts this overture, the intricately wrought and cadenced sonority is so protracted, however, that even sustained murmuring becomes physically exhausting. The reader becomes attuned to Rosa's, Shreve's, and especially Quentin's desire for air and breath in an "airless" (7) enclosure. (The opening of Chapter 8, "There would be no deep breathing tonight," designates an exercise we have long since been needing. It is significant too that the novel contains no landscape descriptions, so deprives us of visual openness.) What happens next for readers with a developed auditory imagination is suggested by the moments in the novel when "listening reneges and hearing-sense self-confounds." We cease speaking aloud and voice moves inward. Voice "disembodies" itself by ceasing to be an acoustical phenomenon, though it remains potently auditory, voiced and heard in the same chamber where Quentin hears his personal commonwealth speak. Sutpen is first evoked in this way when Rosa's voice, "not ceasing but vanishing," summons up a "quiet thunderclap [in which] he would abrupt (man-horse-demon)"—until at length hearing can "reconcile" to the extent that the "two separate Quentins" begin internally "talking to one another in the long silence of notpeople, in notlanguage" (8–9).

It was an analogous performance of the inner sensorium that Keats praised in the ode Faulkner so often cited, as in this Faulknerian version of the piper piping ditties of no tone: "beyond the silence, thin pipes unheard, wild and passionate and sad" (*Mosquitoes* 340). Of course the best-known allusions involve the visual paradox of the Grecian urn. But both paradoxes, hearing the unheard and seeing motion or stillness in its opposite, are part of a larger conception and practice, which involve flooding the physical senses so as to internalize—and, as it were, eternalize—the impressions in the sensorium. In this process, moreover, a kind of synaesthetic conversion of the senses is apparently assumed to occur.

Just as in *Absalom, Absalom!* imaginative vision is said to arise when audible voice disappears into inner audition, so in *Light in August* spectral sound emerges when sight is exhausted: The wagon "seems to hang suspended . . . forever and forever, so infinitesimal is its progress . . . so that in the watching of it the eye loses it as sight and sense drowsily merge and blend. . . . So that at last, as though out of some trivial and unimportant region beyond even distance, the sound of it seems to come slow and terrific and without meaning, as though it were a ghost travelling . . . ahead of its own shape" (7). The perceiver's or reader's overloaded exercise of a sense activates the sensorium, the region "beyond even distance," into sensory transformation. Faulkner obviously has a "Proustian" fascination with alter-sensory evocativeness, as in, for instance, the effect of the heavy odor of honeysuckle on Quentin in *The Sound and the Fury*. But the premier sense for this exercise is hearing.[4]

A cardinal principle of Faulkner's symbolic action reemerges in the evanescent phenomenon that generates power. The principle is that what is transitory and fragile is powerful because it is assimilable by others and in them becomes permanent, "immortal." This principle of permanence achieved through transforming evanescence impels both Judith's transmittal of Bon's letter, his dead tongue speaking, and the rhetorical effect of performing voice. By elaborately creating the conditions for the already transitory physical sensation of sound to become even more evanescent through exhausting voice, Faulkner seeks to make it lasting through assimilation.

And as we have noted in previous novels, a silence or silencing stands at both ends of this vocal process. In thematic terms, it does so because the process begins with the deflection of outcry into the auditorially accentuated style that, when spoken, transforms into a perfected and durable speaking silence. As a counterpart, *Absalom's* textual score seems inexhaustible as it continues for page after page, so that, as insistently rich passages invite our murmuring or even speaking out again, the internalization of voice from silence through speech into silence periodically recurs.

Christopher Middleton has offered the term *endophone* to designate internal sound. "Actual voicing," he points out, "can nourish the inner ear's competence," but "the inner ear is capable of an auditory complexity which exceeds almost any audible vocalizing" (72). Educated by actual voicing but exceeding its powers, inner audition "construes the text as a symbolic analogue of the planes upon and through which the poet's endophone did once move. . . . The reader imaginatively somatizes the vocality of the text, for it has aroused in him various other sense-traces" (73). These, then, are the phases of the process as far as we have traced it: voice "disembodied" through performance, voice assimilated, and voice performatively reembodied in imagination. The sequence, more completely, is the reader's enticement by a stream of sounding words associated with women, then breathless immersion in this flow, then an inner audition that reembodies voice more enduringly and perfectly. Here, it will be recognized, is a reader's variant on Faulkner's enduring parable, the temptation of Sir Galwyn: an enticing drowning in a woman-stream holding the prospect of life as fame. In the tragic reading-enactment of *Absalom, Absalom!* which the score elicits, we yield to a comparable temptation and so experience an analogue to Faulkner's writing himself to life through a death in voices and shades. But unlike Sir Galwyn, who knows what his temptation entails, and more like Faulkner himself, we reanimate the novel's tragic process because we perform and engender for ourselves unforeseen shadows, personified consequences to be endured. In the novel's broadest context, we participate in the problems and troublesome solutions of a specific ongoing cultural shaping of human beings, and we do so as the culture's represented members largely do, through voice and eloquent silence.

We are clearly concerned here with an audition that is distinctly performative but not merely cognitive: Unless the performance is *done,* nothing happens—not at this level, at least. Of course, we understand what we speak, but that understanding is not to the point here. It is not the means of internalizing voices through exercise, exhaustion, and reexercise at the level of endophone. It is only at this level that voice becomes, in principle, inexhaustible for us. Through this inexhaustibility, *Absalom, Absalom!* actively, sensuously implicates the speaking reader in the tragedy of assimilation and the temptation of catharsis. The solution to a problem, that of death and impermanence, is the source of others.

Carolyn Porter has argued that the challenge the novel presents readers is either to involve themselves in Quentin's historically burdened effort to confront his past and present or to remain safely outside his endeavor. To take the first choice, Porter argues, is troubling, but to take the second is to be like Sutpen, a reified abstraction outside historical process (259–76). I am examining here a related but distinct set of alternatives aligning readers with either Quentin or Quentin's version of Sutpen, who is to Quentin as catharsis is to pollution. The first is either to perform the textual score or not. The selection is not a cognitive one, nor as a rule is it consciously made. Speaking readers (sufficiently "endophonic" readers) quickly find themselves implicated in internalized heterophony, to use Bakhtin's term, in a way primarily "eye" readers will not. They do so considerably before they can grasp the novel's issues, including the alternatives Porter persuasively identifies. The experience is recurrent. Because the novel delays and suspends meaning at all levels from sentence to plot structure, these readers will have repeatedly assimilated voices before the import of what they voice begins to dawn.

The further question then becomes how these voices are to be dealt with once they are absorbed. This is the question that has already enveloped Quentin when the novel begins. Quentin is the magnified counterpart of the reader who has more or less unconsciously absorbed the novel's voices through hearing them, long before the significance of this assimilation can be grasped ratiocinatively. "I have heard too much, I have been told too much; I have had to listen to too much, too long" (207). It is no accident that Quentin's characterization in this novel lacks what Henry James called solidity of specification. Rosa has dangling legs, Mr. Compson has his cigar, Shreve his pink body, but Quentin is only a voice and a panting breath. As a physical and psychological individual, Quentin is the most shadowy of the shades who inhabit him and the novel. That itself makes a point.[5]

Exactly in these terms, he is a shadow with considerable substance, as the reader's most spectral shade. Quentin's dilemma as listener serves to amplify the reality of mutual involvement, the oppressive sense of ventriloquism this can produce, and the resulting cathartic desire to disburden oneself of that which in fact makes one a person.

What Quentin as audience does narrate, then, are key episodes of Sutpen's life which further illuminate the management of speaking and hearing, and the reproduction of persons.

V

Quentin listens in tense, mostly silent oppression for six chapters to re-creations of Sutpen by the other narrators, who fill out Rosa's evocation but, notwithstanding their irony about her demonizing, do not free Sutpen from demonhood. In Chapter 7, Quentin tries to transcend Shreve's Rosa-mocking epithet for Sutpen, "the demon," as well as his own burdened "voice . . . with that overtone of sullen bemusement, of smoldering outrage" (218) Quentin at last speaks to adduce for Sutpen a history and motivation that will personalize him. In doing so, Quentin implicitly argues that Sutpen's life project incipiently also sought to make himself and "his kind" free persons. Quentin speaks by telling the story of mortifying shame vindicated, and possession of this story he did not have in the earlier novel gives him the voice he did not have then either. The plot, however, will not hold still for Quentin and end in final vindication; instead, it opens out into repercussive shame.

Quentin, inherently alert to questions of audience, in effect corrects Rosa's statement that Sutpen spoke *"not to us . . . but to the air"* in evoking his *"Camelots and Carcassonnes"* (160). According to Quentin, Sutpen did have an audience, just as heroic figures traditionally have often spoken beyond their immediate listeners by appealing to the gods or future generations to vindicate them. But Quentin's Sutpen is neither Shreve's exotic figure, to be relished and parodied self-protectively, nor Rosa's demon nor Mr. Compson's Greek-tragedy persona and superperson. He is a person addressing others, with an understandable, though self-defeating vocal strategy.

Quentin, relying on his grandfather's testimony of what Sutpen told him, depicts a Sutpen whose vision of his personal value is instantly ignited when he realizes that the planter who insults him by proxy is invulnerable to him:

> *There aint any good or harm either in the living world that I can do to him.* It was like that, he said, like an explosion—a bright glare that vanished and left nothing, no ashes nor refuse; just a limitless flat plain with the severe shape of his intact innocence rising from it like a monument; that innocence instructing him as calm as [his other internal voices] had ever spoken . . . and when it said *them* in place of *he* or *him,* it meant more than all the human puny mortals under the sun that might lie in hammocks all afternoon. (238)

Stung into emulative rivalry, Sutpen transmutes himself into a form matching the scale of what he believes opposes him. In an instant at once of birth, death, and afterlife, he imagines himself as monument.

The fate he opposes is the depersonalized reproduction of himself in his family, as he sees it through the planter's servant's mocking eyes, "creatures heavy and without grace, brutely evacuated into a world without hope or purpose for them, who would in turn spawn with brutish and vicious *prolixity,* . . . fill space and earth with a race . . . with for sole heritage that expression on a balloon face bursting with laughter" (235; my italics).

To conceive the meaninglessly *prolific* as *prolixity* is to associate it with ineffective voices. More important, it is to conceptualize the problem in such a way that this brutish, speechless reproduction can be transformed into Sutpen's desired vocal sublation: Sutpen as vocal monument. The fate he opposes is a family with only meager resources of speech to achieve self-esteem against a pervasive denial of recognition: women with voices like Quentin's, "filled with a quality dark and sullen," and men suddenly breaking out "into harsh recapitulation of [their] own worth, the respect which [their] own physical prowess commands from [their] fellows," or else exulting over having scapegoated the planters' black slaves (230–31). This sort of speech and the "vicious prolixity" of physical reproduction are the related self-negating means of asserting personhood. This is the world of voices and figuratively related symbolic actions in which Sutpen finds himself, a world desperately on the defensive. Defensively sullen, boasting, or exulting, its repertoire in effect dictates that he cannot get a hearing when he goes to speak his message at the planter's front door. The black servant's refusing voice conjures up for Sutpen that incapable family voice and the mentally associated futility of trying to attack the landed classes by proxy of assaulting their slaves, a futility that emerges as the servant's "roaring waves of mellow laughter meaningless and terrifying and loud" (232). For Sutpen there has to be a voice that can still that terrible loudness.

I linger over this well-known episode because what must be stressed is the interplay of vision, action, and voice, each containing the other, as well as the young Sutpen's exceptional susceptibility to voice as the key to escaping a subhuman reproduction. It also needs to be stressed that this is Quentin's Sutpen, a boy whose young creator is revealed in the telling details Quentin ascribes to Sutpen's thoughts, albeit by warrant of "Grandfather said." What sets Quentin's Sutpen apart from Quentin is that Sutpen does not relapse into sullenness or vocal outbursts. His voice delivers him from an excremental sexual reproduction (a genealogy "brutely evacuated") to a bare plain with "no . . . refuse." The explosion of insight Quentin's Sutpen has is a vocal catharsis, brought about by a buildup from calm thinking to the climax that is Sutpen's last agitation: "All of a sudden it was not thinking, it was something shouting . . . all kind of shouting at him at once, boiling out and over him" (237). The sustained calm voice that subsequently emerges with Sutpen's epiphany will be forever innocent of such vocal, or other, indications of vulnerability. From its symbolic action stem the realizing actions designed to make him as invulnerable to voices and mocking eyes as the calm voice already implies he is.

The source of Sutpen's capacity to raise his own monumental destiny in his mind is also what is consecrated in it and his subsequent monumental bearing and voice, "his innocence, his pristine aptitude for platform drama and childlike heroic simplicity" (246). Because of this self-dramatizing aptitude, Sutpen's own imagination can in effect predramatize and impersonate a communal vision. In his epiphany, as in his subsequent life, Sutpen plays both the hero and the commemorators who raise a monument to him, like the child who vocalizes the roar of an imagined crowd as he pretends to score the championship game's winning point.

The "bombastic . . . carven" (189) tombstones Sutpen orders for himself and his wife materialize his envisioned monument of "innocent" self-dramatization. Both the bombastic tombstones and the calm-voiced visionary monolith reveal his desire to take his immortality into his own hands insofar as possible. But the major refinement here is that for Quentin's Sutpen, his prospective audience, the ultimate recognizer and proof of his personal worth, is as real as the all too tangible headstones his troops must drag through their campaigns. The implication of Quentin's presentation is that when Sutpen speaks his calm bombast apparently to the air, he is not, as Rosa believes, absent from the room because in imagination he is diffused throughout his plantation (160). Quentin's Sutpen is absent not in space but in time, for in his deepest self-conception, he addresses the people who are part of his "central I-Am's private own" (139). He speaks to a predramatized renovated family that extends from past to future. Sutpen with his pristine aptitude for platform drama always inhabits a stage before an audience whose magnitude and makeup require his serenely exalted language. This is the style he uses, as Grandfather Compson notes, even to ask for a match or to offer a cigar (240). As his son Henry will later try to oppose "all the voices of his heredity and training" (342), Sutpen does so by performatively transmuting them into an aristocratic equanimity. Thereby he addresses "all the men and women that had died to make him . . . all the dead ones waiting and watching to see if he was going to do it right, fix things right so that he would be able to look in the face not only the old dead ones but all the living ones that would come after him when he would be one of the dead" (220).

In short, Quentin's Sutpen acts in the eyes of his ancestors and the posterity who will immortalize him, and all his House, as human persons: "his descendants who might not even ever hear his . . . name, [who] waited to be born without even having to know that they had once been riven forever free from brutehood just as his own (Sutpen's) children were" (261).

Thus, from Quentin's perspective, Rosa says more than she knows when she describes Sutpen's initial marriage proposal to her: "*I do not know what he looked at while he spoke, save that by the sound of his voice it*

*was not at us nor at anything in that room. . . . That was my courtship . . .
a ukase, a decree, a serene and florid boast like a sentence . . . not to be
spoken and heard but to be read carved in the bland stone which pediments a
forgotten and nameless effigy"* (164). All Sutpen's language is addressed
as if it were a proposal from someone dead to those who, knowingly
or not, will read and be his monument. Quentin's Sutpen acts as if his
words could actually be heard by his family line, "waiting and
watching," as if his line's now-efficacious voice could be read from a
book in which the hero's immortalizing poet had transcribed his
words. Sutpen is in this regard rather like a serious version of Don
Quixote, who enjoys speaking and acting as he imagines his poet will
describe him doing, for posterity's emulation. Sutpen is, to recall the
earlier discussion, like a Hightower who acts to produce this immortalizing posterity nonverbally as well as verbally. More than this,
Quentin's Sutpen speaks like a man in a monumental book whose
fecund words summon up, create, his reader-descendants through
the association of the prolific and the prolix.

Despite what Rosa says, Sutpen does indeed *speak* the elevated
language his heroic un-self-consciousness permits him. Quentin's
narrative sights along the lines of this rhetoric to discover its intended
audience. Insofar as Sutpen's forebears and descendants, as thus conceived by him, constitute his transformed self, he does indeed speak
to them. Projecting in his stilted language an image of books and
reading, Sutpen simultaneously renovates, revenges, and replies to
the illiterate brutish folk who were his poor-white family. It is as if
his calm orotundity, rejecting the sullen or harsh monosyllables of
nonpersons and the wordless "prolixity" of brute fecundity, wishes
to constitute a *humanly* reproductive script.

What distinguishes Sutpen's voice from those of the narrators who
actually speak him into being is that he implicitly understands the
reproduction of persons to be a one-way self-projection. Though
Quentin is right to say that "Thomas Sutpen made us all," Sutpen's
fiat did not make the descendants he imagined and in the way he
imagined. Rather, his monologue piqued and burdened a diverse
series of symbolic descendants into a dialogical exchange that, while
it does not entirely break free from the monologue that provokes
them, at base makes Sutpen as he makes them. Theirs is the two-
way, reciprocal creation of human beings, which is always tempted
to be unidirectional.

Initially, dialogical speech is an unintended, merely entailed casualty of Sutpen's self-invention through voice. What engross Sutpen are the sullen or harsh monosyllables of nonpersons and the muteness of brute fecundity, and these are what his calmly florid rhetoric is set up to oppose, with the resources familiar to him. Prime among them is a bookish voice. In Sutpen, "dialogism" gets caught in the cross fire between this voice and the subpersonal existence it exists to refute.

It is not surprising that Quentin's Sutpen speaks like a book. Quentin's evocation of his Sutpen is doubly bookish and doubly voiced, or "book-voiced." During much of Quentin's account, he stares at and apparently speaks to his father's letter announcing Rosa's death—a letter in turn associated with Bon's (207)—and to the open book on the desk. Further, Quentin discloses that Sutpen's equipment for living was furnished by listening to books.

At one point Quentin depicts a then-illiterate boy Sutpen listening to his teacher read aloud during his brief encounter with school before his youthful crisis. Sutpen learns from this listening "that most of the deeds, good and bad both, incurring opprobrium or plaudits or reward . . . had already been performed and were to be learned about only from books. . . . I did not know that in . . . listening I was equipping myself better for what I should later design to do than if I had learned all the addition and subtraction in the book" (241–42). This listening supplies the materials of Sutpen's heroic self-transformation, since he learns not only of the book-preserved memorable deeds but that the West Indies is a place where fresh deeds could still be done. The Indies form for Quentin's Sutpen an exception to the near exhaustion of action by others' prior performances. Hearing of the West Indies furnishes him with the idea that emulative rivalry is possible. This incident also establishes the association of memorable deeds with getting put into books for others to hear, not literally, of course, but as an encouragement for Sutpen to speak the stilted bookish rhetoric he does.

When Sutpen is affronted at the door, the prior schoolroom listening must have played a large part in his sudden self-recognition, both negatively, in letting him keenly intuit just how despicable "his kind" looked from a grander perspective, and positively, in providing him with the hypothesis of his own personal grandeur and its actualization. Sutpen's fundamental emulative rivalry engages not only with a specific planter and his class but with the all-but-exhausted heroic deeds in books. The parallel is underscored when

Sutpen insists to Grandfather Compson that he was "quite calm" (243) when he confronted the teacher to demand if the teacher read accurately from the book. Sutpen is like an author transmuting inferior materials, "his kind," into a higher genre by a rhetoric confidently addressed to that genre's proper audience. He is involved in transmuting a genre of perceived subpersons by an imitative rivalry with another "kind" that has at one stroke insulted him and inspired him to assimilate it purposefully.

The rhetoric of equanimity, which Sutpen perfects, conveys the impression that the speaker has everything under control because he or she has the self so manifestly under control. In situations where others feel doubt or self-divisive shame or guilt, the equanimous voice and demeanor influence them to identify themselves with and emulate the powerful enacted behavior and thus the actor. The voice controls the field of discourse so that other voices chime in or are inaudible. Sutpen in effect limits and controls his performative identification with others by taking on the exclusive and excluding role of a calm monological voice that can and does refuse others a hearing. Nothing in *Absalom, Absalom!* is more radiantly incongruous than Quentin, sullenly speaking a narrative heavily interlarded with "Grandfather said" and "Father said" about a man who cast off his stultifying sullen ancestral voices and did so with the help of a book-inspired univocality. This voice, like the House, contemplates the end of unwanted assimilation; it is no wonder that Rosa feels that the physical house speaks with an inimical voice when she tries to enter it (138).

But the novel tells us repeatedly that voice—like water, dust, and daughters—creates and infiltrates openings. The crucial paired idea is that, contrary to Sutpen's founding rhetorical principles, audiences are unforeseeable, in the sense that those who are intentionally addressed are not simply equivalent to those who hear. Witness, for example, Shreve as foreign auditor and narrator, Judith's covertly watching her father brutally wrestling with slaves, Rosa's own childhood spent in eavesdropping, and in Quentin's narrative, Wash's overhearing Sutpen's derogatory statement to Milly. Judith's transmission of Bon's "dead tongue speaking" through his letter cooperates with the unforeseeability of audiences. Sutpen, addressing his envisioned human audience, to the exclusion of the human diversity of his active flesh-and-blood listeners, is undone by this unforeseeability.

Wash, for whom Sutpen is his own apotheosis, his living monument, discovers that once he has placed his vulnerability in Sutpen's
safekeeping, the calm voice that radiated invulnerability can harm as
well and return the reproductive transformation to its starting point.
Sutpen stoically passes off the birth of a daughter, when he desperately needs a son, with a calmly unfeeling flippancy that arrogates her
to animal reproduction (286) and touches Wash to the quick. When
this avenger of daughters then attacks "men of Sutpen's own kind"
(280) "with the scythe above his head . . . making . . . no outcry"
(292), this image of silent death symbolically rounds out the undoing
of the House with its monological No to death. And it recalls again
the suppression and transformations of outcry in our reading, which
sustain Sutpen's immortality despite himself.

VI

We have pursued thus far the interplay of three dialectical moments:

personal unaccommodation and mortal outcry, which result from
a Sutpen-like drive to purify one's voices, one's House;

opposing this prospect of incapacity, a mutual accommodation by
weaving a fragile web of language and culture, whose very fragility
and evanescence furnishes a basis for one's empowering assimilation;

the overly susceptible assimilation that itself becomes threatening
and so fosters a desire for catharsis—but this would return the process to the first moment.

Quentin, epitomizing this last phase, adapts Sutpen's story so that
it simultaneously compels and cautions him. He modifies the first
two phases so that brutish reproduction becomes not a result but a
starting point. The second, opposing phase becomes Sutpen's enacted
monological family, not born but cloned in the father's display of
self-sufficiency.

Though these persons never exist in flesh and blood, their more
attenuated counterparts do. From the perspective of *The Sound and the
Fury,* Sutpen is very much the symbolic father of Quentin's un-
acknowledging father. Considered as a parable addressed by Quentin
to himself, Sutpen's story means that the powerful voice Quentin
imagines would make his father hear him, would also only echo the
father's progenitor, repeat his founding life strategy, and end in self-

defeat. Quentin and Quentin's Sutpen face each other as vocal problem and problematic heroic solution. Through Sutpen, Quentin in
effect contemplates, while he enacts, the script of a protracted self-
destruction, one foreshadowed in heroically adopting an excluding,
invulnerable voice.

To put this now in more directly rhetorical terms, both Rosa's
firsthand and Quentin's secondhand account agree in showing that
the fixity of Sutpen's rhetoric renders it "antirhetorical," in the respect that rhetoric entails canvassing an inventory of ways to speak
effectively on particular occasions. Similarly, his "forensic verbiage"
(246) is forensic in the sense that its floridity resembles the traditional
southern courtroom style (which Faulkner recalls [203]): its judgments, attacks, and defenses are locked into one stylization. As
Quentin portrays him, Sutpen constantly addresses only one ur-sit-
uation, the tidewater planter's affront, in the voice (belatedly) selected for that occasion. And only one memorized, eternal audience
governs his, and their, self-justification. That there are really no new
and various occasions or audiences for his voice is both the source of
his personal power to convey an impression of being undisturbably
integral and the limit of his practical effectiveness. If it is his booklike
appearance of being self-contained that makes him outrageously
memorable to others, it is also because they speak this book in their
various tones and for their various purposes, that he has his continuing life and power.

As the Sutpen legend is converted by his unforseen audiences and
narrators into a narrative rhetoric conformably heroic in its magnitude yet invested with narrators' tones very distant from Sutpen's
symmetrical equanimity, he becomes "a thousand times more potent
and alive" than when he lived (280). In thus being conceived and
performed in terms of potency, Sutpen is not alone, and the fact that
he is a dead, "historical" figure only intensifies this basis of personal
relationship. In *Absalom,* as in Faulkner generally, other people and
their personal products (such as letters, books, and houses) are not
essentially regarded as objects to be known. They are chiefly personal
powers—strategic powers transmitting and stimulating inimical, benign, or neutral capacities, powers to ally with or oppose or ignore.
Knowledge too is power, of a crucial kind but after all just one
capacity "which enables man to bear with living" (161). Insofar as
one's knowledge is realistic, one's strategic means to bear with living
can be more efficacious. But to know persons is in significant part to

conjecture, to embellish what is unsaid and unshown, which means to operate even more within a field of power and to be tempted to *know* powers without *acknowledging* persons.

If others are mysterious—as Quentin's motives as listener and speaker immediately strike us—this is largely because mystery is part of personal capacity, especially in an honor-shame culture where honor-preserving reticence is at a premium not only because inscrutability generally enhances interpersonal power (and surely Faulkner is the novelist for whom inscrutable faces are a lodestar). Insofar as the self is a commonwealth, some of whose powers must be marshaled against others within the self in order to function, this strategic reticence and mystery also extends within. Thus the characters not only conjecture about their contempories but puzzle over their own motives and knowledge—as Rosa, Quentin, Henry, and Bon do— just as the narrators conjecture about the dead. When the characters are most deeply conflicted, their embattled decision to act or to know appears as a shadowy force dictating to them, as when Rosa approaches the Sutpen mansion with a "curious terrified yet implacable determination, as though it were not she who had to go and find out but she only the helpless agent of someone or something else who must know" (365).

"As though" is itself the sign of necessary conjectural unfolding, performed by the anonymous transcribing narrator no less than the four represented narrators. This form of elaboration illustrates other confluent principles and functions of amplification besides that noted earlier, the principle of indirectly voicing and transforming the outcry of unaccommodation. The novel's combinations of volubility and reticence are complementary, as one participant speaks what the other cannot or does not say. The dialogical conventions of expression and silence in the honor-shame code and in a still highly oral manuscript culture converge here.

The personal reserve that in many areas of life marks the traditional honor-shame decorum stems from the potentially dangerous face-to-face encounter of oral communication. Shreve and Quentin's joint narration, with its accompanying moments of self-revelation and mutual acknowledgment, underscores the tension of this ambivalent encounter, as when they "glared . . . quiet and profoundly intent . . . almost as a youth and a very young girl might out of virginity itself—a sort of hushed and naked searching" (299). The quasi-sexual sense of a gentle yet potentially shameful exposure which

Quentin and Shreve manifest in questioning and answering each other through one conjectural elaboration after another provides one significant indication of why questions are not asked and declarations not made.

Consider, by way of illustration, a brother's announcement to his sister that he has just killed her fiancé, who is his best friend. When Henry tells Judith that she cannot marry Bon, she asks, "Why not?" But Henry's reply, "Because I killed him" terminates the questioning. Judith is not represented as asking (even if then Henry might refuse to answer) the seemingly inevitable next question: "My God! Why?" Nor does Judith ask Sutpen why when he returns from the war, though the absence of his own surprised question about why Henry would commit murder might be thought to absolutely require that she probe this highly suspicious silence.

The habits and necessity of reticence are stressed constantly. There are certain things that simply must not be declared or asked openly but must be assumed. All the narrators assume that there is an immense margin of actual or presumed unspoken understanding, or simple refusal to question or to speak, between the characters. As a result, constant conjecture and elaboration of the unsaid but inferable are demanded by the conditions of self-respecting reticence. This is "why," as it were, the lengthy narratives are required: to perform the speech complementary to taciturnity. In Shreve and Quentin's speculative version, when Henry, desperate to know if Bon is his half brother, visits Bon's vengeful mother, he must only infer the truth because of *her* harshly mocking inference that Judith loves Bon. In the same context, the conjectural "knowledge" of Bon's paternity shared by Bon and the lawyer "was no secret between them now; it would just be unsaid" (335–37).

Similarly, on this major issue of assumed knowledge and honorable silence, Bon simply cannot approach Sutpen and ask him to confirm and acknowledge his parentage. That Bon refrains from doing so is in fact his major appeal to Sutpen: his very silence should be, from his point of view, a major inducement to Sutpen's recognition, because it indicates that Bon is honorable and can be counted on to do the proper thing and withdraw from Sutpen's life after being recognized as a worthy, honorably silent son. As Bon says to Henry, "He should have told me. He should have told me, myself, himself. I was fair and honorable with him. I waited. . . . I gave him every chance to tell me himself. . . . But he didn't tell me. He just told you, sent me a message like you send a command by a nigger servant to a beggar or a tramp to clear out" (341). We infer, from Quentin's conjectural account, that Bon here feels himself treated just as the boy Sutpen was treated by the plantation owner's servant. On this occasion, however, what is called for is not voice on Bon's part but a pointed silence evocative of Sutpen's voice. Bon's silently anticipatory relation to his presumed father resonates strongly with Judith's transmittal of Bon's letter as a mute appeal of dependence on its receiver.

Clearly, the conventions of silence that acknowledge one's own and another's dignity also require those reticular indirections in which acknowledgment may be only pro forma or doubtful.

The novel's pivotal decision—whether Sutpen will recognize Bon—takes for granted the honor code's requirement of tacit reciprocity wherein one party manifests his or her self-esteem by silence on certain matters while the other party similarly meets the requirement of personal dignity by speaking of them if the occasion warrants. In the dialogue situation assumed by the honor-shame culture, where it is the office of one party to be silent, it is the complementary office of the other to speak. Thus much of the everyday mutual persuasion of this culture is vested in conventions of silence and of the speaking of what another leaves unspoken.

Parallel to this rhetorical reciprocity is the transcriber's expected elaboration and embellishment in the manuscript conventions characteristic of traditional honor-shame culture. The old idea of transcription, the taking down of what is spoken, and the related conception that writing is consequent to primary orality, are to be distinguished from writing as inscription, where writing is conceived as a direct and primary expression of thought, as in a print culture. As Gerald Bruns has demonstrated, in the ethos of a manuscript culture, it is not only permissible but desirable to use the occasion of transcription to adorn and elaborate what the speaker or previous writer said, to reflect what (the transcriber assumes) the speaker meant to say to the greatest effect, or has yet to formulate, even if it was not literally said (*Inventions* 44–59; see also Ong, *Orality* 132). For the sympathetic transcriber to add greater copiousness is to follow one's habitual experience with another's words in conversation. In conversation, obviously the point is not stenographic copying of one participant's monologue by another but the developing and filling out of a joint expression, even if one speaker does most of the speaking.

The two distinguishable but parallel cultural conventions reinforce each other. The one transcriptively treats another's discourse as the occasion for dialogical amplification. The other honorably conjectures or maintains proud reticence in the give and take of personal power. There is additional reinforcement when the territory of discourse (like the subject of Bon's paternity between himself and Sutpen) is a minefield of potential disgrace, requiring extensive rhetorics of silence and conjectural elaborations.

It is on such terms that the narrative convention and rhetoric of *Absalom, Absalom!* can be illuminated. The basic narrative convention is not inscription, with its print-culture ethos of stenographic replication and "scientistic" exactitude, but transcription. That is, *Absalom, Absalom!* presents itself as a transcription, a taking down, of dialogue and oral narratives, to which the transcribing (authorial) narrator adds occasional speculative commentary and judgments, brief descriptions, and necessary connecting matter. The transcribing narrator's own prose is as marked by sonority as that of the oral narrators and is tonally—that is, both stylistically and attitudinally—close to the represented oral narrator of the moment. The other narrators, in turn, all sound like distinguishable variants of the transcribing narrator, so that orality and the act of transcription equally interpenetrate. Again, the act of transcription means amplification, not stenography, by an ethos faithful to every speaker's presumed desire for copiousness and maximum effect. It is an ethos, precisely, of reciprocation and accommodation, furnishing other speakers with what their words lack and the transcriber with what these provide. By this convention of an orally modeled accommodation of sonorous eloquence, the novel can offer itself to the reader as an occasion for consummating performance. Faulkner transfers tragedy from stage play and closet drama for reading, to novel as theater.[6]

The writings represented in *Absalom, Absalom!* are likewise transcriptive—manuscript, not print. (When print is referred to, it is treated orally: Quentin apparently speaks to the book on his desk, and an illiterate young Sutpen is represented as hearing books read aloud to him.) The two letters—Bon's to Judith, and Mr. Compson's to Quentin—manifest the embellished, dialogical style that marks the whole novel. Bon's ornate letter, for example, is punctuated by such oral markers as "*There. They have started firing again,*" the use of "*Yes*" as confirmation of a previous statement, and dialogical questions like "*Stop what? you will say.*" Much of the novel, in fact, appears as a kind of exponentially magnified amplification of the second letter, spoken and transcribed parenthetically between the point at which Mr. Compson's letter expresses uncertainty that there is any comfort in death (174), and his final conjectural hope, two hundred pages later (377), that there is. The conjectural accommodations that fill these pages are as if spoken and transcribed between the lines of Mr. Compson's manuscript memento mori.

Since much critical attention has already been devoted to the reader's conjectural elaboration prompted (supposedly "forced") by the novel's various reticences—especially regarding Quentin's basis for claiming to know the secret of Bon's birth—I will not pursue this further. What is to the point is that these reticences and the reader's corresponding impulse to conjecture, elicit a reading experience cognate with the novel's transcriptive activity as well as the dialogical workings of honor-code silence and speech. But whether this conjecturing will be taken by the reader as a constraint such as Bon is under ("He should have told me") or an opportunity (like Shreve's "Let me play a while now" [280]) is another matter. It bears on the whole question of the novel's burdensome empowering, which in a few pages we will be prepared to take up directly.

Once we understand the transcriptive convention and the novel's corresponding self-presentation as a vocal world for "serious" performative emulation, much else that has puzzled critics about *Absalom*'s mode of discourse is clarified. Chapter 5, continuing Rosa's narration to Quention from Chapter 1, furnishes ready illustrations.

Though she repeatedly claims that she "holds no brief" for herself, she of course presents an apologia coupled with a condemnation of Sutpen, focused upon two things: his unbearable insult and her having placed herself in a situation where she could be thus insulted. In effect, Rosa exculpates herself, as a southern lady, for having made herself liable to the equivalent of psychological rape by Sutpen. As a whole, her implicit defense is that, while she had the normal yearnings of a young southern woman who was dependent on one whom she saw as a war hero, he was a demon with a demon's superhuman powers and subhuman morality.

The chapter has all the verbal markers of being orally addressed to Quentin, and like the first chapter, its speech dialogically anticipates his possible objections to and doubts about her behavior. Unlike the first chapter, however, this apologia is presented in italics until the last page, when it is revealed that Quentin has not been listening because he has been unable in imagination to "pass" Judith's doorway to Henry announcing Bon's death. Further, besides the evidence of italics, as Albert Guerard notes, "even the best southern poetess would not really say to a young man of college age" such things as *"mammalian meat . . . all polymath love's androgynous advocate"* and *"friction's ravishing of the male-furrowed meat also weaponed and panoplied as a man instead of hollow woman"* (145–46).[7]

But just as obvious in Rosa's narration are dialogical indicators like those in Bon's letter, and as a review of the chapter would quickly show, there is a modulation of speech registers throughout. What is indicated by all the evidence is a discourse issuing from actual dialogical speech and bearing its marks, yet not always spoken literally. In fact, it is not even necessarily thought literally by Rosa. The standards to apply here are transcriptive and rhetorical. In Chapter 5 her primary means of apologia is the evocation of herself as a vulnerable and imaginative young woman who, having grown up in a loveless environment and having recently lost her vicarious love, Bon, now feels sexually and idealistically attracted to a heroic mad titan to whom she wishes to provide "sun" and "airy space" (167–68). There is a great deal here that Rosa, as a product of a traditional honor-shame culture, cannot say, but that must be powerfully intimated if her self-defense is to succeed.

This silence is what needs to be filled out transcriptively, yet the apologia must emerge as her own statement reflecting the young Rosa who was mortally affronted by Sutpen and for whom the surviving Rosa donned black mourning clothes. That youthful sensibility can best serve as its own defense, particularly to a young man of college age. Chapter 5, with its youthful, lush romantic lyricism, is on these terms one of the principal resurrections of a dead voice in the novel. But as in all such cases, there is refraction: the dead voice can only speak *as* another, surviving voice. Here the voice is that of an older Rosa, but only *as* imitated elaboratively by the transcribing narrator, who "hears and reports" Rosa even though the characterized audience, Quentin, does not, and who phrases Rosa's poetic speech in a way neither the younger nor the older woman could or would exactly. The strongly sexual, "fleshly," statements, then, represent a dialogism combining a burgeoning youthful physical desire, the older woman's mixture of longing, outrage, and implacability toward the flesh, and a way of capturing these conflicting voices and emotions which suggests the voice of a male transcribing narrator, who verbally gives Rosa the "airy space" she wished to furnish Sutpen.

Such rich dialogism foregrounds the accommodations of amplification. It is equally important to stress the modulated character of speech throughout the chapter, since the total achieved effect of constant modulation interspersed with such moments of strongly foregrounded elaboration is to blur the boundaries that voices "must" observe, the bounds between what an individual speaks and what another speaks for the individual. This blurs in turn the bounds between what is repeated and what is modified—the bounds, in other words, between the inward and the outward dialogism of this vocal world. That this effect exists in pointed contrast to the image of Quentin's self-exclusion at a threshold and his fixation on the announcement of Bon's murder requires, I think, no further elaboration from me. Clearly, moreover, what is said of this chapter can be said to greater or lesser degree about all the narratives. These are always presented as oral, rhetorically purposeful, and dialogical, yet in their sonorous elaborations, intricate syntax, and "precise" rendering of such details as the dialogue of historical characters, they make no pretense of observing the ordinary verisimilitude of oral narration in the realistic novel.

This is a novel murmurous with ventriloquial voices, voices that cannot be confined to one speaker or hearer, whether in "marriage" or conflict or the mutual "haunting" between the transcribing narrator and the others. It is reductive to regard this lack of fixity as merely an issue of decidable or undecidable epistemological authority. This issue is a subset of the power of voice to permeate, to absorb, and to engage in an amplification of give and take in a dialectic with various silences. It is in the context of this immense busy traffic of accommodating yet dangerous voices and listening that the attempt to establish a freestanding monological House has its significance and tragic magnitude.

That magnitude derives from the narrators who help to furnish their own existence from the legendary House and to regulate what it has already furnished them. In the substance and form of their stories, the narrators enact the accommodations that make them and their creations humanly fragile and humanly strong. The tragic edifice they create is their communal project evidencing the precariousness and the necessity of such personally creative effort, which is greater than any of its individual parts, "bigger than any because it was the sum of all" (*Requiem* 42).

VII

How, then, do readers fare, readers potentially implicated in this effort and "the raging and incredulous recounting (which enables man to bear with living) of that feather's balance between victory and disaster"? In the feather's balance between empowering and a demoralizing burden, where is the line between a power that better enables one to bear and that which bears down even more? If, on this novel's own terms, recounting and hearing can constitute an equipment for living as well as Quentin's painful surfeit, who will be accommodated and how will accommodation be sought? Every variant and possibility of reading obviously cannot be traced—that, in fact, is a key point—but the novel maps certain reading communities even as it commits itself to the unforeseeability of individual audiences.

If the novel derives its meaning and creative energies from deficiencies and unmanageable excesses of accommodation, in the three dialectical moments summarized earlier, it is not difficult to designate the middle phase between the extremes as the counterpart of the novel's own inferable "ideal" reading, a function of its blended rhetorical approaches. Bon's letter, as transmitted by Mr. Compson's Judith, represents the rhetorical appeal of fragility and obvious dependency. Its analogues are the power of passivity we have noticed in the earlier novels, the interdependency in personal reciprocity, and the roster of dependents within *Absalom, Absalom!* (the young Rosa, the "boy symbol" of Sutpen, Bon himself, Charles Etienne Bon, etc.). Sutpen's voice represents the antithetical rhetorical appeal of seeming self-sufficiency. The novel's overall rhetoric, as variously performed and scripted for us by the five narrators, resembles Sutpen's to the extent that it resembles an oratory spoken on a vast stage to a large audience. To the degree that this voice is heroically magnified, addressed, and homogeneous, it manages the novel's multiplicity of personal voices and so serves the traditional function of the hero: to demonstrate the adequacy of the culture's (or the novel's) empowerment and thus persuade the audience to adopt it.

But *Absalom*'s rhetoric also moves significantly away from Sutpen's stylized equanimity and toward mutuality. It does so by its obvious transcription of agitation, in a variety of narrative tones. It does so too by its much greater degree of heterogeneity: its greater range of style and reference, its stylistic and structural flexibility and inventiveness, its zestful mixture of vernacular and high eloquence, its touches of humor (especially in the tall tale of the hunting of the architect)—to say nothing of the novel's variously spoken critique of Sutpen and his voice. Thus, measured from the baseline of Sutpen's heroic voice, the novel's overall heroic-sized rhetoric is much more heterogeneous and commodious.

In a subtler rhetorical inducement, as we saw, the reader's vocal performance parallels the permanence-through-transitoriness of Bon's letter and opposes Sutpen's rhetoric of permanence through monumental stasis. Other features of structure and pacing persistently develop this countereffect in additional, nonauditory ways. One feature is the odd rhythm of narrative focus: the allusive flickering over important matters, then the garrulous pausing over apparent commonplaces, minutiae, or repercussions, so that, like Shreve (and partly through his example), we are prompted to call out "Wait!" to this eccentric movement. The complementary feature is the piecemeal and circling method of presentation, which returns us to what has been passed over and recovers what has been lost, but always in some revised form. Related to this technique is the reader's schooling in unfinality and inexhaustibility through long tension-building delays, which result in explosions of insight or action which turn out to be, in fact, not culminating but which leave something more to be resolved.

A rhetorical education in transience and in a preserving transformation thus accompanies the feelings of anticipation and unfinality. The reading experience of this combined pattern prompts a desire not to permit things to pass away wholly and so elicits a cooperative attitude toward the narrative's reconsiderings and revisings. Concordant with this attitude is an educed patience toward inconclusiveness, rather than exclusiveness, and therefore a tolerance for the not-quite-conclusive, for what is "true enough" (335). True enough, that is, to speaker, audience, and occasion. In other words, there is a large rhetorical inducement to value the elaboration and embellishment by which the transient may be retained by being changed and by which reciprocating accommodation can occur.

Further, the thickened webs of language, the syntactical and structural deferments of meaning, and the novel's reticences all call for an unusual intellectual effort of construal, memory, and conjecture, beginning at the sentence level. These same verbal baffles act to contain the very outcry of unaccommodation whose undertone may well additionally spur our opposing energies, especially in emulation of Faulkner's strenuous force. In short, the novel's rhetoric has the potential to exercise the reader's capacities in such an inclusive combination of ways that it would seem to allow reading to enact the cultural construction of human accommodation itself, in knowing or unwitting opposition to the tragic devastation of humanity. In this reading mode we finally say No to catharsis after experiencing its temptation.

If the novel foretells anything about audiences, however, it is that we readers will strategically use reading as we can. We will perform within the extendable range of our existing powers and within the limits of what we feel we must do and be at given points in our lives. Otherwise stated, the question about the book's possible enabling will not be answered by a single "ideal" reading but by various performed reading roles that regulate the novel's vehement rhetoric and that, in *making* it bearable, make it capacitating in different ways. In a novel so populated by characters and narrators who experience outrage and in which communication is so much a feather's balance between the enhancing and the debilitating, the novel's own potential outrageousness will tip the reading balance in different ways, depending on how its potential rhetorical hubris is taken. So much valuable work has been done by scholars and teachers to make *Absalom, Absalom!* accessible within the special circumstances of classroom required reading that it is easy to forget the challenging hubris of what Faulkner called his "illimitable courage for rhetoric" (*Letters* 188). The novel, however, does not forget.

If Quentin's brooding over the open book can be thought of as emblematic, we can begin with a reader's choice no less important for being obvious: to continue confronting the novel's outrageous style and structure or to close the book unfinished. Many readers have not only closed the book but slammed it shut as an affront to reading. And more than one reader—no doubt including many eventually sympathetic to the novel—can appreciate the vengeful riposte (unwittingly celebratory) by Clifton Fadiman that in *Absalom, Absalom!* Faulkner had invented a new form, the life sentence (63). Certainly, whether by closing the book or muttering an imprecation, readers

The House of *Absalom, Absalom!*

who respond sullenly or vengefully to what they perceive as an outrageous narrative are repeating a response within the novel.

Compounding the challenge of style and structure is the novel's fevered tone. This unusually sustained emotional pitch can offer a potential affront to readers' literary or general civil sense of what role they can be fairly asked to play. The novel's persistent courting of a febrile reading sensibility is remarkable, especially in light of Faulkner's more usual and sometimes boldly disparate tonal mixtures. Consequently (to adapt Wittgenstein's terms), its language game is a form of life readers have declined and will decline in irritation or exhaustion. Others continue reading by a self-protective device the novel anticipates in one impulse shared by Shreve, Mr. Compson, and the "cold, implacable" (10) Rosa of the first chapter: a ratiocinative distancing to oppose or moderate the febrility scripted for them. To a further degree, for a related group of other readers, the rhetoric's open emotional power coupled with its deferred meaning will immediately seem a suspicious attempt to overwhelm them, and they will recoil into an increased guarded calmness. Though no reader may approach Sutpen's degree of enacted equanimity, all readers may well share this strategy to some extent at times in reading *Absalom,* as a preventive against emotional exhaustion, if nothing else.

Readers who "renege" by ceasing to read might say to the novel's implied author, in Quentin's words, "Why tell it to me?" The slogan of those who retreat into guarded equanimity at the novelist's combination of feverishness and reticence, might be Bon's "He should have told me. I gave him his chance."

In a more complex kind of reading, comparable to another of Shreve's moods of narration—"Let me play awhile"—one can commit oneself only tentatively to the role of feverish reader or calm ratiocinator without entering fully or predominantly into either role, but following the adventures of these reading roles, so to speak, while remaining at one remove from them in a more spectatorial, experimental auditioning of them. In this case, one dips into and out of reading roles, seeing what results they will yield and perhaps appreciating one or both without wishing to take them on full time.

For still other readers—or occasions of reading—the novel's demands will serve to create an all-or-nothing provocation like that in the ambiguous hubris of the honor-shame code. According to the principle of provocation, rivalry, and empowering identification we have examined, Faulkner will either lose this audience entirely or win them into a strong identification and partisanship. (In this sense, some of those who slam the book shut may have more in common with some of Faulkner's more extreme bardolaters than either group would wish to admit.) Another large fraction of the audience of course will take lesser degrees of this provocation or tonic goading. And this dynamic will contribute its bracing sense of hazardously shared power to whatever else the reader makes of the novel's rhetorical inducements. In fact, lesser degrees of this reading role exist in all reading to the extent that the novel's difficulty serves as a kind of ordeal of initiation into the writer's world, thus helping, as initiation generally does, to bestow value on the world that has been arduously won. A final variant of ardor and arduousness suggests itself here: even the outraged reader who feels closed out of the book and is tempted to close it as the expression of this role, can become the reading insider par excellence once outrage and being kept outside are grasped as a crucial theme that commences in the earliest pages.

No writer with Faulkner's concern for immortality could help being curious about how he would be read. *Absalom*'s well-known reflexivity on this score is continuous with an associated preoccupation: how people respond to powerful communication or displays of power—such as this novel itself constitutes. What this means is that no matter which of the foregoing reading roles, or combination of roles, we enact, we may find ourselves acknowledged, "recognized" implicitly by a prospect for reading which the novel presents in some counterpart strategy, mood, or personal relationship. In a novel that dramatizes not so much the failure to know others as the failure to acknowledge and accommodate others adequately, this sense of being anticipatorily acknowledged, provided for, can encourage the adaptations that bear with reading. On the other hand, not the least part of the book's great curiosity involves what it means not to sense acknowledgment or, in this case, to feel that *Absalom, Absalom!* makes no provision for our personal and/or reading repertoire. When we feel we can make seemingly inexhaustible power like that of *Absalom* our own in some measure, it is a remarkable form of empowering. When we feel that this force has the inexhaustibility of some alien other which makes no provision for our possession, it can be felt as the oppressive tediousness that Rosa describes: word after word, "tomorrow and tomorrow."

In *Absalom, Absalom!* to feel unacknowledged where acknowledgment is important produces a desire to subject the other to one's power. Besides the many instances we have noted, a final one is most relevant here.

It is because of such unacknowledgment, Shreve and Quentin believe, that Bon was tempted to replace Sutpen's paternal self-reproduction in Henry by his own: *"what could I not mold of this malleable and eager clay which that father himself could not"* (318). Yet at the moment Quentin and Shreve thus enact the role of Bon, "this shade whom they . . . existed in" (316), the opposite of such one-way imposition—their "marriage" of mutual acknowledgment in speaking and hearing—enables them. Nothing could make it clearer that the role of overpowering or being overpowered, exists as a possibility within capacitation, and that what causes it to be realized is perhaps above all just this sense of lacking acknowledgment. Whether readers will feel themselves unacknowledged by the novel and treat it as something to be molded like clay or conversely will feel that to experience its power is to be so molded, or whether they will take its power as an incentive to a dialogical reading performance in which to exist—the novel can propose such alternatives and can be understood to prompt the most enabling selection among them. But by its own principles, there are risks either way, and the novel cannot furnish selection itself, any more than anything can furnish itself alone.

From this vantage, then, we can understand the novel as the tragic enlargement and embellishment of Judith's act of transmission and its double impulse to include and counter Sutpen's cathartic act of innocence. The novel transmits a heterogeneous and open House of Faulkner, inviting the stranger-reader's performance and our enduring of and through what we engender. Thus we heed the novel's title and entitlement, and we belie even as we acknowledge the force of the sole proprietorship that another of the novel's posted signs maintains.

Some Limitations of
Deconstructive "Reading"

Notwithstanding the Derridean position that reading, readers, and texts are simply "effects" of *différance*, activities of a "system," but also noting that Jacques Derrida too speaks of readers as risking certain commitments without which one does not *properly* "read at all" (e.g., 63–64), we can observe that there is a typical deconstructive reader, evidenced in Paul de Man's accounts of reading. In contrast to the optional-focus reading, possibly on several levels simultaneously, which I describe in the first chapter and in this book as a whole, the reader assumed by deconstructionists always compares (in the ideal case) all levels of attention with one another. The deconstructionist pretends that in reading novels, for instance, we would constantly compare the relation between the characters with the relation we as interpreters are "made" to have with the text, and these in turn with the implication of figures of speech and their interrelations, and we would sustain this lucid attention without wavering, perhaps over the hundreds of pages of a Rousseau or Proust text. This heroically sustained attention finds, inevitably, that these aspects imply different things, that there is a loose string hanging, and that these anomalies are irreconcilable contradictions.

Who *reads* like that? Nobody. The perusal of even a few pages of the most moderately complex work would drag on unendurably. Such reading is indeed impossible, though not in the sense meant by de Man and his followers. One can learn to analyze like that, for certain purposes, and can do it excellently, as the best deconstructive analysts prove. But since deconstructionists do not want to admit the contingency of this way of doing analysis, they claim they are describing reading—not *a* way to read (improbable though interesting as that might be) but *the* way of all conceivable reading. For this is not just a reading for which its truth or falsity is, as de Man says, "primarily involved"; this is a reading so obsessed with true and false that everything conceivable is seen and compared for its uniformity in these terms, not "primarily" but exclusively. Having falsely essentialized reading in the first place, they indeed find it impossible, in the sense of being riddled with acute contradictions.

The history of criticism in the last few decades makes the problem evident. Deconstructive criticism has hypostasized a way of reading which has, if not thus hypostasized, a quite respectable rational function. That function is exactly to reduce something to absurdity, namely the so-called New Critical model of complete organic unity, which was the major form of reading-as-knowledge preceding the deconstructionist movement. Deconstruction reduces this to absurdity by imagining a hypothetical reading that would constantly, not to say aggressively, try to read as the organicist knowledge model predicts you should be able to, and then shows that this is impossible without finding the contradictions that weren't supposed to be there. Having shown the previous model to be incorrect by doing it the disservice of taking it with entire seriousness and reading not just closely but hyperclosely, the deconstructionist surely should have then disposed of the disposable hypothetical reading, which had done its work. For clearly if the model was wrong then the reading posited by it was no less so. It should have fallen with the framework it had dissolved and on which it depended. Had this been done, the door might have been opened for a more generous conception of reading.

Instead of casting away the hypothetical reading, the deconstructionist ducked inside it. The special "reading" one had cannily seen was the outcome of a claim that literature offers a special knowledge in which subject and object are united—this "reading" imagined *per impossible*—was not only not disposed of but was asserted to be the essence of reading. Extremely able and sophisticated critics like de Man were led to this step because they could not or would not think outside the fundamental idea that reading is knowledge. Since they were committed to the skeptical side of the argument about knowledge and particularly wanted to subvert all special claims to knowledge, the "reading" that could thus powerfully demonstrate absurdity was too precious a tool to discard. Though it was the most basic sort of confusion to do so, this "reading" was promoted from its contingency as a reductio ad absurdum hypothesis to ontological necessity. The absurdity that the "reading" could claim to show, always of course necessarily reflected back upon it as the ghost of a defunct organicist cognitive paradigm, and this state of self-contradictoriness was asserted to reveal something deep about the nature of everything. Mutatis mutandis, a similar argument can be made about deconstructive "reading" in relation to structuralism, on whose language-modeled binary system deconstruction depends and which it dissolves. (See Bruns's illuminating book, especially the chapter "Systems Versus Tongues . . . ," and his review for something like this critique, made on quite different terms from those I apply to the organicist model.) More generally, the deconstructionists' reply that they must occupy the very totality they deconstruct begs the question of how human systems function and whether texts have the kind of systematicity ascribed to them in the first place so it can be deconstructed.

The persuasiveness of deconstructionist accounts of reading is further limited by a Hegelianism transformed into a procedural tic: the inveterate initial allegation that multiplicity, or some heterogeneity, is contradictory, so that straw-oppositions can be the more easily deconstructed. Roland Barthes, for example, does this in *The Pleasure of the Text* regarding the reader's multiple roles (3); Jonathan Culler follows this technique throughout his discussion of reading in *On Deconstruction* (31–84); and de Man and Derrida may often be accused of it, despite—or because of—the greater slipperiness of their practice.

All this said, it should be clear enough that my own critical approach here and in previous work has a certain family resemblance to deconstructionist themes and methods, since I have often benefited from reading in its discourse. I account generally for this resemblance and interest by the fact that I am interested in an open dialectics whose genealogy is also that of deconstruction, a dialectics of which deconstruction is a variant, although Derrida vehemently dissociates his practice from Hegelian *Erinnerung,* sublation, and (presumable) closure. I trust it is clear too that my general project differs from what I understand as a major thrust of much deconstruction: advancing the cause of a radical skepticism, and of "antihumanism." Further, aside from general philosophical leanings of mine which far preceded my acquaintance with poststructuralism, my debt and relationship to

Kenneth Burke's dialectics are prior and greater as regards overall critical stance. (For a compact sample of Burke on dialectics, see "Dialectic in General" in *Grammar*.) It would be unfortunate if critics either shunned or embraced the practice of dialectics by equating it with its best-advertised current variant, deconstruction, and equally unfortunate if dialectical criticism could not borrow and adapt freely from this or any other variant.

Studying Actual Readers

The first chapter notes that three related but distinguishable subjects of study derive from our conception of reading/writing as a
performance involved in a culture's reproduction of, and through,
persons. Throughout this book we consider Faulknerian tragedy
from the complementary standpoints of the author's symbolic action
of a No to mortality and the text's solicitation of a realizing collaborative performance. We attempt to grasp what the texts foresee of
the actual readings, in the last analysis unforeseeable, which engage
them in the lives of culturally accommodated persons. I propose here
to note briefly what might be done in studying the subject that is the
logical continuation of this rhetorical criticism of performance, actual
readers enacting texts as part of living their lives. Our scope must be
general, surveying the larger domain of reading of which Faulkner's
writings are a part.

In this area, Norman Holland, David Bleich, Jacques Leenhardt,
and others have broken ground by examining actual readers. But
they have used an interpretive rather than a performance model and a
narrow time span. (The latter restricts Janice Radway's stimulating
field study.) What is required now is nothing less than field studies of
readers outside the academic setting, covering fairly long-term histo-
ries of individual or group reading and, in the context of particular
cultural and social systems, focusing on person-shaping habits of
performing and evaluating works. One would want to know, for
instance, how both constant and changing styles of one's personal
performance, including playing the role of audience in the enactments

of everyday life, relate to one's favored literary and nonliterary texts, how families and schools use reading to influence children's repertoires of personal roles at various ages, how cultural values are modified in transmission by idiosyncratic and creative appropriations of these roles by child and adult readers, how a "book that changed my life" may affect different people or social groups in different ways, how the actual (not necessarily high culture) textual canon of a given group over a period of two or more generations is related to the group's shared and transmitted performative and rhetorical styles and to individual and collective strategies for coping with death and other insults to personal value, how competition for prepotence in the popular and high cultural literary marketplace relates to economic and other class factors, how this competition between writers and cultural brokers (e.g., nonacademic book reviewers and influential academic critics) influences what authors write. Many more such questions regard reading in the fabric of quotidian personal life, but all these inquiries would have the greatest significance if conducted whenever possible within a cross-cultural framework (e.g., the American and British working classes as readers) and with a supplementary concern for the influence of other media on persons.

The contemporary criticism of reading, having begun by entangling itself obscurely in the limits of an interpretive paradigm that was incorrectly taken to be all-inclusive, is still nascent. Criticism in confronting readers reading has opened the door to a wide new area to know, and teach, and write about.

Notes

Introduction: On Saying No to Death

1. Book reviewers and academic critics have from the beginning used the second honorific approach widely. See many of the items summarized in McHaney 1–47, and see items under "tragedy" in his index. The first, more self-consciously theoretical usage has appeared in, e.g., Scott, O'Donnell, Sullivan, Lind, Sewall, Longley, Brooks, Michel, and Lenson.

On the adjustment of critical theory to Shakespeare, see Koelb, "'Tragedy' and 'The Tragic'": "What happened once in the history of literary theory can (and perhaps inevitably must) happen again. Shakespeare wrote a number of works which could not be tragedies [according to the neoclassical theory of this *literary form*], but displayed in ample measure 'the tragic' [Schlegel's influential coinage, meaning a sensitive experience, in life or literature, of the dire disasters of the world]. Now those works-which-could-not-be-tragedies are among the select few works that are held by the whole western world to be almost the definition of what a tragedy is. It should be no surprise, then, that any other literary work which might be construed as being 'tragic' should make an honest claim upon being a 'tragedy' as well" (284). Similarly, one can see the dialectical pressures in Faulkner criticism to register the impact of "the tragic" and yet to apply to his works the supposed essential requirements of "tragedy." Not surprisingly, the shift in emphasis from the first to second tactic occurs when Faulkner becomes increasingly the subject of academic commentary, beginning with Sullivan in 1951. Both pressures not infrequently appear in a single critic; see, e.g., Howe on the impact of *The Sound and the Fury* (174) and on the failure of Sutpen to qualify as a hero of tragedy because he attains no self-recognition (223). (This is a typical reduction of Aristotle's *anagnorisis* to a putative requirement for the hero's final self-knowledge. See note 2, below.)

For Faulkner's own numerous explicit and implicit claims that he wrote tragedy, see *University* 41–42 and passim, and *Lion* 14 and passim.

227

Notes

2. We will return to this matter in Chapter 3. One feature of these disputes, however, is especially relevant here. English departments, prominently including Faulkner scholars, to a remarkable degree still generalize the notion of "tragic flaw" and its entailments, although this concept has been superseded in Classics scholarship of the past several decades. Indeed, Gerald Else (379n) made a similar observation in his 1957 study of the *Poetics*. From one perspective, this situation is unfortunate, since it directly or indirectly muddles discussions of Faulkner. From a wider perspective, the cultural power of *tragedy* as a storehouse of value is well illustrated here. That is, there is a collective, more or less unconscious attempt by English departments not only to conserve a "tragic flaw" view of tragedy which is charged with the assumptions of a particular secularized theodicy but to pursue this aim to the point of ignoring the contrary testimony of specialists on the subject.

Bremer usefully surveys the history of interpretation of Aristotelian *hamartia* as "moral flaw" or "guilt" and sums up the present consensus among classicists that the word means, rather, " 'mistake,' 'blunder,' i.e. a well-intentioned action (or at least one not maliciously undertaken) which proves harmful" (195). Renaissance scholars made sense of Aristotle's term by interpreting it according to the "belief [that] it was impossible to consider human wrongdoings without attributing them to the wickedness of fallen man, who had trespassed against the divine law" (97). As Bremer notes, this interpretation of Aristotle's theory (which in either version has a number of often-noted limitations) continues to inform the idea of "tragic flaw." It informs, moreover, the continuing deep conviction that, despite other theories, *genuine* tragedy concerns, and concerns only, a noble but flawed figure who, through deserved suffering, comes to acknowledge his flaw. One influential, and in a qualified form valid, application of this view in Faulkner criticism regards the South as Faulkner's tragic hero, with the institution of slavery as its flaw—e.g., Longley 234 and Brooks, *Toward Yoknapatawpha,* 272. Aside from the dubiousness of citing Aristotle as authority, the mischief lies in the cramped exclusivity of this view, which produces what I think of as a "Job's friends" conception of tragedy. Job's friends could recognize him as an honest man only if he acknowledged the guilt that they assumed must have occasioned his suffering. The "tragic flaw" secularized theodicy can recognize tragedy only by a similar logic. By the same token, this demand for the guilty flaw automatically relegates to a lesser "mere pathos" any depiction of innocent suffering, the suffering of the victim. Joe Christmas, for instance, has been understood in ways that directly or indirectly reflect or contend with this "pathetic" assessment of his status.

For a pleasurable "nontheoretical" means of enriching one's conception of the general subject outlined here, see E. R. Dodds's "On Misunderstanding the *Oedipus Rex.*" See also, besides Bremer and the scholarship he cites, Weitz, Kaufmann on tragedy and innocent suffering, and Williams for some modern, socially contested dimensions of this topic. For a provocative treatment of Aristotle, action, and Greek tragedy, see Jones. For Faulkner's familiarity with Greek tragedy, especially Euripides, consult Blotner, *Faulkner's Library.*

228

Finally, not only the critics who invoke Aristotle are prone to sweeping generalizations about Faulkner and the essence of tragedy. John Irwin, e.g., draws on Freud and Nietzsche to claim that, by trying to "get even" with time, Faulkner's work embodies the "very essence of tragedy, for I take it that all tragedies are in a sense revenger's tragedies" (4). Again, we should understand both the impulse to make such assertions about tragedy's ahistorical essence and the historical, genealogical character of these assertions themselves. Then we are prepared to notice judiciously what general perceptions of tragedy are at stake in the works. Then, that is, we can examine the specific transformations of certain aspects of the tragic genealogy proposed by the work, in the face of readers' sometimes concordant and sometimes discordant generalized paradigms of tragedy.

3. See, e.g., Swink's useful article on the devices Faulkner uses to "create an *illusion* of oral quality" whether the prose is "conversational, extravagant, or home-spun" (183, 209). Like others, Swink points out that, for many passages in Faulkner, "in order for the reader to receive a coherent and clear meaning, his consciousness must provide a voice that reads the words with necessary pauses and voice inflection" (189–90). Given the tendency to base generalizations too simply on Faulkner's extravagantly elaborated prose, it is important to keep in mind the actual wide range of Faulkner's language, both between texts and within even such a novel as *Absalom, Absalom!* As Swink does not sufficiently acknowledge, much of this language is beautifully suited to performance through the usual kinds of oral delivery. The most elaborately scored language, too, we will see, is capable of producing other important reading effects when we answer its call to a more unusual enunciation.

Though writers often are not the best performers of their own work, Faulkner's recordings hint at the resources waiting to be tapped when we devote to performing and recording his (and other major) writings something like the proper care that we devote to editing them.

The deconstructive visual bias is represented in Matthews's refinement of Lilly's notion of Faulknerian "silence": "It is Lilly's inference that such silence is wordless. Faulkner's brand of silence, on the contrary, is a worded silence—a silence that corresponds most nearly to the space of writing" (41).

4. As will become increasingly clear, the opposition can also be stated as a reproduction through others versus what Fairchild in *Mosquitoes* calls "reproduction from within." In contrast to sexual reproduction, "in art, a man can create without any assistance at all: what he does is his. A perversion, I grant you, but a perversion that builds Chartres and invents Lear is a pretty good thing" (320). I have been stimulated by Irwin's study, in which the desire for immortality implicit in the idea of self-doubling is one subtheme of his argument. I wish to take admiring exception to this argument by emphasizing the accommodations of reading which stand in dialectical complementarity and opposition to the kind of Faulknerian self-creation, reproduction from within, with which Irwin is concerned (see esp. 159, 165).

For other discussions of the No, see Korenman and Hamblin. For a superabundant collection of data on Faulkner's lifelong concern with death, see Stock. On the general subject of death, I have found Becker, Bataille, and Kucich instructive and suggestive. More particular debts are noted later.

5. For Faulkner's association of his immortality with the fate of the human race, see Grimwood.

CHAPTER 1: Reading and Performance

1. Culler, *Pursuit,* chap. 1. Such predications of the reader's active interpretation appear, e.g., in Holland, Iser, and Rosenblatt. Rosenblatt is distinctive in her concern for broader ranges of the reading experience than the interpretive. Yet for Rosenblatt, as for Bleich, Fish, Jauss, and all other theorists with whom I am familiar, interpretation or some kind of understanding is still considered the end toward which the whole reading experience tends. For the same reason, from the present perspective, the difference between hermeneutics and "antihermeneutics" is neglible.

2. To my concern for voice, or the speaking or performing of texts, cf. Shattuck, Wesling, Hartman, Ong, Bump, and Steiner, " 'Critic'/'Reader' " 450.

Wesling's formulation is representative of a distinction it seems many want to make: "What needed to be destroyed was the idea of original orality, and we must be grateful to Derrida for the immensity of that demonstration. . . . Nevertheless, Derrida's technical-philosophical account of writing should not itself become one of the factors which represses voice. . . . [I]t could be used to justify a fierce restriction of the scope of literature and literary study. To avoid such restriction, we need more explanation of the ways in which Derridian unwritable and unreadable literature remains literature and remains teachable" (77).

3. Besides Gibson and Booth, another well-known study also tangential to my argument is Ong's "The Writer's Audience Is Always a Fiction" in *Interfaces.* For relevant feminist studies see, e.g., Fetterley and Brownstein.

4. See, e.g., Marcus, Chodorow, Flax, the essays by Marianne Hirsch, Ronnie Scharfman, and Alice Jardine in *Feminist Readings,* and in anthropology, Weiner, especially the concluding chapter on the precariousness of "men's attempt to achieve individual immortality . . . [though] an imitation of women's control over the regenesis of human life" (233).

5. For a significant step in this direction, see Smith.

6. See esp. 43–83 and the following chapters: "Ritual and Social Change: A Javanese Example," "Person, Time, and Conduct in Bali," and "Deep Play: Notes on the Balinese Cockfight." For the concordant views of an evolutionary geneticist, a neurobiologist, and a psychologist, see Lewontin et al., *Not in Our Genes.*

7. The borrowing back has been proceeding for some time, but the reexpansion by criticism has been much less observable. An adequate understanding of reading can both do justice to its subject and perhaps repay an interdisciplinary

debt by focusing on interactive persons in a way that social science studies of culture and personality have found difficult to do.

The concept of repaying the debt comes from T. Walter Herbert's work in progress. I have also been stimulated by the adaptation of Kenneth Burke under way in Robert Wess's study of "the human subject," as indicated in his propaedeutic "Notes."

For a wide-ranging psychosocial study of the centrality of dialogical imitation in forming infants into persons, see Kaye, esp. 115–16. A survey of the large, varied, but still nascent field of culture/society and personality would also include Triandis and Lambert, Benedict, Levine, Landfield and Leitner, Williams, Althusser, E. P. Thompson, Gouldner, Jameson, Goffman, Ong, Booth (*Modern Dogma*), Greenblatt, Darnton, and Peacock.

8. See, e.g., Wadlington, "Godly Gamesomeness," and Wadlington and Stephenson for earlier efforts along these lines.

9. For the early "captive" reader's attempt to personally evaluate and resist certain reader's roles, and so consequently "misread," during the school-learning process, see Bettelheim and Zelan, 64–264.

10. Particular attention should be paid to the textual score, the sounds of an enactable language, as a distinctively human invitation to a capacitating exercise and a basic means of assimilating others as voices. At all levels of schooling, the view that it is merely old-fashioned "aestheticism" to read aloud and educate the ear and voice has deafened and silenced a generation and more of readers. This view developed partly from the overzealous simplification of an influential study early in this century recommending more attention to teaching silent reading in the middle grades to improve comprehension. It ended the opposite oversimplifications involved in the McGuffey's readers emphasis on recitation, which dominated in American schooling for approximately forty years, until 1920. See Chall, 165n, 194n, 1–52, 200–262, 282–87. On the other hand, Bettelheim and Zelan also suggest some of the difficulty in having young students read aloud as a reflection of "comprehension" alone (96–103).

CHAPTER 2: Faulkner and the Tragic Potentials of Honor and Shame

1. Cf. Pitt-Rivers, *Fate,* chap. 1, on the "sacredness" of honor.

2. See Else 76–77, 222. A long-standing theme of scholarship is the ambiguity in such honor-related terms between, on the one hand, intrinsic excellence and virtue and, on the other, reputation and social status. This ambiguity is one of a nested set of issues concerning honor-shame and the heroic that I have found most instructively discussed in the following treatments of Greek, Elizabethan, American southern, and other cultures: Dodds (*Greeks*), Adkins, Lloyd-Jones (esp. 15–27), Pitt-Rivers ("Honor" and *Fate*), Peristiany, Redfield, Nagy, Wyatt-Brown, and Whigham. In my discussion of the honor code and tragedy, I draw the implications of, e.g., Adkins's and Lloyd-Jones's concurrence that

Dodds oversimplified matters in his famous second chapter, "From Shame to Guilt," since the Greek shame culture remained vigorous long after the fifth century and persisted in tension with guilt culture.

3. See Pitt-Rivers, "Honor" 503–4. On Renaissance courtly performance, see Rebhorn, and Whigham 32ff.; e.g., 45: "[Count Annibale] Romei notes that 'though it be in our power, to make our selues worthy of honor, yet it is not in our power to receiue or possesse it: seeing through the ingratitude or ignorance of them, in whose hands iust distribution lieth, we are oft times deceiued. . . . if the vertuous man haue not Fortune for his companion, he cannot haue possession of honor: . . . vertue without fortune, is of it selfe vnto it insufficient.' . . . At least the public sort of virtue known as 'estimation' . . . is radically dependent on the eye and voice of the audience."

In a sense, there is some truth to Howe's idea that Faulkner shifts his emphasis from honor to integrity during his career (146–53). But this is much too simple a division, as Howe presents it. Howe notes, for example, that integrity is shown in the key dramatic gestures by which the Faulkner character "declares himself," in opposition to the burden of his life. Nothing, however, could be more indicative of the honor code than such displays, which announce *soy quien soy,* or, in the words of *Pylon,* "I am I." It is noteworthy too that *Intruder in the Dust* (1948) modifies the famous formula to read "the catharsis of pity and shame."

4. See Bezzerides for an account, humorously retrospective, of one reader's outraged and fascinated encounter with Faulkner's work.

In general terms, what has happened is the onset of "monumentalization" or the interference of (literary) honorific *status* with an important element of the hero's *claim* to honor. This is an aspect of the transactive doubleness of honor.

5. See Burke, *Rhetoric,* 131: The "ways of competition have been . . . zealous ways of *conformity*. . . . [W]hat we call 'competition' is better described as men's attempt to *out-imitate* one another." Whigham (78–79) cites this passage, accurately pinpoints the "coincidence of struggle and assimilation" in such cases, and quotes the *Oxford English Dictionary* on the close relationship between *emulate* and *rival*. Cf. Adamowski, "Children," on the psychological principle of identification with the aggressor and on Sartre's notion of shame.

CHAPTER 3: A Logic of Tragedy

1. In her review (6–7), Evelyn Scott apparently made the connection immediately between Krutch's *The Modern Temper* and Faulkner's novel.

Two likely sources for Faulkner's probable familiarity with the debate over modern tragedy were his affiliation with the knowledgeable *Double Dealer* circle in New Orleans and Ludwig Lewisohn's *A Modern Book of Criticism,* which he owned dating from this period. See esp. the articles in *Double Dealer* by Julius Weis Friend and Joseph T. Shipley. For an attack on traditional critical narrowness, and particularly on the New Humanists in the Lewisohn anthology, see

Lewisohn's Introduction and "A Note on Tragedy" and Johannes Volkelt's "The Philosophical Implications of Tragedy."

For Faulkner's ambivalence at the limits put on great art by the modern situation and audience, see "On Criticism" (originally published in *Double Dealer*, 1925) in *Early Prose and Poetry*. Representative views of Faulkner's tragedy in relation to modernism are found in Brooks (*Yoknapatawpha*), Longley, and Kartiganer (*Fragile Thread*).

2. Arnold is explaining why he has eliminated, as not truly tragic, his "Empedocles on Etna" from this edition. For a searching examination of tragedy and the political dimensions of the competing claims of action in nineteenth-century England, see Farrell. For the problem of passivity in modern fiction, including *Light in August*, see Kaplan.

3. A. C. Bradley was probably the most influential contemporary proponent of action as the distinctive mark of tragedy (e.g., *Shakespearean Tragedy*, 1904). Cf. T. S. Eliot's complaint (c. 1919) that Hamlet's passivity and excessive emotion made "a subject of study for pathologists" (126).

Although the tragedy/pathos distinction is commonplace, the latter mode is rarely examined; one such discussion is my "Pathos and Dreiser," which in a somewhat different form extends my present comments, though the discussion is limited by my then ahistorical view of the subject. See also Kaufmann 197–322 and, on the general extensive topos of "agent and patient," Crampton 1–44.

4. For other attempts to define the special tragic status of the novel, see Lawrance Thompson and Mellard.

We are concerned here, it should be noted, with the open-endedness of the novel at the level of represented action, the level relevant to tragedy traditionally conceived. The discussion of closure in contemporary criticism, especially since Kermode's *Sense of an Ending*, offers critics an enhanced awareness of several ways in which a text may be resolved. See Kartiganer, *Fragile Thread*, 190n for useful references to the critical discussion of this subject in *The Sound and the Fury*.

5. As Ong notes, in a totally binary orientation, the proper distinction disappears between a two-*value* system (true versus false) and the two-*place* order of dichotomy (*Ramus* 210).

6. Slatoff's stimulating treatment of contradiction partly misrepresents its subject by overlooking its tragic thematic implications. Slatoff stresses Faulkner's temperamental ambivalence as the source of his fondness for oxymoron and paradox, but I see in these both an inclination to dichotomous thought and a rhetorical corrective to it, a condensed form of the dynamic at work in the novel as a whole.

7. Cf. also Irwin's stress on Quentin's active willing of passivity, associated with Faulkner's art (164 and passim), and see Faulkner's Fairchild on the passive state of creativity (*Mosquitoes* 339) and Faulkner on language as action (*Early Prose and Poetry* 96).

8. Cf. Lloyd's *Polarity* and Ong's extension of it in, e.g., *Fighting for Life*.

Notes

9. For discussions of emotion in this novel, see Wall and Weinstein.

10. For the contrary view that Quentin completely shares his father's Stoic philosophy, see Brooks, *Yoknapatawpha, 344* and Hunt 50.

11. See Solomon for a discussion of the passions as judgments of self-esteem. Cf. Aristotle on the passions as judgments, as noted by Else with specific regard to tragedy, 433 and passim.

12. Again, I part company with the critics who have helped me to understand sound and voice in this novel over their conception that the text remains muted because the reader does not speak it. See Lilly, Ross ("Loud World"), Bleikasten (*Splendid Failure* 189–91), and Zender.

On the related topic of Quentin's theatricality, see, e.g., Bleikasten 141–42 and Kartiganer, "Quentin Compson," 381–94; both critics interpret Quentin's tendency to self-performance as if it were a pointless aesthetic and "formalist" end in itself. I wish to stress, on the contrary, the profoundly audience-oriented impulse in such enactment.

For helpful discussions directly or indirectly bearing on Faulkner's indebtedness to the rhetoric of the oral sermon, see the articles by Rosenberg.

13. Cavell, "Knowing and Acknowledging" and "The Avoidance of Love: A Reading of *King Lear*" in *Must We Mean,* and "Between Acknowledgment and Avoidance" in *Claim.*

14. Sundquist also raises this last objection as one of several charges he makes against the novel. Cf. Bleikasten 194–206.

15. The most sweeping version of Faulkner's idea of reciprocating completion is his statement that God created the world so that man must complete it (*Essays, Speeches* 135).

16. As Robert Hamblin (4n) points out, an almost identical phrase, "saying No to time," appears in Faulkner's writing as early as 1925, in the unfinished manuscript of "Elmer."

CHAPTER 4: Voice as Hero

1. On death ritual or ritual alone, the following have been most helpful: Malinowski, Geertz (esp. "Religion as a Cultural System" and "Ritual and Social Change"), Turner, Huntington and Metcalf, Bloch and Parry, Humphreys and King, Ariès, Hardin, Moore and Myerhoff, and Grimes. For an alternative view of this novel within Faulkner's career, see Stonum.

2. See Adamowski, "Faulkner's Popeye," for a discussion of Popeye's life strategy as an "Actor."

3. Bedient's impressive essay on pride and nakedness has stimulated my tracing of a set of similarly competing impulses.

4. See Ross; Broughton, "Cubist Novels"; and Toles for fuller, different discussions of visual effects and analogues. Another, more sophisticated distraction, or complication, to the performance I highlight here is indicated by questions about vocal authority, as in Ross's essay on this novel or Barthes' well-

known commentary on Balzac's "Sarrasine": "A multivalent text can carry out its basic duplicity only if it subverts the opposition between true and false; if it fails to attribute quotations (even when seeking to discredit them) to explicit authorities, if it flouts all respect for origin, paternity, propriety, if it destroys the voice which could give the text its ('organic') unity, in short, if it coldly and fraudulently abolishes quotation marks which must, as we say, in all *honesty,* enclose a quotation and juridically distribute the ownership of the sentences. . . . The wall of voices must be passed through to reach the writing: this latter eschews any designation of ownership and thus can never be *ironic;* or, at least, its irony is never certain" (*S/Z* 44–45).

Or in a more Bakhtinian perspective closer to our present approach, we may take the "struggle" of the several voices as more salient than their mutual accommodation. My point, to repeat, is, first, that such *taking* on our part has a person-constituting character encompassing the epistemological sense wherein perceptually/cognitively we take something to mean or be something (see Chapters 1 and 2). And second, we may always take the conflict of voices or the question of exact responsibility for particular utterances (as esp. in *Absalom*) to be salient matters that (may) distract us from performing them *as* mutually accommodating with our voice. I am saying that such possibilities are necessary accompanying potential "liabilities" to the particular performance we are discussing.

Along these same lines, we must recall the important distinction between an improvisation like Faulkner's and an existing institution like a confirmed communal narrative or public ritual—more specifically, the religious ritual that in Faulkner's time was thought to be the source of tragedy, which did accompany its classical Greek performance. Previous critical applications of the term *ritualistic* to this novel or to Faulkner's writing, besides overlooking the performative potentials we examine here, err most in missing the optional character of reading accommodation inherent in Faulkner's technique, so that like one early discoverer of ritual effect, Claude-Edmonde Magny, they present a Faulkner who casts what she called a "sacred spell" (71), instead of seeing this spell as one indicated possibility hedged about by its enabling "profanations."

CHAPTER 5: Rest in Peace

1. Another principle of simplification, dichotomy, which we have consistently treated thus far, is so often remarked in this novel that it needs little further discussion here. The novel represents a world literally and figuratively of black and white as Faulkner for the first time fully exploits the racial implications of the cultural mapping of everything into segregated realms. The starkness of the design is illuminated chiefly by introducing a perceived racial anomaly, Joe Christmas, who cannot be categorized by dichotomy, who is imbued with its mental habits, and who struggles internally and externally against it. In his discussion of black-white dualism, Kartiganer unduly neglects the last two features of Joe's psychology in describing him as a tragic hero in Nietzschean terms.

Notes

2. Chase's 1948 article established a pattern in some ways useful, in some ways unfortunate, of sorting all circular and curved images together and treating them in the aggregate, contrasted to a "linearity" seen as simply "modern."

3. In addition to Geertz, I draw upon Lee's discussion of the Trobriands. Cf. Brooks's discussion of Faulkner, time, and history (*Toward Yoknapatawpha* 251–82), where Brooks comments on a passage in *Wild Palms:* "When we become aware of ourselves and of reality, 'time begins,' and is immediately sensed as 'retroactive'; time can only be conceived of as a current flowing *from* somewhere *to* somewhere." For a general discussion that approaches Faulkner and "social time" differently from mine, see Kort. Martin's psychoanalytic treatment of "present time," "changing time," orality, and Faulkner's relation to women generally corroborates some of the points I make in this chapter. My concern here is mainly with spatiotemporal cultural maps as they function in this novel. I am not addressing, except in a limited and suggestive way, the general question of Faulkner and time considered by Brooks and Kort.

4. As I noted in the Introduction, the anthropological study of non-Western arrangements of life has had an appreciable impact on the study of Western cultures both present and historical, partly by highlighting such culturally recessive or vestigial and more diffuse features as we are concerned with here.

5. Among the more recent useful discussions of "immobility," see Pitavy (56–84) on the novel's characters.

6. I am indebted to Broughton's discussion of Joe's rejection of healthy forms of receptiveness and passivity (*Abstract* 97–98). I have also found suggestive Kartiganer's idea that Christmas at once obeys and enlarges an inherited "externally conceived plot" (*Fragile Thread* 42); my development of the idea, however, differs from Kartiganer's on many points.

7. To reflect fully on the rhetorical impact of this passage, it is necessary to recall the order of reading events that build toward and away from Joe's death scene, besides the often-remarked sympathetic appeal constituted by his grandmother's account of his birth. Joe's is one of three experiences in sequence, involving in turn Byron Bunch, Christmas, and Hightower, which illuminate each other by comparison and contrast. First, Byron, believing he must abandon Lena in favor of Lucas Burch, becomes Quentin Compson revisited—but revisited with a sympathetically comic eye. Byron imagines with some relief that he and his mule will ride off a hill into nothingness and burn up like a meteor. On a similarly grand scale, he then imagines that the trees around him make up an indifferent audience who doubt his personal identity and the reality or significance of his pain. Byron rapidly traverses the outskirts of tragedy as he sees Lucas Burch's toylike figure fleeing far below, and a wind "at once violent and peaceful" blows away all Byron's despair and "tragic and vain imagining" (712–13). Byron immediately pursues Lucas, who beats him into temporary peacefulness once more.

This incident of Byron's flirtation with tragedy in Chapter 18 is a comic condensation of the elements of Faulknerian tragedy as we have traced them so far. It compactly draws together the threads of the long, complex series of events

236

preceding and, by this compact reminder, as well as its contrast in tone, prepares us for Joe's tragic death. Subsequently, Byron completes the abandonment of his previous strategy of a Hightower-like peaceful retirement from the world, in favor of a paradoxical disquietude in taking to the road after Lena and the serenity she embodies. It is significant for Faulkner's rhetorical strategy that Byron's actions here are irreducibly amusing in Faulkner's treatment. Faulkner presents Byron as the admirably decent, level-headed, cautious man who is amusingly victimized by not-quite-requited love, and in the last chapter he plays up Byron's comic predicament to help create the closing emphasis on good-natured amusement.

If Joe's catharsis is distinguished from Byron's in that the latter is fundamentally comic and transitory, its most significant features are equally underscored by contrast to the more equivocal status of Hightower's experience at the close of Chapter 20. For all the painful demystification to which Hightower at last wins, including his perhaps excessive debunking of the grandfather as but a "bravo" (760), the phantoms who provide the minister with his life-sustaining drama cannot be exorcised. His still-recurrent vision of the cavalry raid brings his catharsis to a climax by returning him to a drama retaining life-giving honor (763), and it is too much to expect that he would free himself so quickly from this script, if he ever does. But the result is a catharsis with which the reader to a degree is prompted to empathize, without fully undergoing a similar release. That is, Faulkner renders the vision in empathetically sonorous prose, but Hightower's escape to his private myth is as disappointing as it is understandable and pitiable. His artificial "memory" of the raid (even with the bravado of the henhouse death elided) suggests how much Hightower is still caught in an isolating, ruinous escapism as a preventative against inadmissible knowledge and as a symbolic action of life-sustaining pride. It therefore invites in us a state of lingering emotional irresolution, particularly emphasized by the contrasting ending of the preceding chapter, portraying Christmas's death, as well as the final comic relaxation of the subsequent, concluding chapter.

The usefulness of Carole Anne Taylor's solid essay on "tragic paradox" in Bunch, Christmas, and Hightower is limited by facile connections drawn between Byron and Joe and by an unsuccessful attempt to connect her epistemological concerns to Cavell's insights into tragedy and acknowledgment. On the latter, cf. my earlier discussion of *The Sound and the Fury*.

8. E.g., *Mosquitoes* 250, *Early Prose and Poetry* 93. Cf. Martin.

9. See Oates for something like this reaction.

CHAPTER 6: The House of *Absalom, Absalom!*

1. The best, that is, except for those works in which the killing is actually averted by last-minute recognition of another's identity, which Aristotle rates best of all. (There is an often-noted discrepancy between this preference and Aristotle's general insistence that the best tragedy ends in the hero's misfortune.)

Notes

I have presented here a variation of Else's view of Aristotelian catharsis and knowledge by reintroducing catharsis for the audience, in accordance with the usual view of what Aristotle meant. Else, *Poetics*, 423–50 and passim.

2. As Brooks, e.g., has noted (304), Judith's acknowledgment of Bon's son repudiates Sutpen's design. We will be concerned here with the other, subtler symbolic actions that perform—and script for us—the daughter's No to Sutpen's No to death.

3. If we read *Absalom* with *The Sound and the Fury*, it is noteworthy that Judith in this scene is the creation of Mr. Compson, a father whose own daughter undid him and his family, so that Judith's letter transmittal is as it were the sublimation into stoic symbolic action of a sexual "pollution" Caddy was perceived to have visited upon her family's honor. The related fact is that Judith's description of personal entanglement reflects Mr. Compson's perspective on his own times rather than his compensatory view that her era was populated by heroic uninvolved integers.

Robbins discusses the narrators' monological imposition of speech on others and briefly relates this to Judith's actions here, but Robbins scants the reciprocal features of speech.

Matthews's stress on the "marriage" of collaborative storytelling and the "personal, affective 'truth'" of Mr. Compson's and the other narrators' stories (118–61) provides an often persuasive complement to Robbins and to Irwin's emphasis on conflict between generations. What needs to be understood, however, is that the myriad forms of marriage and struggle, merger and division, are mutually entailed and that they are fundamental constituents of empowering in Faulkner's world and his rhetoric.

4. Ross's deconstruction of *Absalom* depends on first establishing that evocation of the past is the novel's aim and article of faith, the source of its cognitive value. Ross points out that the novel repeatedly suggests that evocation depends on both the foregrounding of voice and the "vanishing" of voice. He is able to show, however, that voice never vanishes, primarily because the "narrative voice is too rich" to disappear (143). Thus evocation is rendered dubious. But Ross's whole argument really depends above all on the elimination of the speaking reader in the first place: "Voice . . . in a written document can only be figurative" (137). That is, in effect he must assume a silent eye-reader. But it matters a great deal if a reader takes the large hint from the novel and reads aloud. In this case, voice does vanish in the sense that it often does for the characters: "listening reneges"—"physical" listening by a speaker/listener who has first made an effort to sustain a performance of narrative voice and share its tonic power. Second, as I have been arguing, evocation by itself is not the point.

5. The matter of course can be clarified by transferring, as do Irwin and Matthews, Quentin's "incestuous" preoccupations from *The Sound and the Fury* to *Absalom*. Kartiganer (*Fragile Thread* 195–96 and "Quentin Compson") makes some thoughtful objections to this transfer. But the value of discussing the novels together on these and related terms is, I think, well illustrated by Matthews's explanations of how the narrators both express themselves and address the con-

cerns of their audiences. See also Kartiganer's chapter on *Absalom* for an insightful analysis of Mr. Compson's symbolic action of narration so as to exonerate himself for his life of inaction. Kartiganer, however, does not weigh the implications of the fact that this life of inaction is only clear in the earlier novel, not in *Absalom,* which stresses instead the father's gently sardonic, pessimistic tone, which is compatible with or a counterpart to inaction. Something similar may be said of the earlier and later versions of Quentin.

Although I concentrate on *Absalom* here, reading the novels together is simply another option that Faulkner provides his readers, the two novels presenting us with versions of Quentin as *Absalom* presents us with (much more diverse) versions of Sutpen. We are in fact tracing certain key continuities in these versions of Quentin in terms of what *Absalom* makes salient. It seems to me indisputable that Quentin's connection with incest is, to state it minimally, not at all salient in this later novel (e.g., it is not even mentioned that Quentin has a sister). If we do not attend to both continuity and particularity when we think of the novels together, it is tempting to let the gaudy subject of incest do our interpreting for us. Thus a failing of Irwin's important study is that his understanding of Quentin and incest in *The Sound and the Fury* is not adequately balanced against a sense of the particular issues concerning Quentin in *Absalom,* but simply overwhelms the latter novel.

The theme of incest is one way of dramatizing the logic of self-sufficient exclusiveness taken to its rigorous, disturbing conclusion. The obverse is the comparably disquieting assimilation of others ("miscegenation," figurative or literal) and the need for acknowledgment. These issues we consider at present under different but generally compatible rubrics from incest, which, as Faulkner might put it, is one of his tools, each with its own powers and limitations, to build his house. In *Absalom,* even curiouser tools than incest are linked to Quentin.

6. It seems likely that Faulkner's experience in writing for the movies in the thirties had some effect on his novelistic use of free transcriptive conventions, since literal cinematic scriptwriting typically consists of a sequence of revisions, elaborations, and adaptations by collaborators ranging from, say, the original novelist through the various writers of "treatments" and scripts to the director and the actors, who sometimes change the dialogue.

7. Cf. Guerard, "Innovator," 74–75, and *Triumph* 323.

Works Cited

Adamowski, T. H. "Children of the Idea: Heroes and Family Romances in *Absalom, Absalom!*" *Mosaic* 10 (1976): 115–37.
———. "Faulkner's Popeye: The 'Other' as Self." *Canadian Review of American Studies* 8 (1977): 36–51.
Adkins, Arthur W. H. *Merit and Responsibility: A Study in Greek Values*. London: Oxford University Press, 1960.
Althusser, Louis. *Lenin and Philosophy, and Other Essays*. Trans. Ben Brewster. London: New Left Books, 1971.
Ariès, Philippe. *The Hour of Our Death*. Trans. Helen Weaver. New York: Knopf, 1981.
———. *Western Attitudes toward Death: From the Middle Ages to the Present*. Trans. Patricia M. Ranum. Baltimore: Johns Hopkins University Press, 1974.
Arnold, Matthew. *The Portable Matthew Arnold*. Ed. Lionel Trilling. New York: Viking, 1966.
Austin, J. L. *How to Do Things with Words*. Cambridge: Harvard University Press, 1975.
Bakhtin, Mikhail. *The Dialogic Imagination: Four Essays by M. M. Bakhtin*. Ed. Michael Holquist. Trans. Caryl Emerson and Michael Holquist. Austin: University of Texas Press, 1981.
———. *Problems of Dostoevsky's Poetics*. Ed. and trans. Caryl Emerson. Minneapolis: University of Minnesota Press, 1984.
Bakhtin, Mikhail / V. N. Vološinov. *Marxism and the Philosophy of Language*. Trans. Ladislav Matejka and I. R. Titunik. Cambridge: Harvard University Press, 1986.
Barthes, Roland. *The Pleasure of the Text*. Trans. Richard Miller. New York: Hill and Wang, 1975.
———. *S/Z*. New York: Hill and Wang, 1974.
Bataille, Georges. *Death and Sensuality*. New York: Walker, 1962.
Becker, Ernest. *The Denial of Death*. New York: Free Press, 1973.

Works Cited

Bedient, Calvin. "Pride and Nakedness: *As I Lay Dying.*" *Modern Language Quarterly* 29 (1968): 61–76.

Benedict, Ruth. *Patterns of Culture.* New York: Houghton Mifflin, 1934.

Bettelheim, Bruno, and Karen Zelan. *On Learning to Read: The Child's Fascination with Meaning.* New York: Knopf, 1982.

Bezzerides, A. I. Preface to *William Faulkner: A Life on Paper.* Ed. Ann Abadie. Jackson: University Press of Mississippi, 1980.

Bleich, David. *Subjective Criticism.* Baltimore: Johns Hopkins University Press, 1978.

Bleikasten, André. *Faulkner's "As I Lay Dying."* Rev. ed. Trans. Roger Little. Bloomington: Indiana University Press, 1973.

——. *The Most Splendid Failure: Faulkner's "The Sound and the Fury."* Bloomington: Indiana University Press, 1976.

Bloch, Maurice, and Jonathan Parry, eds. *Death and the Regeneration of Life.* Cambridge: Cambridge University Press, 1982.

Blotner, Joseph. *Faulkner: A Biography.* 2 vols. New York: Random House, 1974.

——. "William Faulkner's Essay on the Composition of *Sartoris.*" *Yale University Library Gazette* 47 (1973): 121–24.

——. *William Faulkner's Library: A Catalogue.* Charlottesville: University Press of Virginia, 1964.

Boose, Lynda E. "An Approach through Theme: Marriage and the Family." In *Approaches to Teaching Shakespeare's "King Lear."* Ed. Robert Ray. New York: Modern Language Association of America, 1986, pp. 59–68.

Booth, Stephen. *King Lear, Macbeth, Indefinition, and Tragedy.* New Haven: Yale University Press, 1983.

Booth, Wayne C. *Modern Dogma and the Rhetoric of Assent.* Chicago: University of Chicago Press, 1974.

——. *The Rhetoric of Fiction.* 2d ed. Chicago: University of Chicago Press, 1983.

Bradley, A. C. *Shakespearean Tragedy.* 1904; rpt. New York: Meridian, 1955.

Bremer, J. M. *Hamartia: Tragic Error in the Poetics of Aristotle and in Greek Tragedy.* Amsterdam: Adolf M. Hakkert, 1969.

Brodhead, Richard H., ed. *Faulkner: New Perspectives.* Englewood Cliffs: Prentice-Hall, 1983.

Brooks, Cleanth. *William Faulkner: The Yoknapatawpha Country.* New Haven: Yale University Press, 1963.

——. *William Faulkner: Toward Yoknapatawpha and Beyond.* New Haven: Yale University Press, 1978.

Broughton, Panthea Reid. "Faulkner's Cubist Novels." In *"A Cosmos of My Own."* Ed. Doreen Fowler and Ann J. Abadie. Jackson: University Press of Mississippi, 1981, pp. 59–94.

——. *William Faulkner: The Abstract and the Actual.* Baton Rouge: Louisiana State University Press, 1974.

Brownstein, Rachel M. *Becoming a Heroine: Reading about Women in Novels.* New York: Viking, 1982.

Bruns, Gerald K. *Inventions: Writing, Textuality, and Understanding in Literary History*. New Haven: Yale University Press, 1982.

———. "Structuralism, Deconstruction, and Hermeneutics." *Diacritics* 14 (1984): 12–23.

Bump, Jerome. "Reading Hopkins: Visual vs. Auditory Paradigms." In *Literature, Arts, and Religion*. Ed. Harry R. Garvin. Lewisburg, Pa.: Bucknell University Press, 1982.

Burke, Kenneth. *Attitudes toward History*. 3d ed. Berkeley: University of California Press, 1984.

———. *Language as Symbolic Action: Essays on Life, Literature and Method*. Berkeley: University of California Press, 1968.

———. *The Philosophy of Literary Form*. Rev. ed. New York: Vintage, 1957.

Castle, Terry. *Clarissa's Ciphers: Meaning and Disruption in Richardson's "Clarissa."* Ithaca: Cornell University Press, 1982.

Cavell, Stanley. *The Claim of Reason: Wittgenstein, Skepticism, Morality, and Tragedy*. New York: Oxford University Press, 1979.

———. *Must We Mean What We Say?* New York: Charles Scribner's Sons, 1969.

Chall, Jeanne S. *Learning to Read: The Great Debate*. Updated ed. New York: McGraw-Hill, 1983.

Chase, Richard. "The Stone and the Crucifixion: Faulkner's *Light in August*." *Kenyon Review* 10 (1949): 539–51.

Chodorow, Nancy. *The Reproduction of Mothering*. Berkeley: University of California Press, 1978.

Crampton, Georgia Renan. *The Condition of Creatures: Suffering and Action in Chaucer and Spenser*. New Haven: Yale University Press, 1974.

Culler, Jonathan. *On Deconstruction: Theory and Criticism after Structuralism*. Ithaca: Cornell University Press, 1982.

———. *The Pursuit of Signs: Semiotics, Literature, Deconstruction*. Ithaca: Cornell University Press, 1981.

———. *Structuralist Poetics: Structuralism, Linguistics, and the Study of Literature*. Ithaca: Cornell University Press, 1975.

Darnton, Robert. *The Great Cat Massacre and Other Episodes in French Cultural History*. New York: Basic Books, 1984.

De Man, Paul. *Allegories of Reading: Figural Language in Rousseau, Nietzsche, Rilke, and Proust*. New Haven: Yale University Press, 1979.

———. Foreword to *The Dissimulating Harmony*. By Carol Jacobs. Baltimore: Johns Hopkins University Press, 1978, pp. vii–xiii.

Derrida, Jacques. *Dissemination*. Chicago: University of Chicago Press, 1982.

Dodds, E. R. *The Greeks and the Irrational*. 1951; rpt. Berkeley: University of California Press, 1971.

———. "On Misunderstanding the *Oedipus Rex*." *Greece and Rome* 13 (1966): 37–49. Rpt. in *Greek Tragedy: Modern Essays in Criticism*. Ed. Erich Segal. New York: Harper and Row, 1983.

Eliot, George. *Middlemarch*. Boston: Houghton Mifflin, 1965.

Eliot, T. S. *Selected Essays*. New York: Harcourt, 1950.

Works Cited

Else, Gerald F. *Aristotle's 'Poetics': The Argument*. Cambridge: Harvard University Press, 1957.

Faber, M. D. "Faulkner's *The Sound and the Fury:* Object Relations and Narrative Structure." *American Imago* 34 (1977): 327–50.

Fadiman, Clifton. "Faulkner, Extra-Special, Double-Distilled." *New Yorker,* 31 Oct. 1936, pp. 62–64.

Farrell, John P. *Revolution as Tragedy: The Dilemma of the Moderate from Scott to Arnold*. Ithaca: Cornell University Press, 1980.

Faulkner, William. *Absalom, Absalom!* New York: Modern Library, 1966.

———. *As I Lay Dying*. In *William Faulkner: Novels, 1930–1935*. New York: Library of America, 1985.

———. *Early Prose and Poetry*. Ed. Carvel Collins. Boston: Little, Brown, 1962.

———. *Essays, Speeches & Public Letters*. Ed. James B. Meriwether. New York: Random House, 1966.

———. *A Fable*. New York: Random House, 1954.

———. *Faulkner in the University: Class Conferences at the University of Virginia, 1957–58*. Ed. Frederick L. Gwynn and Joseph L. Blotner. Charlottesville: University Press of Virginia, 1978.

———. *A Faulkner Miscellany*. Ed. James B. Meriwether. Jackson: University Press of Mississippi, 1974.

———. *Flags in the Dust*. New York: Vintage, 1974.

———. *Helen: A Courtship*. New Orleans and Oxford, Miss.: Tulane University and Yoknapatawpha Press, 1981.

———. "An Introduction for *The Sound and the Fury*." Rpt. *The Southern Review* 8 n.s. (1972): 705–10.

———. *Knight's Gambit*. New York: Random House, 1949.

———. *Light in August*. In *William Faulkner: Novels, 1930–1935*. New York: Library of America, 1985.

———. *Lion in the Garden: Interviews with William Faulkner, 1926–1962*. Ed. James B. Meriwether and Michael Millgate. Lincoln: University of Nebraska Press, 1980.

———. *Mayday*. Notre Dame: University of Notre Dame Press, 1980.

———. *Mosquitoes*. New York: Liveright, 1951.

———. *Pylon*. In *William Faulkner: Novels, 1930–1935*. New York: Library of America, 1985.

———. *Requiem for a Nun*. New York: Random House, 1951.

———. *Sanctuary*. In *William Faulkner: Novels, 1930–1935*. New York: Library of America, 1985.

———. *Selected Letters*. Ed. Joseph Blotner. New York: Random House, 1977.

———. *Soldiers' Pay*. New York: Liveright, 1970.

———. *The Sound and the Fury*. New York: Random House, 1984.

———. *William Faulkner Reads from His Novels*. Listening Library, CX 336.

———. *William Faulkner Reads the Nobel Prize Acceptance Speech and Selections from "As I Lay Dying," "A Fable," "The Old Man."* Caedmon, TC 1035.

Feminist Readings: French Texts/American Contexts. Yale French Studies 62 (1981).

Works Cited

Fetterley, Judith. *The Resisting Reader: A Feminist Approach to American Fiction.* Bloomington: Indiana University Press, 1977.

Fish, Stanley E. *Is There a Text in This Class?* Cambridge: Harvard University Press, 1980.

Flax, Jane. "Mother-Daughter Relationships: Psycho-Dynamics, Politics, and Philosophy." In *The Future of Difference.* Ed. Hester Eisenstein and Alice Jardine. Boston: G. K. Hall, 1980, pp. 20–40.

Fowler, Alastair. *Kinds of Literature: An Introduction to the Theory of Genres and Modes.* Cambridge: Harvard University Press, 1982.

Friend, Julius Weis. "Joseph Conrad: An Appreciation." *Double Dealer* 7 (1924): 3–5.

Gallie, W. B. *Philosophy and the Historical Understanding.* 2d ed. New York: Schocken, 1968.

Geertz, Clifford. *The Interpretation of Cultures.* New York: Harper, 1973.

Gibson, Walker. "Authors, Speakers, Readers, and Mock Readers." In *Reader-Response Criticism: From Formalism to Post-Structuralism.* Ed. Jane P. Tompkins. Baltimore: Johns Hopkins University Press, 1980, pp. 1–6.

Girard, René. *Violence and the Sacred.* Trans. Patrick Gregory. Baltimore: Johns Hopkins University Press, 1977.

Goffman, Erving. *Interaction Ritual: Essays on Face-to-Face Behavior.* Garden City: Doubleday, 1967.

Goldmann, Lucien. *The Hidden God: A Study of Tragic Vision in the Pensées of Pascal and the Tragedies of Racine.* Trans. Philip Thody. New York: Humanities Press, 1964.

Gouldner, Alvin W. *The Dialectic of Ideology and Technology.* New York: Oxford University Press, 1976.

Graff, Gerald. *Literature against Itself: Literary Ideas in Modern Society.* Chicago: University of Chicago Press, 1979.

Greenblatt, Stephen. *Renaissance Self-Fashioning: From More to Shakespeare.* Chicago: University of Chicago Press, 1980.

Grimes, Ronald L. *Beginnings in Ritual Studies.* Washington, D.C.: University Press of America, 1982.

Grimwood, Michael. "The Self-Parodic Context of Faulkner's Nobel Prize Speech." *The Southern Review* 15 (1979): 366–75.

Guerard, Albert J. "The Faulknerian Voice." In *The Maker and the Myth: Faulkner and Yoknapatawpha 1977.* Ed. Evans Harrington and Ann J. Abadie. Jackson: University Press of Mississippi, 1978, pp. 25–42.

———. "Faulkner the Innovator." In *The Maker and the Myth: Faulkner and Yoknapatawpha 1977.* Ed. Evans Harrington and Ann J. Abadie. Jackson: University Press of Mississippi, 1978, pp. 71–88.

———. *The Triumph of the Novel: Dickens, Dostoevsky, Faulkner.* New York: Oxford University Press, 1976.

Hamblin, Robert W. "Saying No to Death: Toward William Faulkner's Theory of Fiction." In *"A Cosmos of My Own."* Ed. Doreen Fowler and Ann J. Abadie. Jackson: University Press of Mississippi, 1981, pp. 3–35.

Works Cited

Hardin, Richard F. " 'Ritual' in Recent Criticism: The Elusive Sense of Community." *PMLA* 98 (1983): 846–62.

Hartman, Geoffrey. *Saving the Text: Literature/Derrida/Philosophy.* Baltimore: Johns Hopkins University Press, 1981.

Holland, Norman. *5 Readers Reading.* New Haven: Yale University Press, 1975.

———. "Unity Identity Text Self." *PMLA* 90 (1975): 813–22.

Howe, Irving. *William Faulkner: A Critical Study.* 3d ed. Chicago: University of Chicago Press, 1975.

Humphries, S. C., and H. King, eds. *Mortality and Immortality.* London: Academic Press, 1981.

Hunt, John W. *William Faulkner: Art in Theological Tension.* Syracuse, N.Y.: Syracuse University Press, 1965.

Huntington, Richard, and Peter Metcalf. *Celebrations of Death: The Anthropology of Mortuary Ritual.* Cambridge: Cambridge University Press, 1979.

Ihde, Don. *Listening and Voice: A Phenomenology of Sound.* Athens: Ohio University Press, 1976.

Irwin, John T. *Doubling and Incest/Repetition and Revenge.* Baltimore: Johns Hopkins University Press, 1975.

Iser, Wolfgang. *The Act of Reading.* Baltimore: Johns Hopkins University Press, 1978.

Jameson, Fredric. *The Political Unconscious: Narrative as a Socially Symbolic Act.* Ithaca: Cornell University Press, 1981.

Jauss, Hans Robert. *Toward an Aesthetic of Reception.* Trans. Timothy Bahti. Minneapolis: University of Minnesota Press, 1982.

Jones, John. *On Aristotle and Greek Tragedy.* London: Chatto & Windus, 1962.

Kaplan, Harold J. *The Passive Voice.* Athens: Ohio University Press, 1966.

Kartiganer, Donald M. *The Fragile Thread: The Meaning of Form in Faulkner's Novels.* Amherst: University of Massachusetts Press, 1979.

———. "Quentin Compson and Faulkner's Drama of the Generations." In *Critical Essays on William Faulkner: The Compson Family.* Ed. Arthur F. Kinney. Boston: G. K. Hall, 1982.

Kaufmann, Walter. *Tragedy and Philosophy.* Garden City: Doubleday, 1968.

Kaye, Kenneth. *The Mental and Social Life of Babies: How Parents Create Persons.* Chicago: University of Chicago Press, 1982.

Kermode, Frank. *The Classic: Literary Images of Permanence and Change.* Cambridge: Harvard University Press, 1983.

———. *The Sense of an Ending.* New York: Oxford University Press, 1967.

Knox, Bernard M. W. *The Heroic Temper: Studies in Sophoclean Tragedy.* Berkeley: University of California Press, 1964.

Koelb, Clayton. "The Problem of Tragedy as a Genre." *Genre* 8 (1975): 248–66.

———. " 'Tragedy' and 'The Tragic': The Shakespearean Connection." *Genre* 13 (1980): 275–86.

———. " 'Tragedy' as an Evaluative Term." *Comparative Literature Studies* 11 (1974): 69–84.

Works Cited

Korenman, Joan S. "Faulkner and 'That Undying Mark.'" *Studies in American Fiction* 4 (1976): 81–91.

Kort, Wesley A. "Social Time in Faulkner's Fiction." *Arizona Quarterly* 37 (1981): 101–15.

Krutch, Joseph Wood. *The Modern Temper*. New York: Harcourt, Brace, 1929.

Kucich, John. "Death Worship among the Victorians: *The Old Curiosity Shop*." *PMLA* 95 (1980): 58–72.

Landfield, A. W., and L. M. Leitner, eds. *Personal Construct Psychology: Psychotherapy and Personality*. New York: Wiley, 1980.

Leaver, Florence. "Faulkner: The Word as Principle and Power." In *William Faulkner: Three Decades of Criticism*. Ed. Frederick J. Hoffman and Olga W. Vickery. New York: Harcourt, 1963, pp. 199–209.

Lee, Dorothy. *Freedom and Culture*. Englewood Cliffs: Prentice-Hall, 1962.

Leenhardt, Jacques. "Toward a Sociology of Reading." In *The Reader in the Text: Essays in Audience and Interpretation*. Ed. Susan Suleiman and Inge Crosman. Princeton: Princeton University Press, 1980, pp. 204–24.

Lenson, David. *Achilles' Choice: Examples of Modern Tragedy*. Princeton: Princeton University Press, 1975.

Levine, Robert A. *Culture, Behavior, and Personality*. 2d ed. New York: Aldine, 1982.

Lewisohn, Ludwig. *A Modern Book of Criticism*. New York: Boni and Liveright, 1919.

Lewontin, R. C., Steven Rose, and Leon J. Kamin. *Not in Our Genes: Biology, Ideology, and Human Nature*. New York: Pantheon, 1984.

Lilly, Paul R., Jr. "Caddy and Addie: Speakers of Faulkner's Impeccable Language." *Journal of Narrative Technique* 3 (1973): 170–82.

Lind, Ilse Dusoir. "The Design and Meaning of *Absalom, Absalom!*" *PMLA* 70 (1955): 887–912.

Lloyd, G. E. R. *Polarity and Analogy: Two Types of Argumentation in Early Greek Thought*. Cambridge: Cambridge University Press, 1966.

Lloyd-Jones, Hugh. *The Justice of Zeus*. 2d ed. Berkeley: University of California Press, 1983.

Longley, John L. *The Tragic Mask: A Study of Faulkner's Heroes*. Chapel Hill: University of North Carolina Press, 1963.

McHaney, Thomas L. *William Faulkner: A Reference Guide*. Boston: G. K. Hall, 1976.

Magny, Claude-Edmonde. "Faulkner or Theological Inversion." In *Faulkner: A Collection of Critical Essays*. Ed. Robert Penn Warren. Englewood Cliffs: Prentice-Hall, 1966, pp. 66–78.

Mailloux, Steven. *Interpretive Conventions: The Reader in the Study of American Fiction*. Ithaca: Cornell University Press, 1982.

Malinowski, Bronislaw. *Magic, Science and Religion*. Boston: Beacon Press, 1948.

Marcus, Jane. "Liberty, Sorority, Misogyny." In *The Representation of Women in Fiction*. Ed. Carolyn G. Heilburn and Margaret R. Higonnet. Baltimore: Johns Hopkins University Press, 1981, pp. 60–97.

247

Works Cited

Martin, Jay. "'The Whole Burden of Man's History of His Impossible Heart's Desire': The Early Life of William Faulkner." *American Literature* 53 (1982): 607–29.

Matthews, John T. *The Play of Faulkner's Language.* Ithaca: Cornell University Press, 1982.

Mead, George Herbert. *Mind, Self, and Society.* Chicago: University of Chicago Press, 1934.

Mellard, James M. "*The Sound and the Fury:* Quentin Compson and Faulkner's 'Tragedy of Passion.'" *Studies in the Novel* 2 (1970): 61–75.

Michel, Laurence. "Faulkner: Saying No to Death." In *The Thing Contained: Theory of the Tragic.* Bloomington: Indiana University Press, 1970.

Middleton, Christopher. *The Pursuit of the Kingfisher.* Manchester: Carcanet Press, 1984.

Minter, David. *William Faulkner: His Life and Work.* Baltimore: Johns Hopkins University Press, 1980.

Moore, Sally F., and Barbara G. Myerhoff, eds. *Secular Ritual.* Amsterdam: Van Gorcum, 1977.

Nagy, Gregory. *The Best of the Achaeans: Concepts of the Hero in Archaic Greek Poetry.* Baltimore: Johns Hopkins University Press, 1979.

Oates, Joyce Carol. "'At Least I Have Made a Woman of Her': Images of Women in Twentieth-Century Literature." *Georgia Review* 37 (1983): 7–30.

O'Donnell, George Marion. "Faulkner's Mythology." *Kenyon Review* 1 (1939): 285–99.

Ong, Walter J. *Fighting for Life: Contest, Sexuality, and Consciousness.* Ithaca: Cornell University Press, 1981.

———. *Interfaces of the Word: Studies in the Evolution of Consciousness and Culture.* Ithaca: Cornell University Press, 1977.

——— *Orality and Literacy: The Technologizing of the Word.* London: Methuen, 1982.

———. *Ramus, Method, and the Decay of Dialogue.* Cambridge: Harvard University Press, 1958.

Peacock, James L. *Consciousness and Change: Symbolic Anthropology in Evolutionary Perspective.* New York: John Wiley and Sons, 1975.

———. *Rites of Modernization: Symbolic and Social Aspects of Indonesian Proletarian Drama.* Chicago: University of Chicago Press, 1968.

Peristiany, J. G., ed. *Honour and Shame: The Values of Mediterranean Society.* Chicago: University of Chicago Press, 1966.

Pitavy, François. *Faulkner's "Light in August."* Rev. ed. Trans. Gillian E. Cook. Bloomington: Indiana University Press, 1973.

Pitt-Rivers, Julian. *The Fate of Schechem; or, The Politics of Sex: Essays in the Anthropology of the Mediterranean.* Cambridge: Cambridge University Press, 1977.

——— "Honor." *International Encyclopedia of the Social Sciences.* Ed. David L. Sills. New York: Macmillan, 1968.

Poirier, Richard. *A World Elsewhere: The Place of Style in American Literature*. New York: Oxford University Press, 1966.

Porter, Carolyn. *Seeing and Being: The Plight of the Participant Observer in Emerson, James, Adams, and Faulkner*. Middletown, Conn.: Wesleyan University Press, 1981.

Radway, Janice A. *Reading the Romance: Women, Patriarchy, and Popular Literature*. Chapel Hill: University of North Carolina Press, 1984.

Rebhorn, Wayne A. *Courtly Performances: Masking and Festivity in Castiglione's "Book of the Courtier."* Detroit: Wayne State University Press, 1978.

Redfield, James M. *Nature and Culture in the "Iliad": The Tragedy of Hector*. Chicago: University of Chicago Press, 1975.

Reiss, Timothy J. *Tragedy and Truth: Studies in the Development of a Renaissance and Neoclassical Discourse*. New Haven: Yale University Press, 1980.

Robbins, Deborah. "The Desperate Eloquence of *Absalom, Absalom!*" *Mississippi Quarterly* 34 (1981): 315–24.

Rorty, Richard. *Consequences of Pragmatism*. Minneapolis: University of Minnesota Press, 1982.

Rosenberg, Bruce A. "The Aesthetics of the Folk Sermon." *Georgia Review* 25 (1971): 424–38.

———. "The Oral Quality of Reverend Shegog's Sermon in William Faulkner's *The Sound and the Fury*." *Literatur in Wissenshaft und Unterricht* 2 (1969): 73–88.

Rosenblatt, Louise M. *The Reader, the Text, the Poem*. Carbondale: Southern Illinois University Press, 1978.

Ross, Stephen M. "The Evocation of Voice in *Absalom, Absalom!*" *Essays in Literature* 8 (1981): 135–49.

———. "The 'Loud World' of Quentin Compson." *Studies in the Novel* 7 (1975): 245–57.

———. "'Voice' in Narrative Texts: The Example of *As I Lay Dying*." *PMLA* 94 (1979): 300–310.

Scott, Evelyn. *On William Faulkner's "The Sound and the Fury."* New York: Cape and Smith, 1929.

Sensibar, Judith L. *The Origins of Faulkner's Art*. Austin: University of Texas Press, 1984.

Sewall, Richard B. *"Absalom, Absalom!": The Vision of Tragedy*. New Haven: Yale University Press, 1959.

Shattuck, Roger. "How to Rescue Literature." *New York Review of Books*, 17 April 1980, pp. 29–35.

Shipley, Joseph T. "The Growth of Tragedy." *Double Dealer* 7 (1925): 191–94.

Slatoff, Walter J. *Quest for Failure: A Study of William Faulkner*. Ithaca: Cornell University Press, 1960.

Smith, Barbara Herrnstein. "Contingencies of Value." *Critical Inquiry* 10 (1983): 1–35.

Solomon, Robert C. *The Passions*. Garden City: Doubleday, 1976.

Sontag, Susan. *Against Interpretation and Other Essays*. New York: Farrar, Straus & Giroux, 1966.

Works Cited

Steiner, George. "'Critic'/'Reader.'" *New Literary History* 10 (1979): 423–52.

—— *The Death of Tragedy*. New York: Hill and Wang, 1961.

Stock, Jerold Howard. "Suggestions of Death-Anxiety in the Life of William Faulkner." Diss., University of West Virginia 1977.

Stonum, Gary Lee. *Faulkner's Career: An Internal Literary History*. Ithaca: Cornell University Press, 1979.

Sullivan, Walter. "The Tragic Design of *Absalom, Absalom!*" *South Atlantic Quarterly* 50 (1951): 552–66.

Sundquist, Eric J. *Faulkner: The House Divided*. Baltimore: Johns Hopkins University Press, 1983.

Swink, Helen. "William Faulkner: The Novelist as Oral Narrator." *Georgia Review* 26 (1972): 183–209.

Taylor, Carole Anne. "*Light in August:* The Epistemology of Tragic Paradox." *Texas Studies in Literature and Language* 22 (1980): 48–68.

Thompson, E. P. *The Poverty of Theory*. New York: Monthly Review Press, 1978.

Thompson, Lawrance. *William Faulkner: An Introduction and Interpretation*. 2d ed. New York: Holt, Rinehart and Winston, 1967.

Toles, George. "The Space Between: A Study of Faulkner's *Sanctuary*." *Texas Studies in Literature and Language* 22 (1980): 22–47.

Tompkins, Jane P. "The Reader in History: The Changing Shape of Literary Response." In *Reader-Response Criticism: From Formalism to Post-Structuralism*. Ed. Jane P. Tompkins. Baltimore: Johns Hopkins University Press, 1980, pp. 201–32.

Triandis, Harry C., and William Wilson Lambert, eds. *Handbook of Cross-cultural Psychology*. Vols. 1, 4, 5, and 6. Boston: Allyn and Bacon, 1980.

Turner, Victor. *Dramas, Fields, and Metaphors: Symbolic Action in Human Society*. Ithaca: Cornell University Press, 1974.

—— *From Ritual to Theatre: The Human Seriousness of Play*. New York: Performing Arts Journal Publications, 1982.

—— *The Ritual Process: Structure and Anti-structure*. Chicago: Aldine, 1969.

Vickery, Olga W. *The Novels of William Faulkner: A Critical Interpretation*. Rev. ed. Baton Rouge: Louisiana State University Press, 1964.

Volkelt, Johannes. "The Philosophical Implications of Tragedy." In *A Modern Book of Criticism*. Ed. Ludwig Lewisohn. New York: Boni and Liveright, 1919.

Vygotsky, Lev. *Thought and Language*. Cambridge: Harvard University Press, 1962.

Wadlington, Warwick, "Godly Gamesomeness: Self-Taste in *Moby-Dick*." In *The Confidence Game in American Literature*. Princeton: Princeton University Press, 1975, pp. 73–103.

—— "Pathos and Dreiser." *Southern Review* 7 n.s. (1971): 411–29.

Wadlington, Warwick, and William C. Stephenson. "'Deep within the Reader's Eye' with Wallace Stevens." *Wallace Stevens Journal* 2 (1978): 21–33.

Works Cited

Waggoner, Hyatt H. *William Faulkner: From Jefferson to the World*. Lexington: University of Kentucky Press, 1959.

Wagner, Linda W. "Language and Act: Caddy Compson." *Southern Literary Journal* 14 (1982): 49–61.

Wall, Carey. "*The Sound and the Fury:* The Emotional Center." *Midwest Quarterly* 2 (1970): 371–87.

Wasserman, Earl R. "The Pleasures of Tragedy." *ELH* 14 (1947): 283–307.

Weiner, Annette B. *Women of Value, Men of Renown*. Austin: University of Texas Press, 1976.

Weinstein, Arnold L. "Vision as Feeling: Bernanos and Faulkner." In *Vision and Response in Modern Fiction*. Ithaca: Cornell University Press, 1974, pp. 91–153.

Weitz, Morris. "Tragedy." *The Encyclopedia of Philosophy*. Ed. Paul Edwards. New York: Macmillan, 1967.

Wesling, Donald. "Difficulties of the Bardic: Literature and the Human Voice." *Critical Inquiry* 8 (1981): 69–81.

Wess, Robert V. "Notes toward a Marxist Rhetoric." *Bucknell Review* 28 (1983): 126–47.

Whigham, Frank. *Ambition and Privilege: The Social Tropes of Elizabethan Courtesy Theory*. Berkeley: University of California Press, 1984.

Williams, Raymond. *Marxism and Literature*. New York: Oxford University Press, 1977.

———. *Modern Tragedy*. Stanford: Stanford University Press, 1966.

Woolf, Virginia. *The Common Reader*. New York: Harcourt, Brace, 1948.

Wyatt, David. *Prodigal Sons: A Study in Authorship and Authority*. Baltimore: Johns Hopkins University Press, 1980.

Wyatt-Brown, Bertram. *Southern Honor: Ethics and Behavior in the Old South*. New York: Oxford University Press, 1982.

Zender, Karl F. "Faulkner and the Power of Sound." *PMLA* 99 (1984): 89–108.

Index

Index

Index

Library of Congress Cataloging-in-Publication Data

Wadlington, Warwick, 1938–
    Reading Faulknerian tragedy.

    Bibliography: p.
    Includes index.
    1. Faulkner, William, 1897–1962—Criticism and
interpretation. 2. Tragic, The, in literature. I. Title.
PS3511.A86Z984 1987   813'.52   86-29166
ISBN 0-8014-2011-3 (alk. paper)